MATHEMATICS
Formative
Assessment

We dedicate this book to the Maine Mathematics and Science Alliance (MMSA). It was the MMSA that brought the authors together almost ten years ago, nurtured our common passion for formative assessment, and left us both with the collaborative spirit and collegiality to continue this work together as our paths diverged.

MATHEMATICS
Formative
Assessment

75 Practical Strategies for Linking
Assessment, Instruction, and Learning

Page Keeley
Cheryl Rose Tobey

A JOINT PUBLICATION

CORWIN
A SAGE Company

NCTM®

NATIONAL COUNCIL OF
TEACHERS OF MATHEMATICS

CORWIN
A SAGE Company

FOR INFORMATION:

Corwin
A SAGE Company
2455 Teller Road
Thousand Oaks, California 91320
(800) 233-9936
Fax: (800) 417-2466
www.corwin.com

SAGE Ltd.
1 Oliver's Yard
55 City Road
London EC1Y 1SP
United Kingdom

SAGE India Pvt. Ltd.
B 1/I 1 Mohan Cooperative
Industrial Area
Mathura Road, New Delhi 110 044
India

SAGE Asia-Pacific Pte. Ltd.
33 Pekin Street #02-01
Far East Square
Singapore 048763

Acquisitions Editor: Cathy Hernandez
Editorial Assistant: Sarah Bartlett
Production Editor: Jane Haenel
Permissions Editor: Adele Hutchinson
Copy Editor: Alan Cook
Typesetter: C&M Digitals (P) Ltd.
Proofreader: Caryne Brown
Indexer: Michael Ferreira
Cover Designer: Karine Hovsepian

Copyright © 2011 by Corwin

Printed in the United States of America

Library of Congress Cataloging-in-Publication Data

Keeley, Page.
Mathematics formative assessment: 75 practical strategies for linking assessment, instruction, and learning/Page Keeley and Cheryl Rose Tobey.

p. cm.
Includes bibliographical references and index.

ISBN 978-1-4129-6812-6 (pbk.)

1. Mathematics—Study and teaching. 2. Educational evaluation. I. Tobey, Cheryl Rose. II. Title.

QA11.2.K44 2011
372.7—dc23   2011019158

This book is printed on acid-free paper.

14 15 16 17 10 9 8 7 6 5

Contents

Preface

The most important single factor influencing learning is what the learner already knows. Ascertain this and teach him accordingly.

—Ausubel, Novak, & Hanesian, 1978

ABOUT THIS BOOK

In 2008 the book *Science Formative Assessment: 75 Practical Strategies for Linking Assessment, Instruction, and Learning* was copublished by Corwin and the National Science Teachers Association (NSTA). The book quickly became a best seller, widely used by teachers, university preservice instructors, and professional learning communities. Science teachers shared the book with other teachers in their schools, including mathematics teachers. While mathematics teachers modified the strategies to fit their subject, many of them expressed the desire to have a parallel book for mathematics educators, using similar strategies from the science version but including examples for mathematics as well as some strategies specific to mathematics. Well, we heard you! This book is designed for mathematics educators, and as with the science formative assessment book that preceded it, many of the strategies in this book can be shared across all content areas.

Like the science version, this book addresses the need to balance opportunity to learn, which includes assessment *for* learning (Black, Harrison, Lee, Marshall, & Wiliam, 2003), with assessment *of* learning. Optimal opportunities to learn exist when mathematics teachers are aware of the variety of different ideas and strategies students are likely to bring to their learning; see the connections between students' thinking, problem-solving skills, and the specific ideas included in standards; and provide learning experiences that build a bridge between their students' thinking and mathematical understanding. What is effective for one purpose—external accountability—may not effectively serve the purpose of informing instructional planning and decision making in the classroom, which is ultimately what affects student learning. A rich repertoire of formative assessment techniques provides the ongoing feedback and stimulus for deep thinking that a high-stakes test once or twice a year cannot provide in time to inform instruction and affect learning.

Teachers are the most important link in the chain that connects assessment, instruction, and learning. The need for a varied repertoire of purposeful techniques that weave mathematics assessment throughout instruction and learning is what led to this book. We hope you can turn the insights and ideas gleaned from this book into practical actions that will transform teaching and learning in your classroom.

Purpose and Need

There is a substantial body of research that indicates formative assessment can significantly improve student learning. Yet this same research shows that the features of formative assessment that affect student achievement are, sadly, missing from many classrooms (Black, Harrison, Lee, Marshall, & Wiliam, 2003). The purpose of this book is to provide teachers with guidance, suggestions, and techniques for using formative assessment to improve teaching and learning in the mathematics classroom. A wide variety of assessment books and resources available to mathematics educators provide the theoretical rationale for formative assessment and its implications for teaching and learning. This book expands on the current literature by identifying and describing content-specific practical techniques teachers can use to build a rich repertoire of formative assessment strategies for the mathematics classroom.

The acronym FACT is used to label the 75 techniques included in this book. FACT stands for Formative Assessment Classroom Technique. Through the varied use of FACTs, explicitly intended to gather information about or promote students' thinking and learning, teachers can focus on what works best for learning and design or modify lessons to fit the needs of the students.

Audience

The primary audience for this book is K–12 mathematics teachers. However, many of the strategies described can be used in other disciplines such as science, social studies, language arts, fine arts, health, and foreign language; these other uses, as well as those for other content areas not listed here, are noted in each of the FACT descriptions. University faculty may also find the FACTs useful in teaching college students or preparing preservice teachers to use formative assessment. Professional developers can use several of the FACTs to design and monitor learning experiences for adult learners, including teachers. Many Professional Learning

Communities (PLCs) are using this book to study formative assessment and to build their capacity to use effective formative strategies to improve student learning.

Organization

The organization of this book follows the same organization as the science version (Keeley, 2008). Where appropriate, we kept the same information so that the two books would parallel each other and could be used together in science and mathematics PLCs or by teams of science and mathematics teachers. Chapter 1 provides an introduction to formative assessment in the mathematics classroom. It describes the inextricable link between assessment, instruction, and learning. It describes what a FACT is and the cognitive research that supports the use of FACTs. It describes the learning environments that support assessment, instruction, and learning. It examines the relationship between teaching and learning and describes new roles and implications for a formative assessment–centered classroom.

Chapter 2 focuses on the use of FACTs to integrate assessment, instruction, and learning. It examines the connection between assessment and instruction and describes a learning cycle model in mathematics called the Mathematics Assessment, Instruction, and Learning (MAIL) cycle, which integrates assessment with instruction and learning and provides a framework for using FACTs. This cycle parallels the SAIL (Science Assessment, Instruction, and Learning) cycle. It describes how formative assessment promotes learning in the mathematics classroom, including the role of metacognition, self-assessment, and reflection. It provides suggestions for strengthening the link between assessment, instruction, and learning.

Chapter 3 addresses considerations for selecting, planning for, and implementing mathematics formative assessment. It also provides suggestions for ways to use this book with PLCs. It includes a matrix for matching FACTs with their main purposes for use in teaching and learning as well as secondary purposes.

Chapter 4 is the heart of the book. It includes a collection of 75 FACTs. Many of the same FACTs are included in the science version of this book, and several new ones, specific to mathematics, have been added. The FACTs are arranged in alphabetical order so that teachers can locate them by name (we found we could not arrange them by use since many of the uses overlapped). They are also numbered on the matrix in Figure 3.5. Each FACT uses a common format that provides a description, how it promotes student learning, how it informs instruction, considerations for design and administration, modifications that can be made to a FACT for different types of students or purposes, caveats for using a particular technique, general attributes, and uses in other disciplines besides science. Each FACT includes an example that shows or describes how the FACT is used in mathematics. Space is provided after each FACT to record your notes on how it worked in your classroom and any modifications or suggestions for further use.

The Appendix contains an annotated list of the resources referred to in Chapter 4, as well as additional resources useful for expanding your knowledge of formative assessment, building a repertoire of strategies, and accessing ready-made probes. In addition, several websites are provided that focus on formative assessment.

Acknowledgments

M ost of the ideas and techniques in this book are not new or unique. They have been drawn from formative assessment techniques used by classroom teachers, professional developers, researchers, and the authors' experiences as former middle and high school science and mathematics teachers. Several of the FACTs are so commonly used that it is hard to trace them back to the original source. In some cases a new name and a new twist have been added to an old technique.

We are indebted to the teachers we have had the honor and pleasure to work with in various projects, both in Maine and nationally, who have shared their repertoire of strategies with us, tried out both new strategies and variations of existing ones, and helped us to understand which FACTs work well in different contexts. In particular we would like to thank all the teachers in the Northern New England Co-mentoring Network (NNECN) Mathematics Access and Teaching in High School (MATHS), Science Content, Conceptual Change, and Collaboration (SC4), Governor's Academy, and Creating a Network of Educators Communicating about Teaching (CNECT), projects for giving us a window into your use of several of these formative assessment strategies. We thank all the teachers who have inspired us through your dedication to the continuous improvement of teaching practice and your keen insights into student learning.

We especially wish to acknowledge our present and former MMSA colleagues who have worked with us for many years on this journey into formative assessment: Lynn Farrin, Joyce Tugel, Chad Dorsey, Nancy Chesley, Mary Dunn, Caroline Arline, Lisa Marchi, Meghan Southworth, Henrietta List, and Leslie Minton. We would also like to express appreciation to EDC colleagues from the Formative Assessment in the Mathematics Classroom: Engaging Teachers and Students (FACETS) project—Susan Jansen, Emily Fagan, Eric Karnowksi, and Fred Gross—for their review and feedback of many of the FACTs. And we extend a huge thank-you to the many school districts and organizations we have worked with to build teachers' capacity to use formative assessment. A special thank-you goes to Jean May-Brett at the Louisiana Department of Education for bringing us both together to share our science and mathematics formative assessment work with Math-Science Partnership leaders throughout Louisiana so that they could include formative techniques into their projects to improve teaching and learning for students in their state.

We gratefully acknowledge our Corwin editor, Cathy Hernandez, for her positive enthusiasm and flexibility in working around our busy schedules. We also wish to acknowledge the outstanding support the staff at Corwin provides to their authors.

The contributions of the following reviewers are gratefully acknowledged:

Barbara Fox, Math Coach
Boston Teacher Residency
Boston, MA

Daniel Kikuji Rubenstein, Executive Director
Brooklyn Prospect Charter School
Brooklyn, NY

Zsuzsanna Laughland, Mathematics Teacher
Kennett High School
Conway, NH

Amanda McKee, Math Teacher
Johnsonville High School/Florence County #5
Johnsonville, SC

Lyneille Meza, Math Teacher
Strickland Middle School
Denton, TX

Edward C. Nolan, PreK–12 Content Specialist, Mathematics
Department of Curriculum and Instruction
Rockville, MD

Debra A. Scarpelli, Math Teacher
Slater Junior High School
Pawtucket, RI

About the Authors

Page Keeley is the Senior Science Program Director at the Maine Mathematics and Science Alliance (MMSA), where she has worked since 1996. She directs projects and provides professional development in the areas of leadership, professional development design, linking standards and research on learning, formative assessment, and mentoring and coaching,. She was the Principal Investigator on three National Science Foundation grants, including the Northern New England Co-Mentoring Network, Curriculum Topic Study: A Systematic Approach to Utilizing National Standards and Cognitive Research, and PRISMS: Phenomena and Representations for Instruction of Science in Middle School. She is the author of eleven nationally published books, including four books in the Curriculum Topic Study Series, six volumes in the Uncovering Student Ideas in Science: 25 Formative Assessment Probes Series, and *Science Formative Assessment: 75 Practical Strategies for Linking Assessment, Instruction, and Learning*. She consults with school districts, State Math-Science Partnership Projects, and organizations throughout the United States on building teachers' capacity to use diagnostic and formative assessment. She is a frequent invited speaker at national conferences, including NSTA, and led the People-to-People Citizen Ambassador Program's Science Education delegation to South Africa in 2009, to China in 2010, and to India in 2011.

Page taught middle and high school science for 15 years, where she used formative assessment strategies and probes long before there was a name attached to them. Many of the strategies in her books come from her experiences as a science teacher. Page was an active teacher leader at the state and national level. She received the Presidential Award for Excellence in Secondary Science Teaching in 1992 and the Milken National Distinguished Educator Award in 1993, and was the AT&T Maine Governor's Fellow for Technology in 1994. She has been an adjunct instructor at the University of Maine, is a Cohort 1 Fellow in the National Academy for Science and

Mathematics Education Leadership, and serves on several national advisory boards. Prior to teaching, she was a research assistant in immunology at the Jackson Laboratory of Mammalian Genetics in Bar Harbor, Maine. She received her BS in life sciences from the University of New Hampshire and her MEd in Secondary Science Education from the University of Maine. Page was elected the 63rd president of the National Science Teachers Association (NSTA) for the 2008–2009 term. In 2009 she was the recipient of the National Staff Development Council's (NSDC) Susan Loucks-Horsley Award for her contributions to science education leadership and professional development. She lives on 25 acres in rural Maine, where she dabbles in gardening and culinary arts.

Cheryl Rose Tobey is a Senior Mathematics Associate at the Education Development Center (EDC). She is the implementation director for the Pathways to Mathematics Achievement Study and a mathematics specialist for the NSF-funded Formative Assessment in the Mathematics Classroom: Engaging Teachers and Students (FACETS) and Differentiated Professional Development: Building Mathematics Knowledge for Teaching Struggling Students (DPD) projects. She also serves as a project director for an Institute for Educational Science (IES) project, Eliciting Mathematics Misconceptions (EM2). Her work is primarily in the areas of formative assessment and professional development. Prior to joining EDC, Tobey was the senior program director for mathematics at the Maine Mathematics and Science Alliance (MMSA), where she served as the co-principal investigator of the mathematics section of the NSF-funded Curriculum Topic Study, and principal investigator and project director of two Title IIa State Mathematics and Science Partnership projects. Prior to working on these projects, Tobey was the co-principal investigator and project director for MMSA's NSF-funded Local Systemic Change Initiative, Broadening Educational Access to Mathematics in Maine (BEAMM), and she was a fellow in Cohort 4 of the National Academy for Science and Mathematics Education Leadership. She is the coauthor of four published Corwin books, including three books in the Uncovering Student Thinking Series and *Mathematics Curriculum Topic Study: Bridging the Gap Between Standards and Practice*. Before joining MMSA in 2001 to begin working with teachers, Tobey was a high school and middle school mathematics educator for 10 years. She received her BS in secondary mathematics education from the University of Maine at Farmington and her MEd from City University in Seattle.

1

An Introduction to Formative Assessment Classroom Techniques (FACTs)

WHAT DOES A FORMATIVE ASSESSMENT–CENTERED CLASSROOM LOOK LIKE?

In a primary classroom, students are having a "math talk" to decide which figures are triangles. After using a *Card Sort* strategy to group picture cards as "triangles" and "not triangles," the teacher encourages the students to develop a list of characteristics that could be used to decide whether a figure is a triangle. As students share their ideas and come to an agreement, the teacher records the characteristic and draws an example and nonexample to further illustrate the idea. She then gives students an opportunity to regroup their cards, using the defining characteristics developed as a class. As the students discuss the results of their sorting process, she listens for and encourages students to use the listed characteristics to justify their choices. Throughout the discussion, the class works together to revise the triangle characteristics already listed and to add additional characteristics that were not included in the initial discussion.

1

In an intermediate classroom, the teacher uses a *Justified List Probe* to uncover students' explanations of how to determine equivalent and non-equivalent sums and differences of various two-digit numbers (for example, is 23 + 42 equal to 42 + 23? Is 23 + 42 equal to 22 + 43? Is 42 − 23 equal to 23 − 42? Is 42 − 23 equal to 43 − 22? Using the *Sticky Bars* strategy to anonymously display students' ideas, the teacher and the class can see that many students believe that both sums and differences are equivalent regardless of the order of the numbers. Knowing that this is a common misunderstanding cited in the research literature and seeing that the data from her own class mirrors that misunderstanding, the teacher designs a lesson that involves the students in using manipulatives to model the addition and subtraction of various two-digit numbers. After students experience modeling the operations, they revisit their original ideas and have an opportunity to revise them. The next day, students are given the task of defining the commutative property of addition. They work in small groups with *Whiteboards* to demonstrate the commutative property for addition and explain why there is no commutative property for subtraction. At the end of the lesson, students use *I Used to Think . . . But Now I Know . . .* to reflect on their original thinking about whether the sums and differences were or were not equivalent.

In a middle school classroom, the students use a *P-E-O Probe* to predict the number line location of the results of a number of multiple multiplication and division problems. Using the *Human Scatter Graph* technique, the teacher quickly sees that students differ in their responses and their confidence in their answers regarding whether multiplication always makes bigger and division always makes smaller. Knowing that this would be a difficult idea to change, the teacher provides students with various visual representations of multiplication and division with whole numbers, decimals, fractions, and integers using an interactive technology-based program. For multiple problems, students observe the modeling of the operation and discuss the pattern of results with various number types. After the demonstration and class discussion, the students use *Thinking Logs* to reflect on their new ideas regarding the effects of multiplication and division.

In a high school geometry class, small groups of students are using a collection of *Examples and Nonexamples* to discuss and reconcile their different ideas about whether the information provided about a figure is sufficient to determine whether that figure is a parallelogram. With the goal of consensus, students within each group justify their choice, trying to persuade others who disagree. As the groups work to produce justifications that will be shared with the whole class, the teacher circulates among the group, probing further and encouraging argumentation. Students write a *Two-Minute Paper* at the end of class to share their thinking with the teacher and describe the information needed to determine whether a figure is a parallelogram. The teacher uses this information to prepare for the next day's lesson on conditions of parallelograms.

What do all of these classroom snapshots have in common? Each of these examples embeds formative assessment techniques into instruction for a specific teaching and learning purpose. Often it is hard to tell whether a particular technique or strategy serves an instructional, assessment, or learning purpose because they are so intertwined. Students are learning while at the same time the teacher is gathering valuable information about their thinking that will inform instruction and provide opportunities for students to surface, examine, and reflect on their learning.

Each of these snapshots gives a brief glimpse into the different techniques teachers can use in their lessons to promote student thinking, uncover students' ideas, and use information about how their students are progressing conceptually to improve their instruction. The teaching strategies in these snapshots are just a few of the 75 formative assessment classroom techniques (FACTs) described in Chapter 4 that, along with the background on formative assessment described in Chapters 1 through 3, will help you understand and effectively use these techniques. While you may be tempted to skip ahead and go directly to Chapter 4 to find FACTs you can use in your classroom, you are encouraged to read all of the chapters in this book. The image and implementation of formative assessment in your classroom will be sharper and more deliberately focused if you have a firm knowledge base about the purposes and uses of formative assessment, including clearly articulated learning goals, before you select a FACT.

WHY USE FACTS?

Every day, mathematics teachers are asking questions, listening carefully to students as they explain their thinking, observing students as they work in groups, examining students' writing and representations, and orchestrating classroom discourse that promotes the public sharing of ideas. These purposeful, planned, and often-spontaneous teacher-to-student, student-to-teacher, and student-to-student oral and written interactions involve a variety of assessment techniques. These techniques are used to engage students in thinking deeply about their ideas in mathematics, uncover the thinking students bring to their learning that can be used as starting points to build upon during instruction, and help teachers determine how well individual students and the class are progressing toward developing mathematical understanding.

The 75 mathematics FACTs described in this book are inextricably linked to assessment, instruction, and learning. The interconnected nature of formative assessment clearly differentiates the types of

> "Assessment for learning is any assessment for which the first priority in its design and practice is to serve the purpose of promoting pupils' learning. It thus differs from assessment designed primarily to serve the purposes of accountability, or of ranking, or of certifying competence" (Hodgen & Wiliam, 2006).

assessments we call assessments *for* learning from assessments *of* learning—the summative assessments used to measure and document student achievement. Figure 1.1 describes the different types and purposes of assessment in the mathematics classroom.

Figure 1.1   Types and Purposes of Assessment

Diagnostic: To identify preconceptions, errors, types of reasoning, and learning difficulties.

Formative: To inform instruction and provide feedback to students on their learning.

Summative: To measure and document the extent to which students have achieved a learning target.

Source: Keeley (2008), p. 4. Used with permission.

Note: Diagnostic assessment becomes formative when the assessment data are used to inform teaching and learning.

Each FACT described in Chapter 4 is a type of question or activity that helps provide teachers and students with information about their factual, conceptual, and procedural understandings in mathematics. These formative assessment techniques inform teaching by allowing the teacher to continuously gather information on student thinking and learning in order to make data-informed decisions to plan for or adjust instructional activities, monitor the pace of instruction, identify misconceptions and common errors that can be barriers as well as springboards for learning, and spend more time on concepts and procedures that students struggle with. Formative assessment is also used to provide feedback to students, engaging them in the assessment of their own or their peers' thinking. In addition to informing instruction and providing feedback, many of the formative assessment techniques included in this book initiate the use of metacognitive skills and promote deeper student thinking.

"When data are used by teachers to make decisions about next steps for a student or group of students, to plan instruction, and to improve their own practice, they help *inform* as well as *form* practice; this is *formative assessment.* When data are collected at certain planned intervals, and are used to show what students have achieved to date, they provide a *summary* of progress and are *summative assessment*" (Carlson, Humphrey, & Reinhardt, 2003, p. 4).

The FACTs described in this book are designed to be easily embedded into classroom instruction. They are primarily used to assess *before* and *throughout* the learning process, rather than at the endpoint of instruction, except when used for purposes of reflection. Their main purpose is to improve student learning and opportunities to learn by gathering data that are then intentionally used to carefully design instruction that takes into account students' ideas and ways of thinking. They generally do not involve grading in the way that marking papers and assigning grades do; those types of grading tend to cast judgment on students' knowledge and skills and set up competition among students, conveying the unintentional message to the learner that "I am not good at mathematics" or "I'm better in mathematics than my classmates." They are generally not used for the summative purpose of documentation and accountability—measuring and reporting student achievement. The versatility of the techniques described in this book accommodates a range of learning styles and can be used to differentiate instruction and assessment for individuals and groups of students. FACTs can be used to spark students' interest, bring ideas to the surface, initiate mathematical explorations, and encourage classroom discourse—all assessment strategies that promote learning rather than measure and report learning. A rich repertoire of FACTs enables learners to interact with assessment in multiple ways—through writing, drawing, speaking, listening, physically moving, and designing and carrying out mathematical explorations. Figure 1.2 lists a variety of purposes for which FACTs can be used in the mathematics classroom.

Figure 1.2   Twenty Purposes for Using FACTs

- Activate thinking and engage students in learning
- Make students' ideas explicit to themselves and the teacher
- Challenge students' existing ideas and encourage intellectual curiosity
- Encourage continuous reflection on teaching and learning
- Help students consider alternative viewpoints
- Provide a stimulus for discussion and mathematical argumentation
- Help students recognize when they have learned or not learned something
- Encourage students to ask better questions and provide thoughtful responses
- Provide starting points for mathematical inquiry
- Aid formal concept development and transfer
- Determine whether students can apply mathematics ideas to new situations
- Differentiate instruction for individuals or groups of students
- Promote the use of academic language in mathematics learning
- Evaluate the effectiveness of a lesson
- Help students develop self-assessment and peer assessment skills
- Give and use feedback (student to student, teacher to student, and student to teacher)
- Encourage social construction of ideas in mathematics
- Inform immediate or later adjustments to instruction
- Encourage and include participation of all learners
- Increase comfort and confidence in making one's own ideas public

Source: Keeley (2008), p. 6. Used with permission.

Regardless of geographic area, type of school, degree of diversity of the student population, or the grade level taught, every teacher shares the same goal. That goal is to provide the highest quality instruction that will ensure that all students have opportunities to learn the concepts, procedures, and skills that will help them become mathematically literate students and adults. Formative assessment provides ongoing opportunities for teachers to elicit students' prior knowledge; to identify the ideas they struggle with, accommodate, or develop as they engage in the process of learning; and to determine the extent to which students are moving toward or have reached mathematical understanding at an appropriate developmental level. FACTs help teachers continuously examine how students' ideas about concepts and procedures form and change over time as well as how students respond to particular teaching approaches. This information is constantly used to adjust instruction and refocus learning to support each student's intellectual growth in mathematics.

HOW DOES RESEARCH
SUPPORT THE USE OF FACTS?

The seminal research report from the National Research Council, *How People Learn: Brain, Mind, Experience, and School* (Bransford, Brown, & Cocking, 1999), followed by the practitioner version, *How Students Learn Mathematics in the Classroom* (Donovan & Bransford, 2005), have significantly contributed to our understanding of how students learn mathematics. This understanding has implications for what content is taught, how the mathematics is taught, how learning is assessed, and how to promote deeper understanding in mathematics. Three core principles from *How People Learn* underscore the value of using FACTs in the mathematics classroom.

> **Principle 1:** If their [students'] initial understanding is not engaged, they may fail to grasp new concepts and information presented in the classroom, or they may learn them for purposes of a test but revert to their preconceptions (Bransford et al., 1999, p. 14).

This principle supports the use of FACTs as a way to elicit the prior ideas students bring to the classroom, making their thinking visible to themselves, their peers, and the teacher. By knowing in advance the ideas students have already formed in their minds, teachers can design targeted instruction and create conditions for learning that take into account and build on students' preconceived ideas. Students' own ideas and the instructional opportunities that use them as springboards provide the starting point from which concepts and procedures in mathematics can be developed. As students engage in learning experiences designed to help them develop mathematical understanding, teachers keep their fingers on the pulse of students' learning, determine when instruction is effective in helping students revise or refine their ideas, and make midcourse corrections as needed.

> **Principle 2:** To develop competence in an area of inquiry, students must (a) have a deep foundation of factual knowledge, (b) understand facts and ideas in the context of a conceptual framework, and (c) organize knowledge in ways that facilitate retrieval and application (Bransford et al., 1999, p. 16).

This principle points out the importance of factual knowledge but cautions that knowledge of a large set of disconnected facts is not sufficient to support conceptual understanding. Several of the FACTs described in Chapter 4 not only provide strategies for teachers to assess students' knowledge of facts and understanding of concepts but actually promote thinking that supports understanding. This thinking and the feedback students receive during the learning process help support the development of a conceptual framework of ideas. Teachers use the information on students' thinking to design opportunities that will help students develop from novice learners into deeper, conceptual learners who can draw upon and retrieve information from their framework. As concept development is monitored, reinforced, and solidified, formative assessment techniques are also used to determine how well students can transfer their new knowledge and skills from one context to another.

> **Principle 3:** A "metacognitive" approach to instruction can help students learn to take control of their own learning by defining learning goals and monitoring their progress in achieving them (Bransford et al., 1999, p. 18).

John Flavel, a Stanford University psychologist, coined the term *metacognition* in the late 1970s to name the process of thinking about one's own thinking and learning. Since then, cognitive science has focused considerable attention on this phenomenon (Walsh & Sattes, 2005). Several FACTs described in this book promote the use of metacognitive strategies for self-regulation of learning. These strategies help students monitor their own learning by helping them predict outcomes, explain ideas to themselves, note areas where they have difficulty understanding mathematical concepts, activate prior knowledge and background information, and recognize experiences that help or hinder their learning. White and Frederiksen (1998) suggest that metacognitive strategies not be taught generically but rather be embedded into the subject matter that students are learning. The FACTs that support metacognition are designed to be seamlessly embedded into the mathematics learning experiences that target students' ideas and thinking in mathematics. They provide opportunities for students to have an internal dialogue that mentally verbalizes their thinking, which can then be shared with others.

Evidence from the research studies described in *How People Learn* (Bransford et al., 1999) indicates that when these three principles are incorporated into instruction, assessment, and learning, student achievement improves. This research is further supported by the metastudy described in *Assessment for Learning* (Black, Harrison, Lee, Marshall, & Wiliam, 2003) that makes a strong case, supported by a significant effect size in the study, for the use of formative assessment to improve learning, particularly to raise the achievement levels of students who have typically been described as low attainers.

CLASSROOM ENVIRONMENTS THAT SUPPORT FORMATIVE ASSESSMENT

In addition to contributing to our understanding of how students learn mathematics, *How People Learn* (Bransford et al., 1999) has also changed our view of how classroom environments should be designed in order to support teaching and learning. These characteristics relate directly to classroom climates and cultures where the use of FACTs is an integral part of teaching and learning. These environments include the following:

Learner-Centered Environments. In learner-centered environments, careful attention is paid to the knowledge, beliefs, attitudes, and skills students bring to the classroom (Bransford et al., 1999, p. 23). In a learner-centered classroom, teachers use FACTs before and throughout instruction, pay careful attention to the progress of each student, and know at all times where their students are in their thinking and learning. All ideas, whether they are right or wrong, are valued in a learner-centered environment. Learners come to value their ideas, knowing that their existing conceptions that surface through the use of FACTs provide the beginning of a pathway to new understandings.

Knowledge-Centered Environment. In a knowledge-centered environment, teachers know what the goals for learning are, the key concepts and ideas that make up the goals, the prerequisites upon which prior and later understandings are built, the types of experiences that support conceptual learning, and the assessments that will provide information about student learning. In addition, these goals, key concepts and ideas, and prerequisite learnings can be made explicit to students so they can monitor their progress toward achieving understanding (Bransford et al., 1999, p. 24). The knowledge-centered environment uses FACTs to understand students' thinking in order to provide the necessary depth of experience students need to develop conceptual understanding. It looks beyond student engagement and how well students enjoy their mathematics activities. There are important differences between mathematics activities that are "fun" and those that encourage learning with

"An important feature of the assessment-centered classroom is assessment that supports learning by providing students with opportunities to revise and improve their thinking" (Donovan & Bransford, 2005, p. 16).

understanding. FACTs support a knowledge-centered environment by promoting and monitoring learning with understanding.

Assessment-Centered Environment. Assessment-centered environments provide opportunities for students to surface, examine, and revise their thinking (Bransford et al., 1999, p. 24). The ongoing use of FACTs makes students' thinking visible to both teachers and students and provides students with opportunities to revise and improve their thinking and monitor their own learning progress. In a formative assessment–centered environment, teachers identify problem learning areas to focus on. They encourage students to examine how their ideas have changed over the course of a unit of study. Having an opportunity to examine their own ideas and share how and why they have changed is a powerful moment that connects the student to the teaching and learning process.

Community-Centered Environment. A community-centered environment is a place where students learn from each other and continually strive to improve their learning. It is a place where social norms are valued in the search for understanding and both teachers and students believe that everyone can learn (Bransford et al., 1999, p. 25). Within this environment, FACTs are used to promote intellectual camaraderie around discussing and learning mathematics. A mathematics community–centered environment that uses FACTs encourages the following:

- Public sharing of all ideas and problem-solving strategies, not just the "right answers"
- Safety in academic risk taking
- Revision of ideas and problem-solving strategies and reflection
- Questioning and clarification of explanations
- Discussions with peers and use of norms for argumentation
- Group and individual feedback on teaching and learning

A classroom with these four overlapping environments is a place where students and teachers both feel part of an intellectual learning community that is continuously improving opportunities to teach and learn. It is a place where students and teachers thrive. It is a place where the connections between assessment, teaching, and learning are inseparable.

CONNECTING TEACHING AND LEARNING

Teaching without learning can happen in mathematics classrooms. Too often, students learn procedural steps and can produce a correct solution without understanding the important conceptual underpinnings of the process. Without conceptual understanding, students are not able to use their knowledge flexibly, cannot apply the procedure or skill within a new context, and are unable to justify and check the appropriateness of a solution.

> "Learning can and often does take place without the benefit of teaching—and sometimes even in spite of it—but there is no such thing as effective teaching in the absence of learning" (Angelo & Cross, 1993, p. 3).

Even our brightest students sometimes "learn" mathematics for the purpose of passing a test but then quickly revert back to their misconceptions and common errors. Gaps often exist between what was taught and what students actually learned. Frequently these gaps do not show up until after students have been summatively assessed through end-of-unit, district, or state assessments. At this point, it is often too late to go back and modify lessons, particularly when assessments given months and even years later point out gaps in student learning.

To stop this inefficient cycle of backfilling the gaps, teachers need better ways of determining where their students are in their thinking and understanding prior to and throughout the instructional process. Students need to be actively involved in the assessment process, so that they are learning through assessment as well as providing useful feedback to the teacher and other students. Good formative assessment practices raise the quality of classroom instruction and promote deeper conceptual learning. Formative assessment ultimately empowers both the teacher and the student to make the best possible decisions regarding teaching and learning.

> "Formative assessment isn't just about strategies to ascertain current knowledge—formative happens after the finding out has taken place. It's about furthering student learning during the learning process" (Clarke, 2005, p. 1).

Linking assessment, instruction, and learning does not merely involve adding some new techniques to teachers' repertoire of strategies. The purposeful use of FACTs, on a continuous basis, provides much more; it organizes the entire classroom around learning and ways teachers can provide more effective learning experiences based on how their own students think and learn. Formative assessment can be used formally or informally, but it is always purposeful. Teachers can take actions based on the information gained from the use of FACTS immediately, the next day, or over the course of a unit; or ideas for action can be shared with and used by teachers who will have the same students the next year.

If information about student learning is collected but not used as data or feedback that leads to action to improve teaching or learning, then it is not formative. It becomes information for information's sake. For example, using a FACT to find out if students have misconceptions similar to the commonly held ideas noted in the mathematics research literature is interesting and important in and of itself. However, just knowing that students have these ideas does not make this a formative assessment activity. It is not merely the collecting of this information, but the making of decisions as a result of careful examination of the data, that makes the activity formative assessment and connects teaching to learning.

MAKING THE SHIFT TO A FORMATIVE ASSESSMENT–CENTERED CLASSROOM

Formative assessment requires a fundamental shift in our beliefs about the role of a teacher. In a formative assessment–centered classroom, teachers interact more frequently and effectively with students on a day-to-day basis, promoting their learning (Black & Harrison, 2004). This interaction requires the teacher to step back from the traditional role of information provider and corrector of misconceptions and errors in order to listen to and encourage a range of ideas and problem-solving strategies

"Even though teachers routinely gather assessment information through homework, quizzes, and tests, from the students' perspective, this type of information is often collected too late to affect their learning. It is very difficult to 'de-program' students who are used to turning in homework, quizzes, and tests, getting grades back, and considering it 'over and done with'" (Angelo & Cross, 1993, p. 7).

among students. The teacher takes all ideas and strategies seriously, whether they are right or wrong, while helping students talk them through and encouraging them to consider the evidence that supports or challenges their thinking. During such interactions, the teacher is continuously thinking about how to shape instruction to meet the learning needs of students and build a bridge between their initial ideas and the mathematics understandings we want all students to successfully achieve.

The teacher also plays a pivotal role in connecting assessment to students' opportunities to identify and understand the role of a mathematically literate citizen.

Mathematical literacy is an individual's capacity to identify and understand the role that mathematics plays in the world, to make well-founded judgments and to use and engage with mathematics in ways that meet the needs of that individual's life as a constructive, concerned and reflective citizen. (Organisation for Economic Cooperation and Development, 2003)

Providing opportunities to discuss, construct and to organize thinking about the principles, properties, and uses of mathematics in solving relevant problems helps students understand the importance of the discipline beyond the school setting.

Traditionally, mathematics teachers were considered the providers of content that students then learned—teachers teach content and, as a result, students learn. The role of the teacher in a formative assessment–centered classroom is more of a facilitator and monitor of conceptual and procedural learning. The teacher's role expands to helping students use strategies to understand how well they are learning. As a result, students become more conscious of the learning process itself and take greater responsibility for their own learning.

"The role of the learner is not to passively receive information, but to actively participate in the construction of new meaning" (Shapiro, 1994, p. 8).

In a formative assessment–centered classroom, students learn to play an active role in the process of learning. They learn that their role is not only to actively engage in their own learning but to support the learning of others as well. They come to realize that learning has to be done *by* them; it cannot be done *for* them. They learn to use various FACTs that help them take charge of their own learning and assess where they stand in relation to identified learning goals. When they know what the learning target is, they use metacognitive skills along with peer and self-assessment strategies that enable them to steer their own learning in the right direction so they can take responsibility for it (Black & Harrison, 2004).

Standards and learning goals have a significant impact on what teachers teach and students learn. Developing content knowledge that includes important mathematics facts, concepts, procedures, and problem-solving abilities is at the heart of mathematics teaching and learning. As a result, teaching, assessing, and learning must take place with a clear target in mind. Standards should not become a checklist of content to be taught and assessed. Rather, they inform thinking about content as an interconnected cluster of learning goals that develop over time. By clarifying the specific ideas and skills described in the standards and articulated as learning goals, teachers are in a better position to uncover the gap between students' existing knowledge or skill and the knowledge or skill described in the learning goal. As a result, they are better able to monitor that gap as it closes (Black et al., 2003). While a particular FACT may determine the approach that teachers take to uncover students' ideas and modify instruction accordingly, the fundamental ideas and skills students need to learn remain the same. The focus of teaching and learning is on meeting goal-oriented learning needs rather than delivering a set of curricula at an established pace or teaching a favorite activity that does little to promote conceptual understanding.

Identifying and targeting learning goals is not the sole purview of the teacher. In a formative assessment–centered classroom, teachers share learning goals with students. This may involve breaking them down into the key ideas and procedures students will learn. Awareness of the goals for learning helps students see the bigger picture of learning and make connections to what they already know about mathematics concepts and procedures.

Another major shift that happens in a formative assessment–centered classroom

"Through communication, ideas become objects of reflection, refinement, discussion, and amendment. The communication process also helps build meaning and permanence for ideas and makes them public" (National Council of Teachers of Mathematics, 2000, p. 60].

is the recognition of the importance of acknowledging students' ideas. Traditional instruction involves the passing on of information from the teacher or the instructional materials, with little thought given to building on students' existing conceptions. Students form many of their ideas in mathematics by generalizing and adapting concepts and procedures learned in a different mathematical context. Often the adapted concept or procedures are no longer applicable within the new context, possibly contributing to a misunderstanding. These misunderstandings are referred to in a variety of ways, including misconceptions, overgeneralizations, conceptual misunderstandings, or common errors. In this book, they will be referred to generically as *misconceptions*, although the term does not necessarily imply that the idea is completely incorrect. In some cases, misconceptions include partially formed correct ideas, but they are not yet put together in a way that is mathematically correct. The nature of these misconceptions is described as follows (Mestre, 2000):

They interfere with learning when students use them to interpret new experiences.

Students are emotionally and intellectually attached to their misconceptions because they have actively constructed them.

Students give up their misconceptions only with great reluctance.

Repeating a lesson or making it clearer will not help students who base their reasoning on strongly held misconceptions.

Students who overcome a misconception after ordinary instruction often return to it only a short time later.

A constructivist approach to teaching and learning posits that students' existing ideas make a difference to their future learning, so effective teaching needs to take these existing ideas into account. Research indicates that misconceptions held by students persist into adulthood if they are left unconfronted and unchallenged (Carre, 1993). However, this does not simply imply that misconceptions are a bad thing and must be confronted on the spot as "wrong ideas." Rather than immediately correcting misconceptions when they surface, teachers should gather information that may reveal how misconceptions can be used as starting points for instruction. Starting with students' ideas and monitoring their progress as they are guided through learning that helps them recognize when their ideas no longer work for them and need to be modified or changed is the essence of an idea-focused, formative assessment classroom that promotes conceptual change.

As you gain a deeper understanding of the purposes and uses of formative assessment, you may find yourself reshaping techniques or developing new ones. You might find some techniques work better than others, depending on the mathematics idea being assessed or the nature of the learners in your classroom. Many of the FACTs described in Chapter 4 may be new to you; others may be ones you use routinely. Regardless of how you use the FACTs or your familiarity with them, one important implication for the mathematics classroom stands out—formative assessment provides an effective way for teachers to create classrooms that reflect current research on learning and provide greater opportunities for all students to achieve deeper levels of learning.

2

Integrating FACTs With Instruction and Learning

I taught a great lesson but the wrong class came.

—Anonymous

INTEGRATING ASSESSMENT AND INSTRUCTION

Formative assessment classroom techniques (FACTs) are rooted in good teaching practice. They offer a variety of ways to seamlessly integrate assessment and instruction by learning more about what students need to be successful learners of mathematics. Teachers who use FACTs start their lessons where their students' ideas are, identifying and monitoring learning paths that will eventually lead students to discover and understand important concepts and procedures in mathematics. Adapting teaching practice to align with the emerging research on formative assessment and how students learn has a reciprocal effect on teaching and learning. As teachers incorporate more FACTs into their

> "The quality of student learning is directly, although not exclusively, related to the quality of teaching. Therefore, one of the most promising ways to improve learning is to improve teaching" (Angelo & Cross, 1993, p. 7).

practice, their understanding of student learning increases, which in turn improves the quality of their teaching and raises student achievement.

Consider how one mathematics teacher reflected on the link between assessment and her teaching:

> Before introducing the unit on computing with percents, I now first probe for student understanding of the meaning of percent. Without understanding the relationship between percents, decimals, and fractions, the taught procedures of setting up a proportion or converting to a decimal and multiplying, just don't make sense to students. Without a true understanding, there is no ability to check answers for reasonableness of the results. (Teacher Sound Bite in Rose et al., 2007, p. 87)

The above reflection clearly shows the need to select the right tool or technique for the right instructional purpose. With 75 FACTs described in Chapter 4 to choose from, it is important to keep in mind that FACTs are not intended to be used as strategies picked at random. To be effectively integrated into one's teaching practice, FACTs must be thoughtfully selected to match the appropriate stage and purpose of instruction.

The teacher's reflection in the above quote indicates that the purpose of formative assessment is to guide teaching rather than assign a grade to students. While some of the FACTs described in Chapter 4 can be graded, their primary purpose is to inform and guide teaching and learning. This requires the teacher to shift instructional approaches from being the deliverer of content and assigner of grades to being a careful gatherer and analyzer of data about student thinking and learning—data that will provide the teacher with information on how to make the content of a lesson more accessible to learners. This requires teachers to keep their fingers on the pulse of student learning by constantly being aware of, supporting, and monitoring students' questions, comments, ideas, feedback, and reflections. When used throughout instruction, formative assessment helps build the type of deeper conceptual knowledge that leads to enduring understanding.

ASSESSMENT THAT PROMOTES THINKING AND LEARNING

"Learning is a consequence of thinking. Retention, understanding, and the active use of knowledge can be brought about by learning experiences in which learners think about and think with what they are learning. . . . Knowledge comes on the coattails of thinking" (Perkins, 1992).

Formative assessment enhances the daily interactions between students and between students and teachers by providing varied opportunities to surface, examine, work through, and reflect upon mathematical ideas related to a learning goal. While FACTs provide valuable information to the teacher to use for making instructional decisions, they also activate, encourage, and deepen student thinking. Students use their existing ideas and build on them to understand and explain mathematics. FACTs encourage the use of thinking skills in mathematics, such as making and investigating conjectures, interpreting and evaluating results, and developing and justifying ideas. Through the act of thinking about the ideas that surface through formative assessment, students actively engage in the process of constructing, modifying, or deepening their knowledge of content and procedures. Therefore, assessment not only serves the purpose of finding out what students are learning but also promotes learning.

> "An assessment activity can help learning if it provides information to be used as feedback by teachers, and by their students in assessing themselves and each other, to modify the teaching and learning activities in which they are engaged. Such assessment becomes *formative assessment* when the evidence is used to adapt the teaching work to meet learning needs" (Black et al., 2003, p. 2).

Metacognition is a key component of assessment that promotes learning. Metacognition involves thinking about one's thinking, including knowledge about oneself as a processor of concepts and ideas. Figure 2.1 lists several indicators of metacognition.

Figure 2.1   Indicators of Metacognition

Students engaged in metacognitive processes . . .

- know what they or the teacher needs to do in order for them to learn effectively;
- monitor their current understanding and recognize the basis for their ideas, procedures, and problem solving strategies;
- recognize how new knowledge relates to or challenges their existing conceptions or approach to solving problems;
- know what questions to ask to further their understanding;
- are able to evaluate mathematical claims and ideas of others; and
- can monitor the extent to which they are able to contribute to others' learning.

Source: Keeley (2008), p. 17. Used with permission.

Appropriate kinds of self-monitoring through metacognitive techniques and reflection have been demonstrated to support learning with understanding in a variety of areas. Helping students become more metacognitive about their own thinking and learning is closely tied to instructional practices that encourage feedback and self-assessment. However, it is important to point out that responding to feedback provided by the teacher or other students is different from students actively seeking feedback from the teacher or other students in order to assess their current thinking and level of understanding (Donovan & Bransford, 2005).

"Supporting students to become aware of and engaged in their own learning will serve them well in all learning endeavors" (Donovan & Bransford, 2005, p. 12).

Providing support for metacognition and peer and self-assessment is an important use of several of the FACTs described in Chapter 4. FACTs can provide opportunities for students to analyze and evaluate their own ideas and the ideas of their peers. Awareness of one's own thinking includes knowing when new knowledge relates to or challenges what one already knows or believes and leads to questions that stimulate further mathematical inquiry. Opportunities to test out ideas after making predictions confront students with the challenge of deciding if their ideas need to be revised, based on their problem-solving strategies, calculations, and observations. Small-group and class discussions provide a forum for students to express their ideas, make their thinking visible to themselves and others, and explore ideas that seem to make the most sense. Graphic organizers help students organize their thinking.

To be effective in promoting thinking and learning, metacognitive and reflection strategies should be explicitly taught in the mathematics classroom. FACTs that incorporate these strategies should be taught in the context of the content students are learning related to a specific learning goal. Teaching FACTs apart from mathematical content is like teaching problem-solving skills without a problem to apply the skills to.

LINKING ASSESSMENT, INSTRUCTION, AND LEARNING: THE MATHEMATICS ASSESSMENT, INSTRUCTION, AND LEARNING CYCLE (MAIL CYCLE)

A continuous assessment, instruction, and learning cycle model for mathematics that can be used with the FACTs in Chapter 4 is the mathematics assessment, instruction, and learning (MAIL) cycle shown in Figure 2.2. This instructional model can help guide mathematics teachers in selecting an appropriate FACT to match the purpose and stage in the instructional or learning process and reinforces the inextricable link between assessment, instruction, and learning. The circular diagram illustrates the cyclical nature of the MAIL in which instruction can loop back and repeat different stages as needed. Self-assessment and reflection are the centerpiece that promotes metacognition and are connected to each stage in the cycle.

"Teacher inquiry into learning and teaching is a powerful process that begins by learning from and about students first hand" (Stepans et al., 2005, p. 43).

In the early 1960s, J. Myron Atkin and Robert Karplus formulated a constructivist instructional model of guided discovery designed to be similar to the way scientists invent and use new concepts to explain the natural world. This instructional model, called the *learning cycle*, was

Figure 2.2   The Mathematics Assessment, Instruction, and Learning (MAIL) Cycle

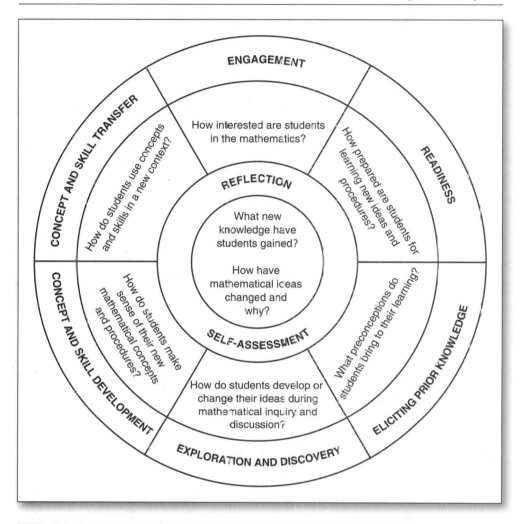

Source: Adapted from Keeley (2008).

designed to allow students an opportunity to surface and examine their prior conceptions. Once their ideas are revealed, students have an opportunity to explore them, arguing about and testing them in the process. When students see that their existing ideas do not fully match their findings, a disequilibrium results that opens the door to the construction of new scientific concepts. When students finally develop the formal scientific understandings and patterns of reasoning that help them make sense of phenomena, they are encouraged to extend their learning and apply their ideas to a new situation or context. While this model was originally developed for science, it is useful in mathematics as well (Fleener, Westbrook, & Rogers, 1995; Siegel, Borasi, & Fonzi, 1998; Stepans et al., 2005).

Throughout the various stages of a learning cycle, teachers design and monitor instruction so that students become increasingly conscious of their own and others' ideas. They gain confidence in their ability to learn, to apply concepts to new situations, and to use mathematical reasoning to construct evidence-based arguments. Teachers orchestrate student learning in different ways at different stages, encouraging a classroom climate in which ideas are openly generated and sufficient time is allowed for sense making and development of new knowledge and skills. While they are facilitating students' development of new ideas, teachers are also conducting formative assessments by monitoring students' changing conceptions and strategies and adapting their teaching and assessment techniques to meet their students' needs.

STAGES IN THE MAIL CYCLE

The FACTs described in Chapter 4 can be used with any instructional model. The advantage of using the FACTs with the MAIL cycle is that it helps provide a framework for seamlessly embedding the assessment techniques into teaching and learning. In addition, the cycle parallels the SAIL (science assessment, instruction, and learning) cycle in science (Keeley, 2008) and builds commonality between instructional and assessment techniques in both disciplines. Each of the stages in the MAIL cycle has an explicit purpose connected to assessment, instruction, and learning, as shown in Figure 2.3 and described below. Figure 2.4 shows the different types of assessment used in each stage of the cycle.

ENGAGEMENT AND READINESS

Using a FACT prior to selecting instructional materials or developing a lesson provides the teacher with a clearer sense of the readiness, motivation, and interest related to the content of the lesson. FACTs provide students with an opportunity to activate their thinking and develop curiosity about the topic. Examples from Chapter 4 include *Friendly Talk Probes* and *Learning Goals Inventory*.

ELICITING PRIOR KNOWLEDGE

Drawing out ideas students have developed through prior learning experiences or intuition provides a starting point from which the teacher can design instruction that will build on those ideas. Probing students' thinking allows teachers to determine where and how ideas may have developed and inform the types of instructional experiences that can build a bridge between where the students are and the mathematical understanding of the concept or procedure. Elicitation strategies promote thinking by

Figure 2.3 MAIL Cycle Connections to Assessing, Teaching, and Learning

Stage in the MAIL Cycle	Connection to Assessment The teacher . . .	Connection to Instruction The teacher . . .	Connection to Learning The student . . .
Engagement and Readiness	• determines students' interest in the content • gathers information about prerequisite learning goals and students' prior experiences that prepare them to learn new ideas and procedures	• interests students in the content and generates curiosity • gets students thinking about what they already know, have previously experienced, and questions they have	• becomes interested in the concept or procedure and is motivated to learn • activates thinking and engages in metacognition • recognizes how prepared he or she is to explore new ideas, procedures, and strategies
Eliciting Prior Knowledge	• elicits and identifies preconceptions students bring to their learning • analyzes students' ways of thinking and reasoning • uses information to design instruction or modify lessons	• gives students an opportunity to identify and voice their preconceived ideas in a nonjudgmental environment • exposes students to others' initial ideas and ways of thinking	• activates own thinking about mathematical ideas • surfaces and examines own ideas • considers others' initial ideas and compares them to own
Exploration and Discovery	• observes and listens to students as they interact • asks probing questions • collects evidence of change in or development of students' ideas • monitors students' progress toward developing understandings and redirects when needed • determines need for differentiation of instruction	• challenges students' existing ideas to facilitate learning • provides stimuli for discussion • initiates mathematical inquiry and idea exploration • provides sufficient time to allow students to work through or test their ideas and problem-solving strategies • encourages explanations using mathematical justification	• investigates own ideas, including testing of predictions and use of evidence to revisit initial conceptions • uses metacognitive processes to think about own ideas and how he or she is learning • experiences cognitive dissonance that may lead to eventually giving up or modifying his or her ideas or problem-solving strategies

(Continued)

21

Figure 2.3 (Continued)

Stage in the MAIL Cycle	Connection to Assessment The teacher . . .	Connection to Instruction The teacher . . .	Connection to Learning The student . . .
Concept and Skill Development	• monitors students' ideas and thinking for evidence of conceptual change • probes deeper to surface hidden misconceptions • identifies a need for additional lessons if there are discrepancies between students' conceptions and the mathematical ideas • assesses for student understanding of targeted concepts and skills	• facilitates construction of new knowledge by helping students examine their ideas, argue mathematically, and put new concepts and procedures together to make sense mathematically • encourages students to explain concepts and procedures in words and symbols and justify their ideas with proof and evidence • builds a bridge between students' initial ideas and procedures and formal mathematics	• examines the connection between own ideas and the mathematical properties that explains one's findings • engages in public sharing, argument, and analysis of ideas • seeks answers to questions, assimilates appropriate terminology and definitions, and clarifies murky understandings • considers alternative explanations and different problem-solving strategies
Concept and Skill Transfer	• analyzes how students use their formal mathematical ideas and skills to develop a progressively more sophisticated knowledge of the concept or use of a skill or procedure and the ability to apply them to different situations • determines the extent to which students can apply concepts and skills to new contexts	• provides further elaboration of the focus concept through additional inquiries or activities • encourages students to build on their previously developed ideas • brings closure to the lessons by having students use the formally developed concepts and procedures they have learned in novel ways	• develops connections and linkages among ideas • recognizes the explanatory power of relevant models, representations, and problem-solving approaches that are applicable to objects, events, and processes encountered in everyday life • applies knowledge and skills in novel situations
Self-Assessment and Reflection	• examines reflections and self-assessments to determine the effectiveness of instruction • provides opportunities for students to give feedback to the teacher on lessons, activities, and instructional strategies that will improve opportunities to learn	• helps students surface what may hinder or support their learning • provides opportunities for students to revisit their initial ideas and skills and compare them to their current use and understandings	• acknowledges own progress in meeting learning goals • identifies areas for improvement or further growth • identifies how confident he or she is in ideas and considers what it might take to change thinking

Source: Adapted from Keeley (2008).

Figure 2.4   MAIL Cycle and General Assessment Types

Stage in the MAIL Cycle	Type of Assessment Used
Engagement and Readiness	Diagnostic* Formative
Eliciting Prior Knowledge	Diagnostic* Formative
Exploration and Discovery	Formative
Concept and Skill Development	Formative
Concept and Skill Transfer	Formative and Summative
Reflection and Self-Assessment	Formative

Source: Adapted from Keeley (2008).

*Diagnostic assessment becomes formative when the data are used to inform teaching and learning.

safely surfacing ideas and challenging students' prior beliefs and knowledge. Discussion that accompanies elicitation allows students to share their thinking with others, which further challenges students' ideas as they consider them in light of their peers' explanations and arguments. Examples from Chapter 4 include *Opposing Views Probes, Commit and Toss,* and *Card Sorts.*

EXPLORATION AND DISCOVERY

The exploration and discovery stage can involve direct experience with concrete or virtual manipulatives, data collection, problem-solving processes, reading text, or uncovering ideas in discussion with peers. This stage often includes prediction and discussion of strategies that initiate mathematical inquiry. Providing opportunities to test their ideas, invent their own procedures, and solve problems gives students a basis of evidence to use in considering mathematical ideas during the concept development stage. This period of exploration and discovery allows the teacher to determine the kinds of understandings and questions students have before developing more structured opportunities for formalizing an understanding of the learning goal. During this stage, FACTs can also reveal how well students are responding to the assigned tasks and considering ideas of others, and whether their original ideas have been challenged by the evidence gathered during their exploratory experiences. Assessment during this stage gives students a chance to share their ideas and receive feedback from the teacher and peers in a nonjudgmental environment. Selected FACTs expose students to others' ideas and thereby help them reflect on their own thinking, which subsequently informs instruction when shared with the teacher. Examples from Chapter 4 include *A & D Statements*, *Strategy Probe*, and *Concept Card Mapping*.

CONCEPT AND SKILL DEVELOPMENT

Assessment of conceptual understanding and use of mathematical skills during sense making, clarification, and development of formal concepts helps both to reinforce student learning and to uncover any difficulties or gaps in understanding that might still exist. FACTs used during this stage help teachers determine the extent to which students have grasped a concept or procedure, and have recognized relationships among ideas. Results inform instruction by identifying needs for additional learning experiences or opportunities to build more sophisticated understandings, and by signaling that students are ready to transfer their mathematical understandings to a new context. In addition, teacher-to-student and student-to-student feedback further enhances opportunities to build conceptual and procedural knowledge. Examples from Chapter 4 include *Mathematicians' Idea Comparison, Always, Sometimes, Never*, and *Odd One Out*.

CONCEPT AND PROCEDURE TRANSFER

Assessment information at this stage is used by the teacher to address impediments that may interfere with transferring learning to a new context or to introduce new and related concepts that build more sophisticated understandings. Assessment information is used to modify learning opportunities so that students can use their newly formed or modified ideas or strategies in a new situation or novel context. Assessment opportunities provide students with an opportunity to think about how they can use their knowledge and skills in new situations. Examples from Chapter 4 include *Justified List, Thought Experiments*, and *Concept Cartoons*.

SELF-ASSESSMENT AND REFLECTION

Encouraging reflection and self-assessment helps students develop essential metacognitive skills that are useful in monitoring their own thinking and learning. Students learn to *think about learning* as well as *think about thinking*. The distinction here is that self-assessment helps students think about whether the *mathematics makes sense*. Reflection helps them think about how they *make sense of the mathematics*. Students' self-assessments and reflections provide valuable feedback to the teacher that shows how well teaching supports metacognition and can point out which students may need differentiated instruction. Reflections on learning activities can be used by the teacher to improve an instructional unit or lesson. Examples from Chapter 4 include *Two Minute Paper, I Used to Think . . . But Now I Know . . .* , and *Muddiest Point.*

SELECTING AND USING FACTS TO STRENGTHEN THE LINK BETWEEN ASSESSMENT, INSTRUCTION, AND LEARNING

Selecting a FACT that informs teaching and promotes thinking is a first step in using assessment *for* learning. The following is a list of suggestions for using FACTs to strengthen the link between assessment, instruction, and learning.

1. *Make students' thinking explicit during problem-solving activities and mathematical investigations.* Use FACTs to draw out students' thinking before and throughout classroom activities.

2. *Create a classroom culture of ideas, not answers.* Use the FACTs to encourage students to share their ideas, regardless of whether they are right or wrong. Many students have been raised in a classroom culture where they are expected to give the "right answer." Thus, they hesitate to share their own ideas when they think they may be "wrong." Hold off on telling students whether they are right or wrong and give them an opportunity to work through their ideas, weighing alternative explanations, evidence, and strategies until they are ready to construct mathematical understanding. The emphasis on surfacing mathematical ideas, inventing procedures, trying different approaches to problems, and revising one's thinking should take precedence over getting the right answer. Getting all ideas, strategies, and solutions out on the table first may take longer, but in the long run, it will lead to deeper, more enduring understanding, and students will be less apt to revert back to their preconceptions after the lesson or unit of instruction ends.

3. *Develop a discourse community.* One of the key features of several of the FACTs described in Chapter 4 is the way they promote learning through discussion and argumentation. When students are talking about their mathematical ideas, whether in a whole-class discussion, in small groups, or in pairs, they are using the language and conventions of mathematics.

Vygotsky (1978) established the *zone of proximal development* as the challenge factor in learning—the difference between what students can do independently and what they can accomplish with the support of others. The constructivist model promotes cooperative situations as essential for effective learning, with much classroom talk—between students and teachers and between students together.

"Talking the talk is an important part of learning" (Black & Harrison, 2004, p. 4). FACTs that encourage "math talk" not only engage students in activating their own thinking; they also provide examples of others' thinking for students to evaluate.

4. *Encourage students to take risks.* Create a climate in which it is acceptable to share an idea without fear of being corrected by or embarrassed in front of the teacher or other students. Create norms of collaboration in the classroom so that everyone's ideas are respected and acknowledged.

5. *Encourage students to listen carefully.* In a formative assessment classroom, different ideas are shared among pairs of students, small groups, and the whole class. Students need to learn to listen carefully to others' ideas and evaluate their reasoning and problem-solving strategies before changing their own ideas. They need to learn not to accept a new idea or strategy just because their peers think it is correct. They need to learn how to critically examine others' ideas before changing their own. Effective formative assessment practices encourage students to think rather than just accept ideas as they are presented.

6. *Use a variety of FACTs in a variety of ways.* Try out different types of FACTs to promote thinking and learning. Vary the ways students can reveal ideas—through writing, drawing, modeling, or speaking. Vary strategies for sharing responses. For example, students can form groups based on similar responses to discuss their ideas, then jigsaw with other groups to consider alternative explanations. Responses can also be shared anonymously by the teacher, allowing the class to discuss and evaluate different explanations.

7. *Use a variety of grouping configurations.* The social context plays a powerful part in motivation and the effectiveness of learning. The social interactions involved when FACTs are used in pairs, small collaborative groups, or whole-class discourse are important for promoting student learning. FACTs can provide a context and focal point for the discussion and argumentation that occur between students. Having to provide justification for one's ideas to a partner or others in a group develops deeper understanding for the student who justifies a response as well as the student who evaluates the justification.

8. *Encourage continuous reflection.* Encourage students to reflect back on their initial ideas related to a learning goal in order to note their own evidence of conceptual change or identify areas where they are still struggling with an idea or procedure. Understanding is an evolving process. It takes time for students to develop mathematical ways of thinking, and students need to understand that there are many steps along the way. Being aware of their own thinking (metacognition) and knowing what learning goal they are striving toward will help students be more

accountable for their own learning. Revisiting their initial response to a FACT and comparing it to where they are in their current understanding is a powerful way to reinforce learning.

Feedback from teachers who have used FACTs to link assessment, instruction, and learning has been overwhelmingly positive. The use of FACTs has considerably elevated teachers' expectations of themselves and their students. The research has been validated for teachers through their own empirical observations as they see evidence of their students becoming more engaged in mathematics, being more metacognitive, increasing their confidence in their mathematical thinking, using higher-level thinking and response skills, valuing feedback and reflection, and, ultimately, improving their performance in mathematics.

All the ingredients are here for you to pay more attention to assessment in the context of effective teaching and learning rather than being distracted by the cloud of coverage and accountability. While coverage of important content and accountability are important, they are achieved appropriately when teachers are truly accountable to students' learning needs and use formative assessment data to continuously inform their teaching so that students have the knowledge and skills to perform well on summative assessments. When student achievement scores improve and long-term retention and understanding replace short-term memorization for standardized testing, then you will know you have successfully linked assessment, instruction, and learning!

Considerations for Selecting, Implementing, and Using Data From FACTs

SELECTING FACTS

A variety of factors need to be considered before selecting a formative assessment classroom technique (FACT). The FACT needs to be an appropriate match to the mathematics content targeted, the needs and teaching styles of the teacher, and the types of students in the class.

SELECTING FACTS TO MATCH LEARNING GOALS

Formative assessment is not the goal; it is a means of achieving a teaching or learning goal.

Selecting a FACT without a teaching or learning goal in mind because it is seems like a fun activity to use in the classroom is analogous to "activitymania"—selecting mathematics activities that are fun and engaging to students but do not necessarily promote learning or inform teaching. Superficially selecting FACTs can result in "FACTmania" and derail their effectiveness in teaching and learning.

Before a FACT is selected, identify and clarify the concept, procedure, or skill the FACT is intended to provide information about. To best assist students in their mathematics learning, a FACT should attend to one of the many facets of learning, including conceptual understanding, knowledge of procedures, use of algorithms, problem-solving processes, and mathematical reasoning skills. There must be a clear match between the FACT and the learning goal it is intended to target. Figure 3.1 includes questions to ask about content and learning goals that can help inform your selection of an appropriate FACT. Using a systematic study process such as Mathematics Curriculum Topic Study, developed by the authors of this book with funding from the National Science Foundation, can help teachers deeply examine the conceptual and procedural content of the topics they teach through the lens of content standards and research on student learning, which in turn informs the appropriate selection of FACTs (see the Appendix).

Figure 3.1   Content Considerations for Selecting FACTs

Before selecting a FACT, ask yourself these questions:

- How well do I understand the content or skill I am teaching?
- What are the meaning and intent of this learning goal?
- What specific ideas provide meaning for the concept?
- What specific skills do students need to solve this problem?
- What content is developmentally appropriate at the level I teach?
- What level of sophistication is appropriate to expect from students at the level I teach?
- What is the mathematical terminology students should know and be able to use with this concept, procedure, or skill?
- What manipulatives can I use to help students understand the concept?
- What context is most appropriate for learning this concept or skill?
- What precursor concepts, skills, or procedures do students need to know first in order to develop understanding?
- What other concepts, skills, or procedures contribute to students' understanding and ability to use these mathematical ideas?
- What misconceptions, common errors, or difficulties should I anticipate related to the content?
- How do the answers to the above questions inform the selection of a FACT?

Source: Adapted from Keeley (2008).

FACTS AND THE COMMON CORE STANDARDS FOR MATHEMATICS

The Common Core State Standards for Mathematics (CCSSI, 2010) define what students should understand and be able to do in K–12 mathematics.

"Asking a student to understand something means asking a teacher to assess whether the student has understood it. But what does mathematical understanding look like? One hallmark of mathematical understanding is the ability to justify, in a way appropriate to the student's mathematical maturity, why a particular mathematical statement is true or where a mathematical rule comes from" (Common Core State Standards Initiative [CCSSI], 2010, p. 4).

As described in the previous section, formative assessment begins by identifying a learning goal, such as a grade level expectation from the Common Core Standards for Mathematics (CCSM). Since the grade level expectations in the CCSM define what students should "understand" or "be able to do," it is important for teachers to select a FACT to find out what students know and can do conceptually or procedurally in relation to the expectation for learning. In addition, an important feature of the CCSM is the Standards for Mathematical Practices. These practices describe a variety of processes, proficiencies, and dispositions that teachers at all grade levels should seek to develop in their students. Since the CCSM do not define the methods and strategies used to determine the readiness and prior knowledge necessary to achieve the standards, the FACTs in this book complement CCSM's eight Standards for Mathematical Practices and their link to mathematical content in the following ways:

1. *Make sense of problems and persevere in solving them.* Several of the FACTs in this book support metacognition by having students identify the extent of their own understanding of a problem and its solution as well as the problem-solving approaches of others. FACTs are also used by the teacher to monitor students' progress in being able to identify and solve a variety of mathematical problems. In addition, several FACTs are used in providing feedback that helps students persevere in solving problems by pointing out areas where they can improve. For example, *Create the Problem* can be used to determine the extent to which students understand the purpose of a mathematical problem and the various ways to solve it.

2. *Reason abstractly and quantitatively.* Many of the FACTs require that students make their thinking explicit, whether orally or in writing. By using these FACTs with mathematical problems and ideas that require students to reason abstractly or quantitatively, teachers can examine students' reasoning abilities to be in a better position to further explore and develop these skills. For example, FACTs incorporating

the use of *Probes* often require students to reason about a concept symbolically, to reason from a set of symbolic statements, or to reason about the quantities being used within the problem.

3. *Construct viable arguments and critique the reasoning of others.* Many of the FACTs require students to justify their answers, either orally or in writing. By using a FACT with a variety of learning goals over time, teachers can monitor students' ability to construct logical arguments using different strategies such as the use of counterexamples, known properties, and concrete referents. For example, *Always, Sometimes, Never True* requires students to determine whether a statement is always true, sometimes true, or never true, and to justify their choice. In addition to allowing the teacher to monitor students' abilities to construct viable arguments, many of the FACTS provide a structured method for students to analyze and critique the reasoning of their peers. For example, *Commit and Toss* is an anonymous technique that allows student ideas to be visible without individual students being identified by their response.

4. *Model with mathematics.* Many of the FACTS require students to create a model, make sense of a mathematical model of a given situation allowing the teacher to assess students' ability to apply known mathematical concepts to a new situation, or describe a symbolic or graphic representation of a given situation. For example, *Thought Experiments* provides a way for students to apply ideas in a novel situation that can't be carried out using a real-life investigation, and *Every Graph Tells a Story* reveals how students make sense of graphical representations.

5. *Use appropriate tools strategically.* By choosing a problem that requires the use of a mathematical tool and by using a FACT to make student thinking visible, teachers can more easily determine whether students are making strategic decisions about the use of a specific tool and whether they are able to use the tool appropriately. For example, *Matching Cards,* by using measurement tools and various items that can be measured, provides a process from which students can share their thinking with classmates and the teacher.

6. *Attend to precision.* Communicating thinking about mathematical concepts, ideas, and procedures is at the heart of many of the FACTS. By establishing an ongoing communication expectation, teachers can elicit and address over time the importance of using accurate terminology, using appropriate and clear labeling, and directly and accurately addressing the question at hand. For example, *Partner Speaks* allows students to talk through a process or solution with another student and to receive feedback before sharing with others. Over time, the feedback can focus on the various components of precision.

7. *Look for and make use of structure.* By using FACTs that require students to express their reasoning, teachers can observe how students apply similar patterns in problems of varying difficulty and make use of the structure of a mathematical representation. For example, *Odd One Out* allows teachers to monitor whether students can analyze relationships between items in a group. Teachers can choose items that are related in structure or by a particular pattern.

8. *Look for and express regularity in repeated reasoning.* Teachers need to be able to determine students' ability to determine general methods, understand generalizations made by others, and evaluate reasonableness of results both during and after the problem-solving process. For example, *Overgeneralization Probes* elicits misconceptions about overgeneralizations and following the probe with the use of *Four Corners* provides an opportunity for students to confront erroneous ideas.

SELECTING FACTS TO MATCH TEACHING GOALS

Formative assessment is closely linked to goals teachers have for improving their instruction. Selecting a FACT that matches an instructional goal can help teachers become more effective at eliciting students' ideas, promoting thinking and rich discussion in the mathematics classroom, monitoring student learning, and improving all students' opportunity to learn mathematics at high levels of understanding. The extensive body of cognitive research literature on students' learning in mathematics has alerted teachers to the fact that even the "brightest" students come to mathematics class with misconceptions or gaps in understanding. They come with theories constructed from their experiences and have actively constructed these theories, an activity crucial to all successful learning. Some of the theories that students use to make sense of the world are, however, incomplete half-truths (Mestre, 1989). The recognition that students come to the classroom with preconceived ideas has encouraged teachers to set teaching goals that will help them grow in their own understanding of their students' ideas and the misconceptions that may impede learning while also serving as springboards upon which to build from their students' ideas. Establishing teaching goals and selecting FACTs that match these teaching goals help teachers teach for understanding and monitor meaningful learning over time, and provide a means of assessing the quality of their teaching in relation to gains in student learning. The mathematics assessment, instruction, and learning (MAIL) cycle described

> There is no one best FACT or collection of FACTs that can improve teaching. Each FACT must be considered critically in terms of how well it matches goals for improving or enhancing instruction.

in Chapter 2 provides a useful framework on which teachers can overlay their teaching goals and select appropriate FACTs. Figure 3.2 lists questions to ask about teaching goals before selecting a FACT.

Figure 3.2   Considerations for Selecting FACTs to Improve Teaching

Before selecting a FACT to improve or enhance teaching, consider these questions:

- Which aspects of instruction and assessment do I need to improve upon?
- Which teaching goal will I focus on to advance my students from where they are now to where they need to be in their conceptual and procedural understanding?
- What types of pedagogy embedded in the FACTS are the best match for the content students are learning?
- How will this FACT help me work smarter, not harder?
- Does the intended purpose of the FACT match my teaching purpose?
- Which FACTs are best used to produce the information I need to inform my teaching?

Source: Adapted from Keeley (2008).

Each FACT described in Chapter 4 provides a description of what it is, how it promotes learning, how it informs instruction, design and administration, modifications, general implementation attributes, caveats for its use, and use in other content areas. Each of these should be carefully read over and considered before selecting a FACT to match a learning or teaching goal. The following suggestions can help you select FACTs that match your instructional context, goals, and style:

- Select a FACT that appropriately matches the mathematics content you are targeting.
- Select a FACT that appropriately matches your teaching or learning purpose and can be easily integrated into the lesson. See the matrix at the end of this chapter that shows both the primary use and other possible uses for each FACT.
- Choose a FACT that you are comfortable with and that appeals to your professional judgment and teaching style.
- The FACTs vary in regard to time required, ease of use, and cognitive demand. If time, ease of use, and demand on students' thinking are concerns, choose a FACT that has a low rating (see general implementation attributes listed with each FACT description in Chapter 4).
- Some FACTs require advance preparation. If preparation is a factor, select a FACT in which you can have all the materials prepared in advance or that uses readily available materials.

THE CRITICAL IMPORTANCE OF CLASSROOM CONTEXT IN SELECTING FACTS

Every teacher knows that within each class, individual students are unique. As a whole, they make up a classroom context with its own personality and set of dynamics. Some days you can teach the same lessons and use the same FACTs with different students or different classes of students, and they will feel like very different students or classes.

> There is no one best FACT or system of FACTs. What works best in one classroom may not work well in another.

Each student and class creates an environment that brings diverse cultural backgrounds, developmental readiness, prior experiences, language issues, prior content knowledge and skills, attitudes, learning and social styles, and habits of mind that affect their learning and the interactions that take place between students and between teachers and students. For this reason, teachers are encouraged to *adapt* FACTs, rather than *adopt* them as is (Angelo & Cross, 1993). In essence, selecting a FACT is a first step in differentiating instruction and assessment for diverse students and unique classroom contexts.

The classroom climate has a major impact on how well students engage with the FACTs. To use the FACTs effectively, teachers need to take into account not only the diverse kinds of students who come to their classroom but also the kind of classroom climate the teacher creates and how it affects learning for each student. A classroom climate in which all students' ideas are valued and where it is safe for them to surface ideas

> "The learning environment which a teacher creates has a profound impact on the success of the assessment strategies used" (Naylor, Keogh, & Goldworthy, 2004, p. 15).

whether they are right or wrong, creativity in thinking and generating ideas is promoted, all students are encouraged to engage in discussion with other students and the teacher, and confidence building and collaborative work are valued can significantly affect how well FACTs are used to inform instruction and promote learning.

The following suggestions can help guide your selection of FACTs to match the context of your classroom:

- Be sensitive to the cultural and social backgrounds of your students when selecting a FACT. Set classroom norms that promote respect for and value each others' ideas and the background knowledge and experiences they bring to their learning.
- Select FACTs that accommodate modifications for English language learners.
- If public sharing of ideas is initially uncomfortable for some students, ease them in by selecting anonymous strategies that do not identify individuals with their responses.

- Select FACTs that engage all students in the learning process and do not make it easy for students to "opt out" by letting the most active or vocal students carry the discussions or answer the questions.
- Don't grade FACTs. Use them to as learning tools that raise the confidence level of students and stimulate further thinking and discussion without judging the ideas as right or wrong.
- Create a climate in which engaging in mathematical reasoning and argumentation is the norm. Choose FACTs that will help all students feel comfortable debating and defending their ideas, listening to the reasoning of others, and acknowledging and evaluating alternative strategies.
- Select FACTs that encourage social interaction and collaboration in an emotionally safe environment.
- Select FACTs that provide opportunities for students to interact with diverse types of students who have different learning styles rather than with one classmate only.

PLANNING TO USE AND IMPLEMENT FACTS

After a FACT or set of FACTs has been selected, teachers need to consider various factors that support or hinder implementation in the classroom. Chapter 4 provides a description of implementation attributes; considerations for designing and administering a FACT, including modifications; and cautions to be aware of when using a FACT. These considerations and suggestions should be examined carefully before implementing any of the FACTs. In addition,

> "A good idea—poorly implemented—is a bad idea" (Ainsworth & Viegut, 2006, p. 109).

successful implementation requires an understanding of the mathematics content and mathematical reasoning. Overlooking the critical need to thoroughly understand the content and ways of reasoning before implementing a FACT can significantly affect its use and impact.

Before using a FACT, it is important to distinguish between two types of formative assessment: *planned formative assessment* and *interactive formative assessment* (Hall & Burke, 2003). Planned formative assessment is a type of formal or semiformal assessment that is planned for ahead of time in order to collect or provide evidence of student thinking and learning. Often it is curriculum driven. Assessment information is gathered through a FACT, interpreted, and acted upon. On the other hand, interactive formative assessment tends to be incidental and unanticipated, and it usually arises out of an instructional activity. It has the potential to occur at any time during student-to-student or student-to-teacher interactions and is more student or teacher driven than curriculum driven. While it is more difficult to plan for interactive formative assessment, one can do so by providing opportunities for classroom observation, discussion, and exchange of ideas. The following considerations will help you plan for and implement the FACTs described in the next chapter:

- Try out some of the FACTs on yourself first to see if they work in the instructional context you have chosen. Make sure you are able to come up with a response or example. If you have difficulty coming up with a response, then you can be sure your students will too.
- Introduce the FACT to students and explain the directions clearly, particularly if it is new to them. Consider modeling it for them the first time it is used.
- If a FACT is new, decide whether to teach the technique first, providing practice and feedback to students in trying out the FACT.
- Decide whether you want students' responses to be anonymous or identified with an individual.
- Modify a FACT for a "teachable moment" or when there is a need to differentiate for particular students or groups of students.
- Vary your use of FACTs. Students can quickly tire of using the same technique repeatedly, and the FACT will lose its effectiveness.
- When using a FACT for the first time, plan on it taking more time than you had anticipated. As with using any new tool or technique, as FACTs become more familiar to students and to you, the amount of time it takes to use it well will decrease.
- Let students know why you are using a particular FACT. When the purpose is made explicit to them and they understand how it helps their learning, the quality of responses to a FACT will be higher.
- Elicit students' ideas in a context that is familiar to them when selecting a FACT. Avoid the use of mathematics terminology students may be unfamiliar with, particularly during the elicitation phase.
- Be careful that you don't cue or lead students toward the answer too soon after they respond to a FACT. Allowing time for students to ponder and "hang out in uncertainty" can actually promote learning.
- Don't ignore incorrect ideas. However, in most cases it is best to refrain from immediately correcting misconceptions and common errors when they surface from using a FACT. Research shows students will revert right back to their misconceptions if they haven't worked through them. Use students' ideas as springboards for learning that you can build upon so that they recognize the error in their thinking.
- Encourage students to share as many ideas as possible in response to a FACT. Generate a list of class ideas. Make sure they give reasons or cite evidence for their ideas.
- Provide adequate time for sense making after ideas have been activated and surfaced.

- Involve students. Ask them for their opinions about the FACTs you have used.
- Involve parents. Produce parent-friendly descriptions of the FACTs you are using so that parents are informed and encouraged to further promote student thinking and sharing of ideas, procedures, and problem-solving strategies.

STARTING OFF WITH SMALL STEPS

If FACTs are new to you, start small by "dipping your toe into the water" and trying out one or two easy-to-use FACTs. Be sure to record your notes on how it worked in the spaces provided with each FACT description in Chapter 4. After trying out a new technique, thoughtfully reflect on how it worked for you by asking these questions:

- Were your students engaged?
- Were you confident and excited about using the FACT?
- How did use of the FACT affect the student-to-student or student-teacher dynamic?
- Was the information gained from the FACT useful to you?
- Would you have gotten the same information without using the FACT?
- What added value did the FACT bring to teaching and learning?
- Did using the FACT cause you to do something differently or think differently about teaching and learning?
- Would you use this FACT again?
- Are there modifications you could make to this FACT to improve its usefulness?

MAINTAINING AND EXTENDING IMPLEMENTATION

Formative assessment can make a significant impact on teaching and learning when used purposefully and over time. Dabbling here and there does not produce significant gains in student learning or teacher performance. Instead, it is the purposeful commitment on the part of the teacher to making formative assessment a regular feature of classroom practice that leads to results. In addition, extending the use of formative assessment beyond an individual teacher's classroom and making it part of a schoolwide commitment to improving student learning will lead to gains at a systemic level.

> "The ongoing identification, collection, and use of information in the classroom is a complex business" (Sato, 2003, p. 109).

Formative assessment is an ideal topic on which professional learning communities (PLCs) can base research, study, implementation, observation of others' classrooms, and shared results. Figure 3.3 provides examples of questions mathematics PLCs can use that link to their use of formative assessment.

Figure 3.3   Questions for Mathematics Professional Learning Communities

Examining Instruction and Assessment in a Professional Learning Community

Questions About Learning Mathematics Concepts, Procedures, and Skills

1. What preconceptions seem to be most prevalent among our students?
2. Do our students exhibit any of the common misconceptions or learning difficulties noted in the research on learning?
3. Which concepts, procedures, or skills seem to be most problematic for our students?
4. What terminology do our students use to describe their ideas? Can they use mathematical terms with understanding?
5. Are our students sufficiently engaged with the content?

Questions About Students

6. Which students seem to be progressing well toward the mathematical ideas?
7. Are there particular students who are having more difficulty than others? Who are they?
8. Which students have an understanding of the mathematics that could be used to support learning for other students?
9. How can we use formative assessment to differentiate instruction for particular students?

Questions About Teaching

10. Are our students responding positively to instruction?
11. Is the pace of our instruction appropriate?
12. What does formative assessment indicate with respect to how well our curriculum matches our teaching and learning goals?
13. What do we need to do to improve our lessons so there is greater opportunity to learn?
14. Do some FACTs embed more easily in our teaching than others? Which FACTs produced the greatest results?
15. What changes or modifications do we need to make to the FACTs to improve their effectiveness?
16. What new FACTs can we add to the ones we have read about or used?

Source: Adapted from Keeley (2008).

This book can serve as a resource that mathematics PLCs can use to improve upon and examine their formative assessment practices as well as a resource for PLCs made up of cross-disciplinary teams. Since there is also a science version of this book, science and mathematics teachers can form PLCs to learn more about the FACTs together.

Each of the FACT descriptions in Chapter 4 provides connections to other subject areas, such as science, language arts, social studies, performing arts, health, and foreign languages. There is a science version of this book, *Science Formative Assessment: 75 Practical Strategies for Linking Assessment, Instruction, and Learning* (Keeley, 2008), that includes several of the same FACTs used in this book. The following are suggestions for maintaining the momentum of implementation and extending the impact of formative assessment outward to other teachers in your school:

> "Formative assessment is relevant to all school subjects and, although different techniques may be more or less useful in different subjects, all the broad strategies are applicable to all subjects. Provided they are open to new ideas, teachers can learn a great deal by observing good formative assessment practice in other subjects" (Black et al., 2003, p. 74).

- Don't go it alone! Work collaboratively with other mathematics teachers to try out and evaluate the use of FACTs. Collaborate with science teachers who are using the science version of this book.
- Encourage schoolwide support of formative assessment. Inform other teachers and administrators about the FACTs in this book. Many of them are applicable to disciplines besides mathematics and science. Start with a small group of colleagues interested in trying out the FACTs. As you (and your students) share successes, other colleagues will want to join you in using FACTs.
- Realize that it takes time to change assessment and instructional practices. Don't expect immediate changes in practice and student engagement.
- Don't treat formative assessment as another new initiative to come down the pike. Formative assessment is not a fad du jour. Recognize where teachers are already using formative assessment and extend everyone's repertoire of strategies by trying out some new FACTs and reflecting on how they worked.
- Encourage an environment in which teachers can watch other teachers in action. Visit each other's classrooms. Seeing how formative assessment plays out with others' students helps teachers understand how they can use FACTs in their own classroom.
- Use "critical friends" protocols as sounding boards to give feedback on formative assessment practices.
- Build time into team, schoolwide, department, or professional learning community meetings to examine and discuss formative assessment.

USING DATA FROM THE FACTS

Even with careful selection, planning, and implementation, assessment is not formative unless the information is used to inform teaching or guide learning. FACTs provide a variety of raw student learning data that can be analyzed in various ways for different purposes.

"It is important to emphasize the critical criterion—formative assessment—is a process, one in which information about learning is *evoked* and then *used* to modify the teaching and learning activities in which teachers and students are engaged" (Black et al., 2003, p. 74).

The techniques described in this book are not formative unless teachers use the data to take action in some way. After teachers have collected formative assessment data, the important task of constructing meaning from the data and using it to inform teaching and learning is the essence of formative assessment. Data are not just the sets of test scores that often reside in a central office. There is a treasure trove of data being mined every day in the classroom that comes from listening to students interact, observing their actions, and analyzing their responses to questions posed. The challenge is not only in systematically collecting these data but understanding what to do with them. The use of formative assessment data can be described as helping teachers to "challenge their assumptions, investigate their own questions, uncover inequities, discover previously unrecognized strengths in their students, question their practice, improve instruction, and see the world anew" (Love, 2002, p. xxiv).

The following suggestions can help you use the assessment data you collect in a formative way:

"Working to analyze student responses, for example, math strategies, written work, and other representations in terms of what it shows about the status of learning relative to desired goals, or what misconceptions or gaps in learning are revealed, is an extremely useful way to increase analytic skills, and very likely content knowledge as well" (Heritage, 2010, p. 111).

- If the FACT involves feedback to students, provide that feedback as soon after the assessment as possible.
- Decide whether feedback will be written or shared through discussion. Allow adequate time to discuss FACT feedback with students.
- Let students know how you plan to use the data from the FACTs to improve your teaching and provide better opportunities for them to learn.
- Select an appropriate question that can be answered by analysis of the type of data generated by the FACT.
- Decide whether your analysis will be a qualitative "temperature taking" or a quantitative data analysis including crunching numbers of responses and percentages of students.
- Present analyzed response data to students—engage them in examining the class data and coming up with suggestions for improving teaching and learning.

- Avoid being overwhelmed with too much data. Often you will not have the time to analyze all of the student response data. Choose "samples" of student responses to examine and share with the class, or select FACTs that lend themselves to a quick scan and analysis.
- Be prepared for negative feedback. Do not feel professionally hurt if you find students' responses reveal that your instruction was not as effective as you may have thought. View it as an opportunity to formulate student learning needs more clearly and build on your existing practice.
- Focus on facts from the data, not the inferences. Don't try to read too much between the lines. Be aware that further probing is often necessary.
- Don't just gloss over results. Spend time reflecting on the data and considering what actions you need to take to improve teaching and learning. Then, take action!
- Share data with others and take collective action to improve teaching and learning.
- Take time to further explore the research on learning and suggested interventions that can help students learn concepts and procedures that the data indicate they are struggling with. Generic instructional strategies may not be as helpful as mathematics-specific strategies. Use the student data to inform areas of research you may want to learn more about.
- Consider being a researcher in your own classroom. Use the FACTs to collect and triangulate data that can be used to investigate problems related to teaching and learning.

As suggested above, using the FACTS in conjunction with becoming a researcher in your own classroom can help improve the learning and teaching of mathematics content. Rose et al. (2007), in *Uncovering Student Thinking in Mathematics*, designed an action research cycle called a QUEST (see Figure 3.4), which readily adapts to the uses of FACTs. The QUEST cycle consists of the following 5 components:

- **Q**uestion: Design a question pertaining to particular mathematics concept.
- **U**ncover: Elicit understandings and misunderstandings *using a FACT.*
- **E**xamine: Analyze and interpret the evidence collected.
- **S**eek links to cognitive research: Review available literature to drive next steps in instruction.
- **T**each the lesson: Plan and implement instruction based on findings and determine the impact on learning by asking an additional question.

Ultimately, how you select, plan for, implement, and use data from FACTs depends on the purpose for which you are using them. As you try out the FACTs, you may discover other ways to use them to inform teaching

Figure 3.4   QUEST Cycle

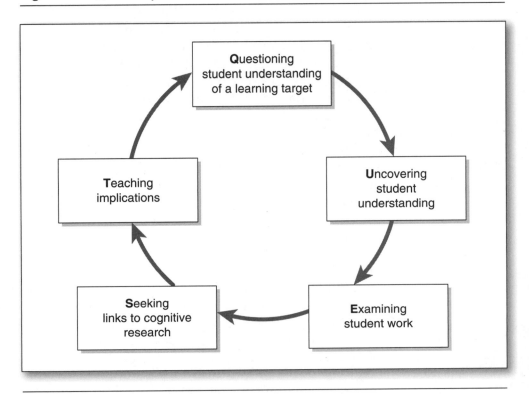

Source: Rose, Minton, & Arline (2007), p. 14. Used with permission.

and learning, including ways to adapt them for use in other disciplines such as science, social studies, health, language arts, visual and performing arts, and foreign languages.

Examine the list of FACTs and their purposes for promoting learning and informing teaching as described in the matrix in Figure 3.5. The matrix identifies the primary purposes with an uppercase X. That is the main purpose for which the probe was designed. The matrix identifies secondary purposes with a lowercase x. These are other purposes for which the probe can be used in some contexts. You may also find other purposes not listed or identified on the matrix.

Find a few techniques that pique your interest and resonate with your instructional style and purpose, and read the descriptions in Chapter 4. Choose one to try out. The most important take-home message of this book is to commit to trying at least one FACT and evaluating its success. It is through that first small step that large strides will soon follow!

Figure 3.5 75 FACTs and Their Use in Teaching and Learning

FACT (Formative Assessment Classroom Technique)	Elicit & Identify Preconceptions	Engage & Motivate Students	Activate Thinking & Promote Metacognition	Provide Stimuli for Mathematical Discussion	Initiate Exploring of Mathematical Ideas	Formal Concept Development & Transfer	Improve Questioning & Responses	Provide Feedback to Teacher or Student	Peer & Self-Assessment	Reflection
1. A & D Statements (page 52)	X	x	X		X					
2. Agreement Circles (page 54)	x	x	X	X		X				
3. Always, Sometimes, or Never True (page 57)	X	x	X	X	x	X				
4. Card Sorts (page 59)	X	x	X	X		X				
5. CCC: Collaborative Clued Corrections (page 63)		x	x	x				X	x	
6. Comments-Only Marking (page 66)		x	x					X	x	
7. Commit and Toss (page 68)	X	x	x	x		x				
8. Concept Attainment Cards (page 71)	x	x	X	x		X		x		
9. Concept Card Mapping (page 74)	X	x	X	x		X		x	x	X
10. Concept Cartoons (page 77)	X	X	X	X	x	x				
11. Create the Problem (page 80)	x	x	X	x		X				
12. Every Graph Tells a Story (page 82)	X	x	X	x		X				
13. Example, Nonexample (page 85)	x	x	X	x		X		x		
14. Fact-First Questioning (page 87)		x	x			X	X			
15. Feedback to Feed-Forward (page 89)		x	x			x		X	X	X
16. Fist to Five (page 92)		x	x					X	X	
17. Four Corners (page 94)	X	x		x	x	x				

(Continued)

43

Figure 3.5 (Continued)

FACT (Formative Assessment Classroom Technique)	Elicit & Identify Preconceptions	Engage & Motivate Students	Activate Thinking & Promote Metacognition	Provide Stimuli for Mathematical Discussion	Initiate Exploring of Mathematical Ideas	Formal Concept Development & Transfer	Improve Questioning & Responses	Provide Feedback to Teacher or Student	Peer & Self-Assessment	Reflection
18. Frayer Model (page 96)	X	x	X			X				
19. Friendly Talk Probes (page 99)	X	X	X	x	x	X				X
20. Give Me Five (page 101)		x								
21. Hot Seat Questioning (page 103)		x	x	x		x	X			X
22. Human Scatter Graph (page 105)	X	x	X	x	x	x				x
23. Is It Fair? (page 108)	x	x	X	x	x	x				
24. I Used to Think . . . But Now I Know . . . (page 109)		x	X						X	X
25. Justified List (page 111)	X	x	X	x		X				x
26. Justified True or False Statements (page 114)	X	x	X	x	x	X				
27. K-W-L Variations (page 116)	X	x	X							x
28. Learning Goals Inventory (LGI) (page 119)	x	x	X						x	x
29. Look Back (page 121)		x	x					x		X
30. Matching Cards (page 123)	X	x	X	X	x	X				
31. Mathematicians' Ideas Comparison (page 125)	x	x	X	x	x	X		x		

FACT (Formative Assessment Classroom Technique)	Elicit & Identify Preconceptions	Engage & Motivate Students	Activate Thinking & Promote Metacognition	Provide Stimuli for Mathematical Discussion	Initiate Exploring of Mathematical Ideas	Formal Concept Development & Transfer	Improve Questioning & Responses	Provide Feedback to Teacher or Student	Peer & Self-Assessment	Reflection
32. More A–More B Probes (page 130)	X	X	X	X	X	X				
33. Muddiest Point (page 132)		X	X					X	X	X
34. No-Hands Questioning (page 134)	X	X	X				X			
35. Odd One Out (page 137)	X	X	X	X		X				
36. Opposing Views Probes (page 139)	X	X	X	X	X	X				
37. Over-generalization Probe (page 141)	X	X	X	X	X	X				
38. Partner Speaks (page 143)		X	X	X		X	X	X	X	
39. Pass the Problem (page 145)		X	X	X		X	X	X		
40. P-E-O Probes (page 147)	X	X	X	X	X	X				
41. Peer-to-Peer Focused Feedback (page 151)		X	X			X	X	X	X	X
42. A Picture Tells a Thousand Words (page 153)		X	X		X	X	X	X		X
43. POMS: Point of Most Significance (page 155)		X	X					X	X	X
44. Popsicle Stick Questioning (page 157)		X	X				X	X		
45. PVF: Paired Verbal Fluency (page 159)	X	X	X					X	X	X

(Continued)

Figure 3.5 (Continued)

FACT (Formative Assessment Classroom Technique)	Elicit & Identify Preconceptions	Engage & Motivate Students	Activate Thinking & Promote Metacognition	Provide Stimuli for Mathematical Discussion	Initiate Exploring of Mathematical Ideas	Formal Concept Development & Transfer	Improve Questioning & Responses	Provide Feedback to Teacher or Student	Peer & Self-Assessment	Reflection
46. Question Generating (page 161)	×	×	×	×		×	×			
47. Response Cards (page 163)		×	×	×		×	×	×		
48. Same A–Same B Probes (page 165)	×	×	×	×	×	×				×
49. Sequencing Cards (page 167)	×	×	×			×			×	×
50. Sticky Bars (page 169)	×	×	×	×	×	×				
51. Strategy Harvest (page 172)	×	×	×	×	×	×		×	×	×
52. Strategy Probe (page 174)	×	×	×	×		×				×
53. Student Evaluation of Learning Gains (page 177)		×	×					×	×	×
54. Student Interviews (page 179)	×	×	×				×			
55. Terminology Inventory Probe (page 181)	×	×	×			×			×	×
56. Ten–Two (page 184)		×	×			×		×	×	×
57. Thinking Log (page 186)		×	×				×		×	×
58. Think Alouds (page 188)	×	×	×			×		×	×	×
59. Think–Pair–Share (page 190)	×	×	×	×	×	×	×	×	×	×
60. Thought Experiments (page 191)	×	×	×	×	×	×				
61. Three-Minute Pause (page 193)		×	×			×		×	×	
62. Three-Two-One (page 195)	×	×	×						×	×

FACT (Formative Assessment Classroom Technique)	Elicit & Identify Preconceptions	Engage & Motivate Students	Activate Thinking & Promote Metacognition	Provide Stimuli for Mathematical Discussion	Initiate Exploring of Mathematical Ideas	Formal Concept Development & Transfer	Improve Questioning & Responses	Provide Feedback to Teacher or Student	Peer & Self-Assessment	Reflection
63. Thumbs Up, Thumbs Down (page 197)	X	x	x			x		X	X	
64. Traffic Light Cards (page 199)	X	x	x			x		X	X	x
65. Traffic Light Cups (page 201)		x	x					X	X	
66. Traffic Light Dots (page 203)		x	x			x		X	X	x
67. Two-Minute Paper (page 204)		x	x			x		X	X	x
68. Two or Three Before Me (page 206)		x	x			x	X			
69. Two Stars and a Wish (page 207)		x	x			x	x	X	X	x
70. Two Thirds Testing (page 210)		x	X			x	x	X	X	
71. Volleyball, Not Ping-Pong! (page 211)	x	X	X	x		x	X			
72. Wait Time Variations (page 213)	x	x	X			x	X			
73. What Are You Doing and Why? (page 217)		x	x			x		X	x	
74. Whiteboarding (page 218)	X	X	X	x	x	X	x	x		
75. Word Sort (page 221)	X	X	X	X		X		x		x

X: *main purpose*
x: *secondary purposes*

4

Get the FACTs!

75 Mathematics Formative Assessment Classroom Techniques (FACTs)

The 75 mathematics FACTs selected for this chapter were gathered from a variety of sources. Many of the techniques described in this section were developed, practiced, or refined by the authors during their many years as classroom teachers and teacher educators. Some were contributed by practicing classroom teachers or are strategies that have been in popular use for many years. Others were adapted from the literature on formative assessment. In selecting a FACT for inclusion in this chapter, each one was reviewed against a set of considerations:

1. *Content Validity:* Is the FACT valid for eliciting information about students' mathematical ideas and ways of thinking?

2. *Engagement:* Is the FACT engaging to students? Would students readily respond to the assessment technique?

3. *Flexibility:* Can the FACT be used in a range of classroom configurations, including individual learning, small groups, and whole-class discussions and activities? Can it be adapted to fit a range of classroom contexts and diversity of students?

4. *Inquiry Based*: Does the FACT promote the spirit of mathematical inquiry and launch into exploration and development of students' mathematical ideas?

5. *Ease of Use:* Is the FACT easy to administer and respond to? Does it use minimal class time? Are the materials readily available? Can the data be quickly collected and analyzed?

6. *Reciprocal Benefits:* Does the FACT benefit students by promoting thinking as well as benefit teachers by informing instruction?

7. *Impact on Opportunity to Learn:* Will the FACT make a difference in the classroom learning environment? Will it increase opportunities for all students to learn mathematics when used effectively?

As you peruse this collection of 75 FACTs, make note of the ones that seem most appropriate for your classroom situation, experience, and instructional goals. Carefully read the information and example provided for each FACT. After using a FACT, add your own notes at the end of the description to describe how it worked in your setting, including any modifications or suggestions that would improve its use in the classroom.

The FACTs are listed alphabetically. Ideally the FACTs would be grouped by similar purpose. Since the purposes of each FACT are multiple and overlapping (as seen in Figure 3.5), it was not possible to group them in this way. If you are looking for FACTs that can be used for a specific purpose, scroll down the column on the matrix (Figure 3.5) for that particular purpose and note the FACTS that are listed there. These can then be quickly located alphabetically or by using the list in the Contents.

Each FACT follows a format that includes the following:

Description. This short paragraph provides a brief snapshot of the FACT—a concise overview describing what it is and how it is used.

How This FACT Promotes Student Learning. This section highlights the impact of the FACT on the student. It describes ways in which the FACT enhances learning, including stimulating metacognition, encouraging mathematical discourse, providing a mechanism for feedback, using "think time" to increase opportunities for students to respond to questions, and promoting self-assessment and reflection. As you use a FACT, note the ways in which your students respond to it and connect it to what they are learning.

How This FACT Informs Instruction. This section highlights the impact of the FACT on teaching practice. It describes ways in which the FACT can be used to support classroom discussion and inform instruction, such as eliciting answers, gathering information on students' thinking that is used to modify lessons, improving questioning, differentiating for individuals or groups of students, obtaining student feedback on effectiveness of lessons, monitoring learning over time, providing feedback to students, and encouraging mathematical discourse. As you use a FACT, note the extent to which it affects your teaching philosophy, beliefs about student learning, and repertoire of teaching strategies.

Design and Administration. This description provides information on selecting content and the preparation needed to use a FACT, including materials, time, modeling, and group work configurations. It also describes how to implement the FACT, including what both the teacher and the student are doing during its use.

General Implementation Attributes. This section describes three general attributes for implementing a FACT in the classroom, each of which ranges from low to high. *Ease of Use* rates the general mechanics of using a FACT, such as availability and preparation of materials, amount of practice students need before using it, and extent of teacher facilitation needed to use it effectively with students. *Time Demand* rates how quickly and efficiently a FACT can be used relative to the benefits gained from its use. A high rating does not necessarily mean the FACT is not useful, but rather that considerable time needs to be invested in using it effectively. *Cognitive Demand* describes the level of complexity of a FACT in terms of how much is required from the students to think and respond to the FACT. This may vary depending on the content used with a particular FACT.

Modifications. This section provides suggestions for modifying a FACT for different audiences. For example, it may describe ways to adjust the cognitive load for students depending on their age and developmental level. It also describes ways to modify the way the FACT is used, such as changing the ways students are grouped for discussion or adapting a paper-and-pencil technique to fit an oral discussion format.

Caveats. With every good technique, there are always cautions to consider when using that technique to improve teaching and learning. This section describes immediate as well as long-term cautions and pitfalls to be aware of when using a particular FACT.

Use With Other Disciplines. While the FACTs in this chapter are described according to how they are used in mathematics, many of the FACTs are readily applicable to other content areas, either as is or with modification. Some, where noted, are specific to the discipline of mathematics. As teachers work within interdisciplinary teams in their schools or in a self-contained classroom, it is helpful to use common techniques across disciplines, creating a classroom or school culture that values and uses a common language, strategies, and routines for formative assessment. When applicable, connections to the disciplines of science, health, social studies, language arts, foreign language, and the visual and performing arts are noted. However, these connections are not set in stone. You may see ways to use a FACT with other disciplines not noted by the authors. In addition, *science indicates the FACT is also included in the science version of this book, *Science Formative Assessment: 75 Practical Strategies for Linking Assessment, Instruction, and Learning* (Keeley, 2008).

Examples. Embedded in each of the 75 FACT descriptions is an illustrative content-specific example showing how the FACT can be used with students in the mathematics classroom. Examples may be K–12 or grade-level specific. They may include authentic student responses, a sample response sheet or template, or a scenario or description that illustrates its use. The examples are intended to give the user a glimpse into what a FACT actually looks like in practice.

My Notes. This is a blank area for you to record notes after you try out a FACT. Some things to record might include the date, which class you used it with, successes or challenges in using it, suggestions for modifying or improving its use, insights you gained from your students, or reflections on how it affected your teaching. In addition, we suggest that you build a file or three-ring binder of the materials you create to use with each FACT (for example, specific worksheets for student replies, sample questions, or reflection prompts) as well as student artifacts that can be shared with others in your professional learning community to gain insights into the use of formative assessment to enhance teaching and learning. Furthermore, we encourage you to share ways you have used different FACTs, made modifications, or developed new FACTs. Please visit the website www .uncoveringstudentideas.org to share your ideas or learn more about ways others are using FACTs.

Now it's time to get the FACTs! The FACTs are organized alphabetically and numbered on the matrix on Figure 3.5. The matrix can help you select FACTs that match a specific purpose or stage in your instructional cycle. Some FACTs will appeal to your style of instruction while others may not. There are plenty of techniques to choose from. In order to use a FACT effectively, it must resonate with your teaching philosophy and instructional style and be an appropriate match to the content you are teaching. As you come across FACTs you might try out in your classroom, consider placing sticky notes on the pages so you can go back and revisit them. Start small by selecting one or two FACTs to try out. Make notes on how well the technique worked for you. Continue adding more techniques that fit your instructional style and teaching goals as you assimilate new techniques into your practice. As you become more proficient in using the FACTs, your repertoire of instructional strategies will increase; this will make a significant impact on your teaching and, ultimately, improve student learning.

#1. A & D STATEMENTS

Description

Students use *A & D Statements* to analyze a set of "fact or fiction" statements. In the first part of *A & D Statements*, students may choose to agree or disagree with a statement or to state that they need more information. In addition, they are asked to describe their thinking about why they agree, disagree, or are unsure. In the second part of the FACT, students describe what they can do to investigate the statement by testing their ideas, examining what is already known, or using other means of mathematical inquiry. Figure 4.1 shows an example of *A & D Statements* for the topic *Fractions*.

Figure 4.1   Fraction *A & D Statements*

Statement	How Can You Find Out?
1. 9/16 is larger than 5/8. ___ agree ___ disagree ___ it depends on ___ not sure My thoughts:	
2. Denominators must be larger than numerators. ___ agree ___ disagree ___ it depends on ___ not sure My thoughts:	
3. Decimals can be written as fractions. ___ agree ___ disagree ___ it depends on ___ not sure My thoughts:	
4. Dividing a number by a fraction makes a larger number. ___ agree ___ disagree ___ it depends on ___ not sure My thoughts:	

How This FACT Promotes Student Learning

A & D Statements provide an opportunity for students to practice meta-cognition (thinking about their own understanding). In addition, this FACT "primes the pump" for mathematical inquiry by having students describe how they could prove each statement using concrete or virtual manipulatives or mathematical procedures, or identify information sources that would help them determine the validity of the statement. When used in small groups, *A & D Statements* encourages mathematical discussion and argumentation. Through the process of defending their ideas or challenging the ideas of others, students may solidify their own thinking, consider the alternative views of others, or modify their own thinking as new information replaces or becomes assimilated into their existing knowledge and beliefs.

How This FACT Informs Instruction

A & D Statements can be used at the beginning of a learning cycle to elicit students' ideas about a mathematical topic. The information helps teachers identify areas where students may need targeted instructional experiences that will challenge their preconceptions and increase confidence in their own ideas. The results can be used to differentiate instruction for selected groups of students who have similar ideas about the topic. Students' descriptions of how they can find out whether the statements are correct provide data the teacher can use regarding their ability to prove their ideas or identify appropriate sources of information that confirm their ideas.

Design and Administration

Select *A & D Statements* that focus on specific concepts or procedures that students will encounter in the mathematics curriculum. Develop statements that can launch into mathematical inquiry using manipulatives, learned or invented algorithms and procedures, or use of various information sources. Examine the research on learning to find common errors or misconceptions related to the topic. Use some of these common errors and misconceptions to develop the statements. Try to develop at least one statement each for the *agree, disagree,* and *it depends on* choices.

Students should first be given the opportunity to respond to the FACT individually. If they choose *disagree* or *it depends on*, ask them to provide an example that refutes the statement or makes the statement true in some cases but not in others. Then, have students discuss their ideas in small groups, coming to consensus on why they agree or disagree with the statement while noting any disagreements among group members. After they have had time to consider others' ideas and design a way to conduct further tests, solve problems, or research the information, allow time for small groups to investigate the statements as exploratory activities. These activities provide a common experience for whole-class discussion aimed at resolving discrepancies between students' initial ideas and discoveries made during their explorations. The teacher should listen carefully as the class shares its findings, building off the students' ideas to provide guidance and clarification that will help students accommodate new mathematical understandings.

General Implementation Attributes

Ease of Use: Medium   Cognitive Demand: Medium/High
Time Demand: Medium

Modifications

This FACT can be modified for younger students by focusing on one statement at a time, rather than a set of statements.

Caveats

This FACT should not be used solely as a true-or-false assessment. It is important to provide follow-up experiences for students to investigate the statements, particularly those in which there is a conflict between students' existing ideas and the correct mathematical idea.

Use With Other Disciplines

This FACT can also be used in *science*, social studies, language arts, health, foreign language, and visual and performing arts.

My Notes

_____

_____

_____

#2. AGREEMENT CIRCLES

Description

Agreement Circles provide a kinesthetic way to activate thinking and engage students in discussing and defending their mathematical ideas. Students stand in a large circle as the teacher reads a statement. The students who agree with the statement step to the center of the circle. Those who disagree remain standing on the outside of the circle. Those in the inner circle face their peers still standing around the outside circle and then divide themselves into small groups of students who agree and disagree. The small groups then engage in discussion to defend their thinking. This is repeated with several rounds of statements relating to the same topic, each time with students starting by standing around the large circle.

How This FACT Promotes Student Learning

Agreement Circles activate students' thinking about mathematical ideas related to a topic they are studying. As the statements are made, students access their existing knowledge. They must justify their thinking to their peers about why they agree or disagree with the statement. As they engage in discussion with their opposing partners, either group may modify their ideas as new information convinces them that their original ideas may need adjustment.

How This FACT Informs Instruction

This FACT can be used prior to instruction or during the conceptual development stage, when formally introduced concepts may need reinforcement. The teacher can get a quick visual sense of students' understanding according to which part of the circle students are standing in. As the teacher circulates and listens to students explain why they agree or disagree, information about students' thinking is revealed that can be used to design further learning experiences or revisit prior experiences aimed at developing conceptual understanding.

Design and Administration

Develop a set of three to five conceptual statements related to the topic of instruction. Some of the statements should be true, others false. False statements can be developed by examining the research on students' commonly held ideas. For example, a set of statements about quadrilaterals might be the following:

1. All squares are rectangles.
2. All rhombuses are quadrilaterals.
3. The opposite sides of a trapezoid are parallel.
4. All rhombuses have right angles.
5. Parallelograms cannot have angles greater than 90 degrees.

Begin by having students form a large circle. Read the first statement; then give students 5 to 10 seconds to think. Ask students to move to the center of the circle if they agree with the statement and stay on the outside if they disagree. Match students up one to two, one to three, one to four, one to five, two to three, three to five, or whatever the proportion of agreement to disagreement indicates, and give them a few minutes to defend their ideas in small groups. Call time, and have students go back to the circle for another round. When finished with all rounds, the next step depends on the stage of instruction. If the FACT was used to activate and elicit student thinking, then the next step is to plan and provide lessons that will help students explore their ideas further and formulate understandings. If the FACT is used during the concept development stage, provide an opportunity for a whole-class discussion to resolve conceptual conflicts, formalize development of the key ideas, and solidify understanding.

General Implementation Attributes

Ease of Use: Medium/High   Cognitive Demand: Medium/High
Time Demand: Medium

Modifications

For younger students, limit the number of statements. If all students end up in either the middle or outside of the circle, have them pair up to explain why they agree or disagree. Often there are differences in the justification of their ideas, even if both students agree or disagree with the statement. If students' arguments can be supported by drawings, provide each student with an individual whiteboard or paper to write on when they discuss and defend their ideas in the circle. As students work through the set of statements and discussions, their initial ideas may change toward the end of the set of questions. Consider providing one more repeat round at the end of the full set or after each statement to allow students the opportunity to change their position if their initial ideas were modified during the discussion.

Caveats

Students need to be confident in their own ideas when using this strategy. Encourage students to refrain from changing their answer because they see a majority of students move to the inside or outside of the circle.

Use With Other Disciplines

This FACT can also be used in *science*, social studies, language arts, health, foreign language, and visual and performing arts.

My Notes

_____

_____

_____

#3. ALWAYS, SOMETIMES, OR NEVER TRUE

Description

Always, Sometimes, or Never True involves a set of statements that students examine and decide if they are always true, sometimes true, or never true. This strategy is useful in revealing whether students overgeneralize or undergeneralize a mathematical concept. In addition, they are asked to provide a justification for their answer. Figure 4.2 shows an example of *Always, Sometimes, or Never True* for a lesson on multiples.

How This FACT Promotes Student Learning

Always, Sometimes, or Never True provides an opportunity for students to practice metacognition (thinking about their own understanding). In addition, this FACT helps students understand that whenever a mathematical assertion is made, it should be checked out to determine whether it always applies, applies in some cases, or never applies. The FACT also encourages mathematical thinking by having students come up with examples and counterexamples to support their answers. When used in small groups, this FACT encourages mathematical discussion and argumentation.

How This FACT Informs Instruction

Always, Sometimes, or Never True can be used at the beginning of a learning cycle to elicit students' prior ideas about a mathematical topic, or it can be used to check for understanding after students have had opportunities to learn about the topic. This FACT is helpful in revealing whether students over-apply or misapply a concept and may point out the limitations of the context in which students learned the idea. The probe encourages teachers to ask students to examine the validity of statements and get into the habit of identifying examples that work and counterexamples that do not work.

Figure 4.2   *Always, Sometimes, or Never True*

1. Multiples of 5 end in 5. ☐ Always ☐ Sometimes ☐ Never	Justify your answer.
2. Multiples of 2 end in an odd number. ☐ Always ☐ Sometimes ☐ Never	Justify your answer.
3. If you add the digits together in a number made up of two or more digits, it will be a multiple of 3. ☐ Always ☐ Sometimes ☐ Never	Justify your answer.
4. Multiples of 7 are odd numbers. ☐ Always ☐ Sometimes ☐ Never	Justify your answer.
5. Multiples of 10 end in 0. ☐ Always ☐ Sometimes ☐ Never	Justify your answer.
6. Multiples of 4 end in either 2, 4, 6, or 8. ☐ Always ☐ Sometimes ☐ Never	Justify your answer.

Design and Administration

If used before instruction, select statements that focus on specific concepts or procedures students will encounter in the mathematics curriculum. If used after instruction, choose statements that address the concepts students have had opportunities to develop. Examine the research on learning to find common errors or misconceptions related to the topic. Use some of these common errors and misconceptions to develop the statements. Develop a statement set that includes at least one of each choice: *always*, *sometimes*, and *never*.

Students should first be given the opportunity to respond to the FACT individually. Then have students discuss their ideas in small groups, coming to consensus on whether they agree that it is always, sometimes, or never true, and providing examples to support their ideas. Follow up with a whole-class discussion, share the examples students came up with, probe and guide students toward other examples that may not have surfaced, and develop a final class consensus on the validity of each statement, justified by examples.

General Implementation Attributes

Ease of Use: High   Cognitive Demand: High
Time Demand: Medium

Modifications

This FACT can be modified for younger students by focusing on one statement at a time rather than on a set of statements. To encourage justification, ask students to describe how they would convince someone that it is always true, sometimes true, or never true.

Caveats

Make sure students try out multiple examples for each statement before deciding whether it is always, sometimes, or never true.

Use With Other Disciplines

This FACT can also be used in science, social studies, language arts, health, foreign language, and visual and performing arts.

My Notes

_____

_____

_____

#4. CARD SORTS

Description

Card Sorts is a sorting activity in which students collaboratively sort a set of cards with pictures, numbers, symbols, or words according to a specific characteristic or category. Students sort the cards based on their preexisting knowledge about the concept or procedure. As students sort the cards, they discuss their reasons for placing each card into a designated group.

How This FACT Promotes Student Learning

Card Sorts provide an opportunity for students to access their prior knowledge. In addition, they promote metacognition by surfacing what they think they understand as well as any uncertainties in their thinking. As students work in pairs or small groups to sort the cards, they put forth their own ideas for others to consider, strengthen their skills at explaining and justifying their ideas, evaluate the thinking of others, and modify their own thinking as new information persuades them to reconsider their original ideas. Since card sorts can often have a variety of outcomes, this helps students recognize that there can sometimes be more than one right answer in mathematics. Card sorts can also be used to help students revisit material they learned previously in order to scaffold their learning for the next lesson.

How This FACT Informs Instruction

Card Sorts provide a way for the teacher to elicit students' preconceptions, assess students' ability to transfer knowledge when provided with new examples or contexts, and look for areas of uncertainty or disagreement among students that may signify the need for further instructional opportunities. *Card Sorts* are best used in small groups to encourage students to share their thinking with their peers. While students discuss their ideas, the teacher circulates around the classroom listening to students agree, disagree, or express their uncertainty. By probing further as students lay out their cards, the teacher gains specific insights into students' levels of understanding. Using this FACT, if the teacher knows how many cards should go into each category, he or she can in effect observe students' ideas from a distance and quickly evaluate the progress of the different groups. The teacher notes ways of thinking or examples that seem to be problematic to make them the focus for subsequent lessons.

The cards can also be used to orchestrate whole-class discussion. The discourse that ensues provides feedback to learners to help resolve conceptual difficulties, while the teacher maintains a nonjudgmental role as listener and clarifier, guiding students toward the accepted mathematical ideas.

Figure 4.3 is an example of a card sort used to determine whether students can choose all the correct values of various digits in a given decimal (Rose & Arline, 2009). The card sort allows the teacher to observe how well the students understand the role of the decimal point and the relationship among the digits in the ones, tenths, and hundredths place. As students discuss their ideas, the teacher can see whether students are able to move beyond just naming digits in various places to recognizing the value of the digit in relationship to the number.

Figure 4.3 Concept Cards

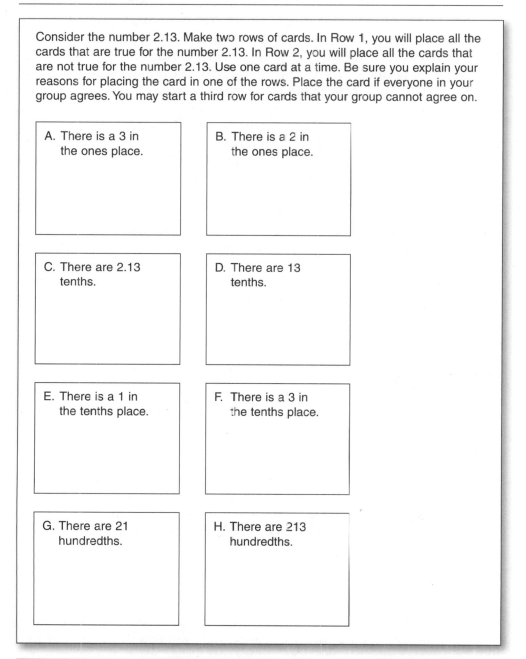

Source: Adapted from Rose & Arline (2009).

Design and Administration

Prepare sets of cards that align with the content goal of the lesson or cluster of lessons students will encounter. It is helpful to use tools such as *Mathematics Curriculum Topic Study* (Keeley & Rose, 2006) to examine the research on student learning in order to identify common errors and misconceptions that may be used as examples on the cards (see Appendix). You can place text on index cards or make cards from preprinted matchbook-size squares on a sheet of paper, cut out and sorted into zip-lock bags (or have students cut out the squares). Provide students with category headers under which to sort their cards. Encourage students to lay out the cards in a row or column under the category header rather than on top of each other so you can see how students sort each individual item. Have students work in small groups to discuss each card and come to a common agreement on which category to place it in. Listen carefully to students as they discuss and argue their ideas. Note cases in which you may need to provide additional instructional opportunities to address students' misunderstandings. If a record of student thinking is needed, provide individual students or small groups with a recording sheet to note where each card was placed along with a justification for its placement, or glue cards onto paper. A *Justified List* probe can be easily turned into a *Card Sort* by placing each of the statements, words, numbers, symbols, or shapes listed on a card. (See Appendix for a source of assessment probes that can be used as card sorts.)

General Implementation Attributes

Ease of Use: High   Cognitive Demand: Medium/High
Time Demand: Medium

Modifications

Consider adding a third category of *it depends on* or *we're not sure yet*. For younger students or less fluent readers, use pictures to accompany words, where possible. For younger students, limit to no more than two sorting categories for younger students—those that fit the concept and those that do not. For older students, consider using multiple categories where appropriate.

Caveats

This FACT can turn into a vocabulary exercise if the words are unfamiliar to students. Some students, particularly English language learners, may need help reading the cards or require visual cues. Emphasize that students need to talk about each card before they assign it to a category.

Discourage students from quickly sorting all the cards first and then discussing them after the sort. Watch for students who dominate the sorting and discussion and intervene if necessary to provide all students in a group with the opportunity to contribute.

Use With Other Disciplines

This FACT can also be used in *science*, social studies, language arts, health, foreign language, and visual and performing arts.

My Notes

#5. CCC: COLLABORATIVE CLUED CORRECTIONS

Description

CCC provides an alternative way to mark student papers with comments that encourage revision. Students complete and submit an assignment made up of selected responses or short answers. The teacher purposely selects a sample of student papers that includes incorrect or partially correct responses. The teacher reviews the samples and provides feedback regarding the number and types of errors or areas for improvement. However, the specific questions or area for correction in each question are not explicitly identified by the teacher. They are only "clued." The sample set of "clued" papers are distributed to small groups of students, who work together to collaboratively seek out the problem areas and revise them.

How This FACT Promotes Student Learning

The purpose of this FACT is to provide feedback to students on homework or class assignments, which typically get corrected, passed back, and quickly forgotten. The *CCC* technique is supported by Black and Wiliam's (1998) research on how learning improves when students are given feedback on their work that encourages revision rather than marking wrong answers and giving a grade, which has been noted to sometimes have a negative effect on students. Working together as a group provides all students with an opportunity to activate and discuss their own ideas and modify them based on peer feedback. The task of identifying the areas that need improvement, based on the teacher's clues, provides greater content engagement in learning than passing back marked assignments. Marked assignments, particularly when students have multiple errors, are often ignored if there is no opportunity for feedback, thus contributing little to furthering content understanding.

How This FACT Informs Instruction

CCC is an example of a technique in which passing back classwork or homework assignments can be used as a learning opportunity while helping teachers manage feedback on student work in an efficient way. Not every student paper needs to be corrected and commented on by the teacher. By selecting representative samples of work which small groups of students then collaborate on to revise, the teacher is free to circulate among groups to provide additional feedback that will support student learning.

Design and Administration

CCCs are best used with a problem-solving assignment of just a few questions that offer a springboard into engaging learning opportunities for students to activate and explain their thinking. Select papers for the CCC that include common errors made by students in the class. Provide useful comments on the paper, but do not explicitly point out where the error or area for improvement lies.

Feedback and revision groups should be formed based on the learning needs and social interaction of the individuals in the group. Each small group should include the student whose paper was marked with clues. Students work together in their small groups to identify the areas of correction or improvement, discuss their ideas related to the questions on the assignment, and collaboratively revise the work once all members of the group accept the corrections. The work is resubmitted and then becomes representative of the group rather than the individual. This encourages others to participate even though the student work is not their own. After submitting the group's work, the teacher returns the remaining unmarked papers for students to revise individually or with a partner. Students become more interested in reviewing their unmarked papers and looking for areas to change or improve on after having an opportunity to first analyze another student's work.

It is important to provide time to teach this strategy and allow students an opportunity to practice it. One way of doing this is to choose one or two samples of anonymous student work to copy, write clues, and use with the whole class in examining the clues, looking for the areas that need revision, and discussing and making revisions to improve the quality and accuracy of the work.

General Implementation Attributes

Ease of Use: Medium
Time Demand: Medium

Cognitive Demand: Medium/High

Modifications

Use short-answer, basic statements with students who have a difficult time deciphering handwriting or reading a lot of student handwritten text. Even though the questions and responses in a selected-response format or basic computation problems are not as robust as a problem-solving format, the discussions that ensue during the CCC provide an opportunity for rich content-focused dialogue. Another way to use this strategy is to pass back student tests marked with the number of correct responses rather than a grade. Students then use their returned tests to find and correct the responses that have errors. Teachers may provide clues to guide students in finding their errors; students can work in small groups to help each other and consult their notes, books, or other classroom resources they may have used.

Caveats

Be careful that students do not use this as an opportunity to put less effort into their own work if they know that only a few papers will be selected for revision. Set norms so that a student whose paper is selected does not feel that the strategy is a negative critique. This FACT works best in classroom environments where students embrace the idea that their own work is an important means of helping *all* students improve the quality of their work. Make sure that all students have an opportunity to review their own work after the CCC, regardless of whether their papers were the ones selected to be clued.

Use With Other Disciplines

This FACT can also be used in *science*, social studies, language arts, health, foreign language, and visual and performing arts.

My Notes

_____

_____

_____

#6. COMMENTS-ONLY MARKING

Description

Comments-Only Marking is a way to provide feedback to students that research has shown is more effective in getting students to use feedback to improve their work. In a study described in the book *Assessment for Learning* (Black et al., 2003), randomly selected students were given an assessment task to complete and then received one of three types of feedback. The first group received tailored, written comments only; the second group received marks (answers marked right or wrong, often accompanied by a grade) only; and the third group received both marks and comments. On subsequent tasks, the students who received comments only performed better than the other two groups. The research indicates that feedback that emphasizes only ways to improve versus feedback that passes judgment on students' abilities (marks and grades), even though comments were provided with the marks and grade in the third group, is more effective at getting students to consider and use the feedback for improvement.

How This FACT Promotes Student Learning

The purpose of this FACT is to provide feedback to students on ways they can improve their work. Making comments only is nonjudgmental; on the other hand, students who often receive a marked-up paper with a poor grade (with or without comments) may feel that they aren't "good at math" and fail to use any comments made to improve their work. Likewise, students who get a good grade but can still improve will often ignore the comments when the grade is good, because they feel their work is "good enough." Providing only the feedback they need to improve, without marks and grades affecting their self-esteem, whether it is high or low, provides students with what they need to further develop their understanding and make progress in their learning.

How This FACT Informs Instruction

The primary purpose of this FACT is to provide an alternative to feedback when a grade is not essential. Seeing the difference it makes in learning for their students when comments only are used helps teachers break the cycle of correcting and grading every piece of work.

Design and Administration

This FACT is time-consuming, because teachers need to provide substantive feedback that can be used by the student. The feedback needs to provide guidance to students on how to improve. Comments in the margin or Post-it notes next to an area of improvement can indicate to the student areas where he or she can improve.

General Implementation Attributes

Ease of Use: Medium   Cognitive Demand: Medium
Time Demand: High

Modifications

This FACT can be combined with FACT #69, *Two Stars and a Wish*. The teacher does not always have to be the source of the comments. Have students work in groups to provide comments on other students' papers. As you build a repertoire of comment types, consider creating a poster of codes for common feedback prompts and add new codes as needed.

Example Feedback Prompts and Codes

- Met Success Criteria (SC): This section provides evidence of meeting one of the criteria for success.
- Unclear Process (UP): Correct answer but am unsure of your process.
- Computation Error (CE): Find and correct calculation error.
- Use Word Wall (WW): Incorporate words from our unit word wall.
- Replace Term (RT): Incorrect use of the math term; can you find a different term to use?
- Number Correct (NC #): You have correctly answered this number of problems. Determine which are correct and incorrect. For the incorrect problems, find and fix your mistake.

Caveats

The comments are useful only if they are substantive enough to provide guidance for students to improve their work or see areas where they did well without actually doing the work for the student. Avoid vague comments like "Good job here," "You could improve here," "Be careful with your calculation," "Check your work," and symbols such as smiling and sad faces. They do little to provide useful feedback.

Use With Other Disciplines

This FACT can also be used in science, social studies, language arts, health, foreign language, and visual and performing arts.

My Notes

_____

_____

_____

#7. COMMIT AND TOSS

Description

Commit and Toss is an anonymous elicitation technique used to make students' thinking visible to the class. It provides a safe, fun, and engaging way for all students to make their ideas known without individual students being identified by their answers. Students are given an assessment probe. After completing the probe, students crumple their papers into a ball and, upon a signal from the teacher, toss the paper balls around the room until the teacher instructs them to stop and pick up or hold on to one paper. Students take the paper they end up with and share the answer and explanation that is described on the paper they are holding. They read only from the paper that is in their hand and do not present their own ideas.

How This FACT Promotes Student Learning

Commit and Toss incorporates an essential component of conceptual change teaching and learning—committing to an answer that best matches one's own thinking and providing an explanation for why that answer was chosen. Before students crumple and toss their papers, they must think about the question posed, commit to a response, and explain the thinking that informed the answer they selected. Once answers are anonymously shared, this FACT helps students recognize that it is common for students in a class to have different ideas. Confidence is built when a student realizes that he or she is not the only one to have a different answer. It helps students see that "wrong" answers can be just as valuable for informing learning opportunities and constructing new ideas as "right" answers. It provides a nonthreatening opportunity to make everyone's ideas public regardless of whether they are right or wrong. It allows students to tap into others' thinking, comparing their own ideas with those of others in the class. Since the technique is anonymous, individual students are more likely to reveal their own ideas rather than providing a "safe" answer they think the teacher wants to hear, which may not be what they actually believe.

How This FACT Informs Instruction

Commit and Toss allows the teacher to get a quick read on ideas and explanations held by the class. It is a very engaging way to get a class snapshot of student thinking. The information is used to design and provide targeted learning opportunities for the development of mathematical ideas; these should include opportunities for students to test their ideas or gather more information that will support or modify their thinking.

Design and Administration

Choose a content goal. Design or select a forced-choice assessment item that requires students to commit to a selected answer and provide a justification for the answer they selected, such as the *What's the Area?* probe example in Figure 4.4.

Figure 4.4 Example of a Probe Used With *Commit and Toss*

What's the Area?

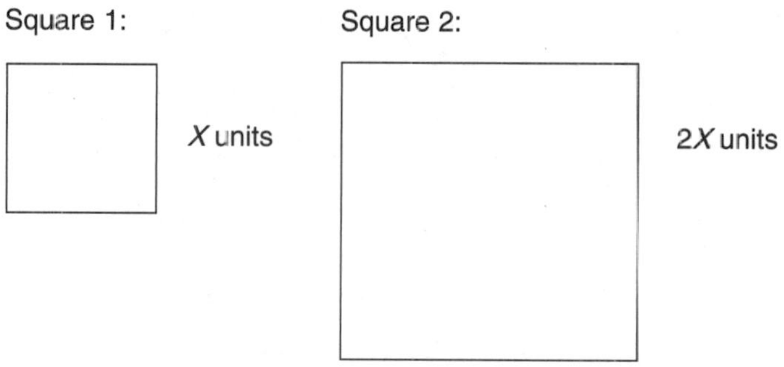

Square 1:

X units

Square 2:

$2X$ units

Circle the letter of the statement that describes how the area of square 1 compares to the area of square 2:

    A. Doubles in size
    B. Same size
    C. Quadruples in size
    D. Not enough information to compare

Explain your reasoning:

Source: Rose & Arline (2009), p. 117. Used with permission.

Remind students not to write their names on their papers. Give students time to think about and record their responses, encouraging them to explain their ideas as best they can so that another student can understand their thinking. When everyone is ready, give the cue to crumple their papers into a ball, stand up, and toss them back and forth to other students. Students keep tossing and catching until the teacher tells them to stop. Make sure all students have a paper. Remind students that the paper they have in their hand will be the one they talk about, not the answer and explanation they wrote on their own paper.

After students catch a paper, give them time to read the response and try to "get into the other student's head" by making sense of what the student was thinking. Ask for a show of hands or use the *Four Corners* strategy to visually show the number of students who selected a particular response. You can have students form small groups according to the selected response on their papers and discuss the similarities or differences in the explanations provided and report out to the class. The teacher can list the ideas mentioned, avoiding any judgments, while noting the different ideas students have that will inform the instructional opportunities that will follow.

Once all the ideas have been made public and discussed, proceed with the targeted lesson. Or, if the FACT is used to lead into a class discussion, engage students in deciding which ideas they believe are most plausible and providing justification for their thinking. This is the time when they can share their own ideas. After providing an opportunity to examine the class's thinking, ask for a show of hands indicating how many students modified or completely changed their ideas. Also ask how many students are sticking with their original ideas. With consensus from the class, discard ideas that are no longer accepted by the class. If more than one idea is still accepted, decide how to investigate which ones are mathematically correct. Provide opportunities for students to use concepts and procedures they are familiar with to test their ideas or research information that will help them figure out the answer. Revisit these ideas again during the formal concept development stage to help students build a bridge between their commonly held ideas and the mathematically correct ideas. Ask students to consider what else it would take to convince them mathematically if they are still experiencing a dissonance between their ideas and the mathematically correct ones. See the Appendix for sources of assessment probes that can be used with this strategy.

General Implementation Attributes

Ease of Use: High   Cognitive Demand: Medium
Time Demand: Low

Modifications

This FACT can be modified to be a less rambunctious activity (but not nearly as much fun!) by changing it to a "commit, fold, and pass" where students fold their papers in half and pass it them around the room until the teacher gives the signal to stop passing. It can also be modified by having all students toss their papers into a receptacle such as a box or wastebasket. Once the receptacle is full, have each student reach in and take out a paper. The *Sticky Bars* strategy also works well with this FACT. After students have tossed their papers and looked at the one they caught, ask them to jot down the answer from the selected response part. The students can then bring their sticky notes up to the wall or whiteboard and create a class bar graph of the results. This visual display is followed by a discussion of the different explanations on their tossed and caught papers.

Caveats

This is a fun, engaging technique; for that reason, be careful not to overuse it, or it will lose its effectiveness. Remind students to honor anonymity even if they recognize someone's handwriting or get their own paper back. It is also important to establish the norm that disparaging or other types of belittling comments should never be made about the student paper they end up with.

Use With Other Disciplines

This FACT can also be used in *science*, social studies, language arts, health, foreign language, and visual and performing arts.

My Notes

_____

_____

_____

#8. CONCEPT ATTAINMENT CARDS

Description

Based on the landmark work of Jerome Bruner (Bruner, Goodnow, & Austin, 1956) on concept attainment, this FACT encourages students to develop their own definition of a concept by examining labeled cards showing examples and nonexamples of a concept. By comparing and contrasting various characteristics and attributes of the examples and nonexamples provided, students identify the defining features of the concept and apply those features to create a definition and additional examples and nonexamples (Joyce, Weil, & Calhoun, 2009).

How This FACT Promotes Student Learning

Coming up with defining features by examining examples and nonexamples requires different cognitive skills from those used to memorize a rule or definition. Students need to carefully consider the numbers or objects in terms of their characteristics and attributes. In this FACT, students are asked to generate their own rules or definitions as well as generate additional examples and nonexamples to demonstrate their understanding of a particular concept. By asking students to come up with their own rules, definitions, and additional examples, this FACT supports students in learning to generate examples, a critical skill they will use throughout their study of mathematics.

How This FACT Informs Instruction

An understanding of mathematical concepts and terminology is crucial to students' ability to understand and solve problems This FACT can help teachers assess the extent to which students are able to generate a rule or definition presented to them when learning about a new concept or mathematical term.

Design and Administration

This FACT is used after students have been introduced to the concept or term but before they have been given a formal definition. Students are asked to think about what they previously learned about a concept, examine labeled examples and nonexamples, and provide a supporting rule or operational definition for the concept. First, identify the concept or mathematical term for which you want to determine how well students are able to generate a rule or definition. Develop a list of examples and nonexamples for each of the various defining characteristics and attributes. Present the examples and nonexamples on individual cards so students can sort as needed. Figure 4.5 is an example used to assess students' understanding of the concept *polygon*.

Students can work individually, in pairs, or in small groups. Have students share the attributes of the examples as well as feedback on operational rules or definitions. The teacher can select certain attributes for a whole-class discussion and develop a class consensus on a rule or definition used to define the word or explain the concept. Reinforce the developed rule or definition by having students generate additional examples and nonexamples.

Figure 4.5   Example *Concept Attainment Cards*

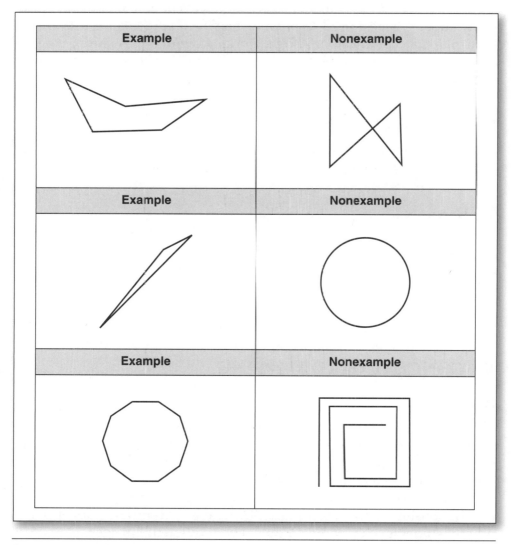

Source: Adapted from Rose Tobey & Minton (2010).

General Implementation Attributes

Ease of Use: Medium   Cognitive Demand: Medium
Time Demand: Medium

Modifications

This FACT can be used with the *Frayer Model*. It is particularly helpful for students who may need visual cues. For students not able to identify attributes with the initial sets of cards, have additional examples and non-examples ready.

Caveats

While this FACT could be used as an elicitation to identify prior knowledge, it is best used to monitor how well students have learned a particular concept or can develop a working definition as part of the concept development stage. Be sure to build in time to provide students with feedback.

Use With Other Disciplines

This FACT can also be used in science, social studies, language arts, health, foreign languages, and visual and performing arts.

My Notes

_____

_____

_____

#9. CONCEPT CARD MAPPING

Description

Concept Card Mapping is a variation on the familiar strategy of concept mapping (Novak, 1998). Instead of constructing their own concept maps from scratch, students are given cards with the concepts written on them. They move the cards around and arrange them as a connected web of knowledge. They create linkages between the concept cards that describe the relationship between concepts. Moving the cards provides an opportunity for students to explore and think about different linkages.

How This FACT Promotes Student Learning

Concept Card Mapping provides an opportunity for students to activate their prior knowledge, think about the relationships between familiar concepts, and make a visual representation of the connections in their own knowledge network. When students create maps collaboratively in small groups, the maps promote discussion. Individuals become more aware of their own ideas and may modify them accordingly as a result of the discussion generated in their group. Because there is no one "right answer," this FACT provides an open entry point for all learners. In the process of exploring their own and others' ideas about ways to arrange the cards, they use that information to connect concepts and terminology together in a coherent way, deepening their understanding of the structure of a topic. Students who tend not to speak up in class have been found to contribute freely in the nonthreatening activity of concept map-making (White & Gunstone, 1992).

How This FACT Informs Instruction

Teachers can use *Concept Card Mapping* as an elicitation prior to instruction or at key points in a sequence of lessons to gather information about how students make linkages among a connected set of concepts and terminology. Using a common set of predetermined words or phrases allows the teacher to see how different students or groups of students make conceptual sense of the same ideas in different ways. The student-generated sentences are examined carefully by the teacher to reveal any conceptual understandings or misunderstandings. The linkages made by students reveal the level of sophistication of their ideas, accuracy of content knowledge, and depth and breadth of their thinking. The information is used to inform the development of lessons that will provide students with an opportunity to explore and solidify important connections.

Different maps can be selected by the teacher to provide teacher-to-student and student-to-student feedback during the formal concept development phase of whole-class instruction. Discussion focuses on whether students agree or disagree with the connections made on the map and ways they may have made different linkages. The maps can also be used by the teacher to initiate questions that probe deeper for student understanding. *Concept Card Mapping* can be used again at the end of an instructional unit to help students reflect on the extent to which their conceptual connections changed since making their original map.

Design and Administration

For the purpose of this technique, a concept is a defined as a simple one- to three-word mental construct or short phrase that represents or categorizes a mathematical idea, such as center of spread, quadrilateral, rational number, or area of a circle (Carey, 2000; Erickson, 1998). Choose concepts central to the topic of instruction and place them in squares that students cut out from a sheet of paper. See the Appendix for a description of Mathematics Curriculum Topic Study, a process that uncovers the essential concepts in a standards-based topic (Keeley & Rose, 2006). If students have never created a concept map, start by introducing concept mapping with a familiar topic. Engage the class in practicing concept mapping through an interactive demonstration. Model and emphasize the importance of creating clear, connecting sentences. For example, in mapping the topic *Angles,* the *obtuse angle* card and the *90 degrees* card might be connected by the phrase *is more than.*

Concept cards can be used as an individual activity or with pairs or small groups of students. When using this FACT with pairs or small groups, encourage students to think first about their own connections and then discuss them with others. Students decide which connections best represent the pairs' or groups' thinking. Once students are satisfied with their maps, they can glue down their cards, write in their linkages to form sentences, and share their maps with others for feedback or practice in giving constructive feedback. Figure 4.6 shows an example of cards used for a concept mapping activity on *Angles.*

Figure 4.6   Concept Cards for Angles

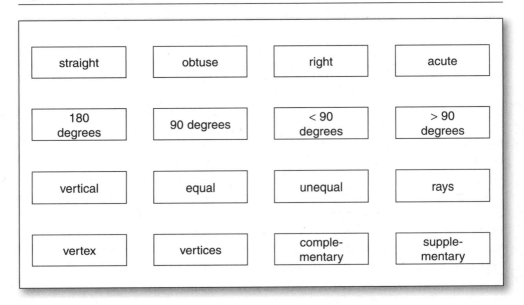

General Implementation Attributes

Ease of Use: Medium   Cognitive Demand: High
Time Demand: Medium

Modifications

Combine pictures with words for younger students. Include a few blank cards for students to write in their own concepts to include on their map. If students struggle with determining the connecting words or phrases, consider providing examples of different connectors that can be used with the topic chosen. Concept card maps can also be used as a pre- and post-assessment. Collect students' initial concept card maps. After students have had opportunities to learn about the concepts and develop deeper conceptual and procedural knowledge, return their original concept card maps and provide an opportunity for them to make changes using pens or pencils of a different color.

Caveats

The level of cognitive demand of this FACT depends on the concrete or abstract nature of the concepts selected and the number of cards to map. Choose the appropriate level of demand that matches the grade level of the students and complexity of the topic they are learning about.

Use With Other Disciplines

This FACT can also be used in *science, social studies, language arts, and health.

My Notes

_____

_____

_____

#10. CONCEPT CARTOONS

Description

Concept Cartoons were originally developed in the United Kingdom as cartoon drawings that visually depict children or adults sharing their ideas about common, everyday science phenomena or mathematical ideas (Dabell, Naylor, & Keogh, 2008; Naylor & Keogh, 2000). Students decide which character in the cartoon they agree with most and why. Cartoon characters' comments about the situation presented in the cartoon include an idea that is more mathematically acceptable than the others as well as alternative ideas based on common misconceptions and errors. Figure 4.7 shows an example of a *Concept Cartoon*–type assessment probe developed for *Uncovering Student Thinking in Mathematics* (Rose, Minton, & Arline, 2007) on the topic of percentages and estimation. See the Appendix for information on the *Concept Cartoons* web site and research reports that support the use of *Concept Cartoons*.

Figure 4.7   Type of *Concept Cartoon*

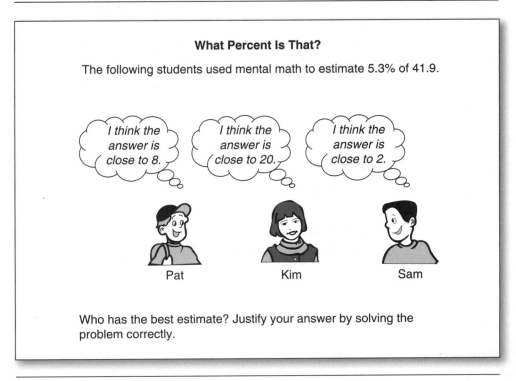

What Percent Is That?

The following students used mental math to estimate 5.3% of 41.9.

> I think the answer is close to 8.

> I think the answer is close to 20.

> I think the answer is close to 2.

Pat   Kim   Sam

Who has the best estimate? Justify your answer by solving the problem correctly.

Source: Rose, Minton, & Arline (2007, p. 84). Used with permission.

How This FACT Promotes Student Learning

Concept Cartoons are designed to engage and motivate students, uncover students' thinking about their own ideas, and encourage mathematical discussion. This FACT is particularly effective with struggling readers or English language learners because the concepts are set in a visual context and contain limited text. Showing cartoon characters with differing points of view reinforces the value placed in mathematics on evaluating others' thinking. Students examine ideas and work to resolve differences in order to come up with an acceptable explanation. *Concept Cartoons* help students develop confidence and trust in making their viewpoints public. As the developers of the original cartoons note, "After all, if they get one wrong, then they can always blame the cartoon character for putting forward that idea!" (Naylor & Keogh, 2000, p. 7). It is the process of surfacing and discussing one's own thinking that makes this a highly engaging and effective technique for promoting student learning.

How This FACT Informs Instruction

Concept Cartoons are most often used at the beginning of a learning cycle to surface students' ideas and engage them in wanting to learn more about the mathematics related to the cartoon situation. The ideas that surface when students respond to the cartoon provide valuable information for the teacher to use in designing instructional experiences that will confront students with their mathematical ideas about the situation presented in the cartoon.

Concept Cartoons can also be used throughout instruction to initiate starting points for mathematical inquiry, solidify concepts learned, and transfer and apply the mathematical concepts students learned to a new context. The cartoons are a particularly useful medium for engaging students in argumentation, providing an opportunity for teachers to listen to students discuss their ideas and use the information to modify lessons or plan for further instruction and assessment. Each cartoon provides an opportunity for students to justify their thinking by explaining the concept or showing how they solved the problem.

Design and Administration

Concept Cartoons are designed to probe students' thinking about common mathematical ideas, often set in situations they encounter every day that involve the use of mathematics. Teachers can use concept cartoons that are already published and available or create their own. If you create your own *Concept Cartoons*, limit the amount of text in the bubbles. Check to be sure there are no contextual clues that might cue the right answer, such as happier facial expressions or one character having a more technical and detailed explanation. Before showing the cartoon, introduce the topic to students. You can provide the cartoon as a printed handout or a projected image, or you can sketch it out for students on a poster chart or whiteboard.

Concept Cartoons work well as a small-group or whole-class discussion stimulus as long as individual students first have an opportunity to activate their own thinking.

Give students time to individually think about their own ideas and then have small groups of students discuss their ideas and try to come to some consensus. At this point the teacher is circulating and listening to ideas being discussed but not passing judgment on students' ideas. Have each group share with the whole class the ideas they came up with, perhaps followed by voting on the one that seems most acceptable to the class. When possible, follow up the discussion by providing students with the opportunity to justify their ideas through use of algorithms, manipulatives, or invented strategies and share the outcomes of their problem-solving processes. Use the results to draw students into a whole-group discussion to share their findings, consider what they have learned, and explain how their ideas have changed or been modified in some way. Probe further to find out what evidence led students to modify or change their ideas.

General Implementation Attributes

Ease of Use: High   Cognitive Demand: Medium
Time Demand: Medium

Modifications

Consider whiting out the bubbles that contain the characters' ideas and adding your own examples of commonly held ideas you may have observed with your own students. An alternative way to generate distracters is to ask students to work in small groups to fill in the bubbles with ideas they think the characters may have and exchange them with other groups for discussion. Students can also create their own cartoons to depict mathematical ideas. A fun and engaging strategy shared on the www.conceptcartoons.com website is to digitally photograph several teachers in the school, paste them into a cartoon format, and include thought bubbles that depict different ideas seemingly coming from the teachers. You can also use digital photos from the Internet of famous people and add bubbles describing their mathematical ideas. One middle school teacher reported that she used digital photos of Bon Jovi, Bono, and Lady Gaga to create a concept cartoon and said she had never seen her students so engaged with a question!

Caveats

Make sure the cartoons are used to stimulate discussion about the various ideas and that students do not disparage the cartoon characters' ways of thinking, because there may be students in the class who have the same or similar ideas as the cartoon characters.

Use With Other Disciplines

This FACT can also be used in *science*, social studies, language arts, health, foreign language, and visual and performing arts.

My Notes

_____

_____

_____

#11. CREATE THE PROBLEM

Description

Create the Problem is a reverse problem-solving FACT. Instead of performing the computation, students are given the solution and are asked to figure out what the real-world problem might be.

How This FACT Promotes Student Learning

Create the Problem helps students think about the purpose of performing certain computations and order of operations to solve problems. It moves students beyond performing rote computations to understanding the variety of problems the computation can be used to solve. It also helps students see the ways mathematics can be used in a variety of contexts.

How This FACT Informs Instruction

This FACT helps teachers see if students understand the purpose of a computational problem. Rather than always asking students to perform a computation, they are asked to tell in their own words what problem the computation might be used to solve. The examples students generate reveal whether they know why a computation is performed versus knowing the procedures used to perform a computation. The information may reveal the need to help students see the real-world applications of performing mathematical procedures, not just how they are used in math class.

Design and Administration

Create the Problem can be designed using basic computational problems or more complex problem-solving tasks. Choose a mathematical equation and have students work backwards from the end result to what they think the initial problem could be. For example, the teacher might give students the equation *2/3 of 15 = 10*. Students are asked to come up with problems that may have been solved with this equation, such as:

- John's mother gave him $15 to spend at the fair. She told him he could only spend 2/3 of it on rides. How much money could John spend on the rides?
- Felix had 15 homework problems. He was 2/3 finished before bedtime. How many problems did he finish before he went to bed?
- Sarah wondered how many pieces in a 15-slice box of pizza would be left if 2/3 of the pieces were not eaten.

Students share their examples and describe how their "story" matches the equation. The teacher asks the class for feedback on whether the "story" is a match to the equation. If not, how could it be changed to match?

General Implementation Attributes

Ease of Use: High   Cognitive Demand: Medium
Time Demand: Medium

Modifications

Use expressions instead of equations and in addition to creating the problem scenario, ask students to describe how they solved it. For example, instead of using the equation given above, give students the expression *2/3 of 15* and ask them to come up with situations where they might use this. Have them share the answer and describe how they found it. Ask students to create problem scenarios to show the need for using grouping symbols. For example, students write a problem for *3 • (5 + 7)* and another problem for *3 • 5 + 7*. (*Note:* Elementary teachers often prefer to use the × symbol for multiplication.)

Caveats

Use simple expressions or equations when you first start using this FACT. Once students are comfortable with it, you can add more complex equations or expressions.

Use With Other Disciplines

This FACT can be used with science in contexts where mathematics is used to solve problems in science.

My Notes

_____

_____

_____

#12. EVERY GRAPH TELLS A STORY

Description

Every Graph Tells a Story reveals how students make sense of graphic representations. Research indicates that students of all ages often interpret graphs of situations as literal pictures rather than as symbolic representations of the situations (Leinhardt, Zaslavsky, & Stein, 1990; McDermott, Rosenquist, & Van Zee, 1987). Students are given a graph and asked to choose the statement that best tells the story of the graph. Their answers reveal whether they interpreted the features of the graph literally (for example, an upward slope interpreted as climbing a hill) or consider the data points and the relationships they describe.

How This FACT Promotes Student Learning

The ability to interpret graphs is an important skill in mathematics and other disciplines, especially science. This probe encourages students to use their understanding of graphic representation in order to interpret a graph. It moves students beyond the procedural skills of constructing graphs to analyzing graphic data in order to understand what graphic data reveal.

How This FACT Informs Instruction

Every Graph Tells a Story helps teachers identify the common errors students make when interpreting a graph. Visuality is a key source of difficulty for students using graphs, particularly in physics situations that involve time and distance. The FACT helps teachers see whether students respond to the visual attributes of the graph by interpreting it literally (for example, interpreting an upward slope as going uphill) or conceptually understand how one type of data in a graph depends upon or is related to another. The information also reveals how well students consider the context of a given graph.

Design and Administration

Choose from a variety of graphic data and types of graphs, preferably representing real-world situations that students are familiar with. Present students with the graph and labeled axes, and develop statements that (1) partially mirror the actual data, (2) mirror literal interpretations of the visual components, and (3) accurately describe the data. Distance-time or position-time graphs are particularly useful for this type of FACT. Have students describe why they selected a particular statement to tell the story of the graph. Provide an opportunity for students to give feedback on others' interpretations. Figure 4.8 is an example of a position-time graph from *Uncovering Student Ideas in Physical Science: 45 Force and Motion Assessment Probes* (Keeley & Harrington, 2010).

General Implementation Attributes

Ease of Use: Medium   Cognitive Demand: High
Time Demand: Medium

Modifications

This FACT can be modified by using an open-ended approach where students are provided with a graph and have to come up with their own stories that describe what is happening on the graph. Have students critique each other's interpretations.

Figure 4.8   Example of *Every Graph Tells a Story*

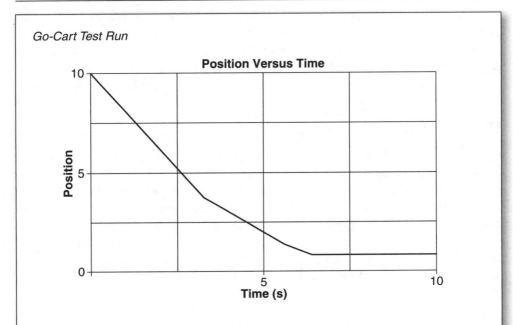

Go-Cart Test Run

Jim and Karen have built a go-cart. They take their go-cart for a test run and graph its motion. Their graph is shown above. They show the graph to their friends. This is what their friends say:

Bill: "Wow, that was a steep hill! You must have been going very fast at the bottom."

Patti: "I think you were going fast at first, but then you slowed down at the end."

Karl: "I think you must have hit something along the way and come to a full stop."

Mort: "It looks like you were going downhill and then the road flattened out."

Circle the name of the friend you think best describes the motion of the go-cart, based on the graph. Explain why you agree with that friend.

Source: Keeley and Harrington (2010). Used with permission.

Caveats

Make sure students are familiar with the labeled axes. For example, if acceleration is graphed and students don't know the difference between acceleration and speed, then the learning problem may be with the vocabulary, not the graph.

Use With Other Disciplines

This FACT can also be used in science and social studies.

My Notes

_____

_____

_____

#13. EXAMPLE, NONEXAMPLE

Description

Successful mathematics students are able to generate examples and non-examples to support their mathematical understanding. Identifying and examining examples and nonexamples reveal students' understanding of a concept as well as how they interpret definitions of mathematical terms.

How This FACT Promotes Student Learning

Coming up with examples and nonexamples requires different cognitive skills from those used to carry out a procedure or memorize a definition. Students need to carefully consider the numbers or objects in terms of their attributes. Often the question asked in the classroom is "Is this an example of . . . ?" In this FACT, students are asked to generate their own examples and describe why they are or are not examples of a particular concept or mathematical term. By asking students to come up with their own examples rather than providing them with examples selected by the teacher, this FACT supports students in learning to generate examples, a critical skill they will use throughout mathematics.

How This FACT Informs Instruction

An understanding of mathematical concepts and terminology is crucial to students' ability to understand and solve problems This FACT can help teachers assess the extent to which students are able to apply a rule or definition presented to them when learning about a new concept or mathematical term.

Design and Administration

This FACT is used after students have been introduced to the concept or term. Examples and nonexamples may have previously been used for instructional purposes to introduce and explain a new concept or word. Students are asked to think about what they previously learned about a word or concept, identify their own examples and nonexamples, and provide a supporting rule or operational definition for the examples and nonexamples they chose. First, identify the concept or mathematical term for which you want to determine how well students are able to identify their own examples and nonexamples. Provide students with a chart to fill in their examples and nonexamples. At the bottom of the chart, provide a space for students to describe the rule or definition they used. Figure 4.9 is an example used to assess students' understanding of the concept and mathematical term *rectangle*.

Figure 4.9   *Example, Nonexample*

Shapes With Four Sides That Are Rectangles	Shapes With Four Sides That Are Not Rectangles
Draw as many different examples as you can here.	Draw as many different nonexamples as you can here.
State the rule you used to decide whether a four-sided shape is a rectangle:	

Students can work individually or in small groups. Have students share their examples and provide feedback to each other on whether they are examples or nonexamples as well as feedback on their operational rule or definition. How well do the examples meet the rule or definition? The teacher can select certain examples for a whole-class discussion on how well they illustrate the *Example, Nonexample* category and develop a class consensus on a rule or definition used to define the word or explain the concept.

General Implementation Attributes

Ease of Use: High   Cognitive Demand: Medium
Time Demand: Medium

Modifications

This FACT can be used as a card sort. It is particularly helpful for students who may need visual cues. Provide examples and nonexamples on cards and have students sort them into the two categories. It can also be used with Venn diagrams.

Caveats

While this FACT could be used as an elicitation to identify prior knowledge, it is best used to monitor how well students have learned a particular concept or can apply a definition. Be sure to build in time to provide students with feedback.

Use With Other Disciplines

This FACT can also be used in science, social studies, language arts, health, foreign languages, and visual and performing arts.

My Notes

_____

_____

_____

#14. FACT-FIRST QUESTIONING

Description

Quality questions provide insight into students' ideas and growing knowledge base. *Fact-First Questioning* is a higher-order questioning technique used to draw out student knowledge beyond recall level. It takes a factual "what is" question and turns it into a deeper "how" or "why" question by stating the fact first and asking students to elaborate.

How This FACT Promotes Student Learning

Students, including high achievers, can memorize, recall, and recount information with very little conceptual understanding. By stating the fact first and asking students to explain or elaborate on it, students tap into deeper thinking processes that lead to a more enduring understanding of mathematical concepts. Stating the fact first and then allowing for wait time provides an opportunity for students to activate their thinking before being asked the higher-level question.

How This FACT Informs Instruction

This FACT helps teachers expand their repertoire of questioning strategies for the purpose of finding out what their students know and understand. A simple change in the way factual questions are asked and responded to can open the door to providing valuable information to teachers about student understanding of the conceptual ideas related to an important mathematical fact. The information helps teachers determine whether students recall important knowledge at a superficial level or have developed deeper conceptual understanding. The information can be used to examine whether terminology and facts are overemphasized at the expense of mathematical understanding and adjust instruction accordingly to focus on concepts instead of terminology and definitions.

Design and Administration

Any factual question can be thoughtfully turned into a *Fact-First Question*. Use the general template: State the fact followed by a question such as "Why is *X* an example of *Y*?" (Black et al., 2003). For example, instead of showing students a picture of a triangle and asking them to identify what kind of triangle it is, turn the question around to ask, "This is an example of an isosceles triangle [show picture]. Why is this triangle called an isosceles triangle?" Instead of the factual recall answer—isosceles triangle, from the first question, the *Fact-First Question* produces a much deeper response that involves describing two equal angles and two equal sides. Another example might be instead of asking the students what sign the product of two negative numbers is, turn the question around to ask, "When a negative number is multiplied by a negative number it results in a positive number. Why does multiplying two negative numbers result in a positive number?"

General Implementation Attributes

Ease of Use: High   Cognitive Demand: Medium
Time Demand: Low

Modifications

Consider modifying traditional textbook recall questions into *Fact-First Questions*. Have older students come up with their own *Fact-First Questions* and responses.

Caveats

Use *Fact-First Questions* after students have been introduced to the terminology and concepts.

Use With Other Disciplines

This FACT can also be used in *science*, social studies, language arts, health, foreign languages, and visual and performing arts.

My Notes

_____

_____

_____

#15. FEEDBACK TO FEED-FORWARD

Description

Formative feedback represents information communicated to the learner that is intended to modify the learner's thinking or behavior for the purpose of improving learning (Shute, 2008, p. 1). *Feedback to Feed-Forward* is a technique used as a follow-up to *Comments-Only Marking*. It is used to encourage students to reflect both on how they used formative feedback (provided by teacher or a peer) to improve the task at hand and how the feedback will affect future work beyond the task itself.

How This FACT Promotes Student Learning

In order for feedback to move students' learning forward, time must be allowed for students to make revisions. The *Feedback to Feed-Forward* technique provides an opportunity for students to reflect on how they use feedback received during a revision process. Because the particular feedback a student receives should be based on the criteria for success laid out in class, the particular feedback to any student will vary depending on those criteria. Therefore, providing multiple opportunities to reflect on the use of feedback builds a student's ability to interpret the feedback, to act on it, and to internalize it. Try to provide multiple opportunities for students to respond to the feedback by revising their work accordingly, rather than simply reading the feedback to them.

How This Fact Informs Instruction

Teachers who use this strategy support the culture needed in a classroom to focus on success and the belief that all students can achieve when given opportunities to use feedback that focuses on the criteria needed to successfully meet a learning target. Since making revisions in mathematics is often a novel approach for students, using the *Feedback to Feed-Forward* reflection sheet allows teachers to determine a student's interpretation of feedback that was provided and whether the feedback moved students' learning forward.

Design and Administration

Use with assignments that provide an opportunity for students to demonstrate their conceptual understanding. Such assignments may require solving multistep problems and explaining solution steps, making and justifying conjectures, or providing examples and nonexamples. Instead of marking students' work right or wrong, look for areas throughout the work where you can identify features that do and do not meet established criteria for success. Frame the feedback so that it points out to students the progress being made toward the goals and what needs to be undertaken to make more progress (Hattie & Timperley, 2007, p. 86). Be sure to frame what needs to be undertaken in a way that directs students but does not do the work for them. An example of a *Feedback to Feed-Forward* template is shown in Figure 4.10. Students complete the Using Feedback section prior to completing the revisions to the task and the Feed-Forward section after the revisions are complete.

General Implementation Attributes

Ease of Use: High   Cognitive Demand: High
Time Demand: Medium

Modifications

This FACT can also be used after feedback is provided using *Two Stars and a Wish, Collaborative Cued Corrections (CCC),* or comment coding used in *Comments Only Marking.*

Figure 4.10 *Feedback to Feed-Forward* Template

Using FEEDBACK   to   FEED-FORWARD

How I will use the feedback to revise my work:

1. What did the feedback tell me?

2. Here are the changes I will make to my work (you can just make a list of things you will do):

3. What parts of the feedback do I not understand yet? (List them. Then ask the person who gave you the feedback to explain it more clearly.)

How this feedback will help me with future work:

Complete these prompts as best you can:

1. One piece of feedback I got that I can remember to use in other work is:

2. I will help myself remember this feedback next time I do an assignment by (doing what?):

Caveats

This is a comments-only FACT. Research indicates a less positive effect on student learning when grades are given in addition to comments (Black & Harrison, 2004). Because this strategy reinforces the notion that the teacher wants students to improve their work and that their improvement is being monitored by the teacher, time should be provided in class for students to read and react to the comments. If possible, provide time in class for students to work on their revisions and reflections.

Use With Other Disciplines

This FACT can also be used in science, social studies, language arts, health, foreign language, and visual and performing arts.

My Notes

_____

_____

_____

#16. FIST TO FIVE

Description

Fist to Five asks students to indicate the extent of their understanding of a concept, mathematical procedure, or directions for an activity by holding up a closed fist (no understanding), one finger (very little understanding), and a range up to five fingers (I understand it completely and can easily explain it to someone else). For example, after giving instructions for a mathematical game, teachers might ask for a *fist to five* to do a quick check on whether students understand the directions before proceeding with the game.

How This FACT Promotes Student Learning

Fist to Five provides an opportunity for all students in a class to indicate when they do not understand a concept, procedure, or set of directions and need additional support for their learning. It is especially effective with individual students who are reluctant to let the teacher know that they are experiencing difficulty during a lesson. It encourages metacognition by raising self-awareness of how ready students feel to proceed with their learning.

How This FACT Informs Instruction

Fist to Five is a monitoring technique used to check understanding of concepts, procedures, or directions at any point in a lesson. It is particularly useful when new material is presented, a new procedure is introduced, or directions for a task are given. It allows the teacher to direct the challenge and pace of lessons toward the needs of the students rather than following a prescribed instructional plan. The quick read of the class provides teachers with the feedback they need to modify the lesson or pair students up to help each other.

Design and Administration

At any time during a lesson, ask students to hold up their hand for a check of understanding.

The closed fist indicates "I have no idea."

One finger indicates "I barely understand."

Two fingers indicate "I understand parts of it but I need help."

Three fingers indicate "I understand most of it but I'm not sure I can explain it well enough to others."

Four fingers indicate "I understand it and can do an adequate job explaining it."

Five fingers indicate "I understand it completely and can easily explain it to someone else."

Some teachers post a *Fist to Five* chart in the room so students remember how many fingers to hold up. Make sure all students hold up their hands. It can be used to group students for peer assistance by putting the students who hold up two or three fingers with the students who hold up four or five fingers. The teacher can then take the closed-fist and one-finger responses aside for differentiated assistance.

General Implementation Attributes

Ease of Use: High   Cognitive Demand: Low
Time Demand: Low

Modifications

This FACT can be modified to a three-finger strategy: one finger means "I don't get it," two fingers means "I partially get it," and three fingers means "I get it." Likewise, you can use thumbs up—I get it; thumbs sideways—I'm not sure I understand; thumbs down—I don't get it.

Caveats

When matching students who claim to understand with students who need help, make sure that the students who held up four or five fingers really do understand well enough to explain it to others before putting them into peer assistance groups.

Use With Other Disciplines

This FACT can also be used in *science*, social studies, language arts, health, foreign languages, and visual and performing arts.

My Notes

_____

_____

_____

#17. FOUR CORNERS

Description

Four Corners is used with selected-response questions to identify and group students who have similar responses to the question asked. Students move to a corner of the room designated to match their response or similar way of thinking.

How This FACT Promotes Student Learning

Four Corners provides an opportunity for students to make their ideas public. By meeting "in the corner" with students who have similar ideas, students can further discuss and clarify their own thinking with others before returning to their seats and engaging in mathematical discussions with the class or small groups of students in which students have a range of conflicting ideas. Members of each corner group can also defend their ideas to the entire class. In the process of explaining their thinking and getting feedback from the teacher and class, students sometimes notice gaps or inconsistencies in their own reasoning and change their ideas to reflect newly accepted information.

How This FACT Informs Instruction

Teachers can visually see which response individual students selected as well as the most prevalent response. By circulating among the corners while students are sharing their thinking, the teacher gains insight into students' *foothold* ideas—those ideas students assume to be true at that point in time (Hammer & Van Zee, 2006). The information is used to inform instructional strategies that can help students gradually move toward acceptable mathematical ideas and thinking.

Design and Administration

Choose a selected-response assessment that includes an explanation and label the four corners of a room with the letter or name that matches the response. Examples of FACTs in this chapter that can be used with the *Four Corners* strategy include *Concept Cartoons, Friendly Talk Probes,* and *P-E-O Probes.* Ask students to individually think through their responses, commit to an answer, and write their explanations. When students are finished with the probe, have them go to the corner of the room that matches the response they have selected. Give students time (usually 5 to 10 minutes) to share and discuss their thinking with others who selected the same response. Teachers can follow up the discussion at the *Four Corners* with a class debate about the ideas by having students return to their seats for mixed small-group and whole-class discussion. Another alternative is to have students remain in their respective corners and work together as a group or subgroups to support their arguments in preparation for a presentation to the groups in the other corners. As students listen to and consider the arguments of other groups, they may move to a different corner when they give up their idea in favor of a new one. The challenge is to try to get all students over to one corner (ideally, the one that represents the mathematically correct response).

General Implementation Attributes

Ease of Use: High   Cognitive Demand: High
Time Demand: Low

Modifications

Use different areas of the room or designated tables for more than four responses, or use only three corners for items that include fewer than four selected responses.

Caveats

This FACT works best in a classroom environment where students feel comfortable expressing and defending their own ideas without being influenced by others' responses.

Use With Other Disciplines

This FACT can also be used in *science,* social studies, language arts, health, foreign languages, and visual and performing arts.

My Notes

_____

_____

_____

#18. FRAYER MODEL

Description

The *Frayer Model* was first developed by Dorothy Frayer and her colleagues at the University of Wisconsin. The *Frayer Model* graphically organizes prior knowledge about a concept or mathematical term into an operational definition, characteristics, examples, and nonexamples (Buell, 2001). An example of a *Frayer Model* template is shown in Figure 4.11.

How This FACT Promotes Student Learning

The *Frayer Model* helps activate students' prior knowledge about a mathematical concept or word. It provides students with the opportunity to clarify a concept or mathematical term and communicate their understanding by providing an operational definition, describe characteristics (or properties), and list examples and nonexamples from their own prior knowledge of the concept or familiarity with the term. This FACT can also be used to help solidify conceptual understanding after students have had an opportunity to learn about the concept or use the term.

How This FACT Informs Instruction

Frayer Models have typically been used to introduce new terminology. However, for formative assessment purposes, they can be used to determine students' prior knowledge about a concept or mathematical term before planning a lesson. Barriers that can hinder learning may be uncovered with this FACT. Students' completed *Frayer Models* provide a starting point with an operational definition and understandings gained through prior instructional experiences that can be further refined through class discussion and formal clarification of the concept. *Frayer Models* can also be used during the conceptual development phase of instruction to monitor the extent to which students can describe a concept or mathematical term they have used throughout their instructional experiences.

Figure 4.11 *Frayer Model* Template

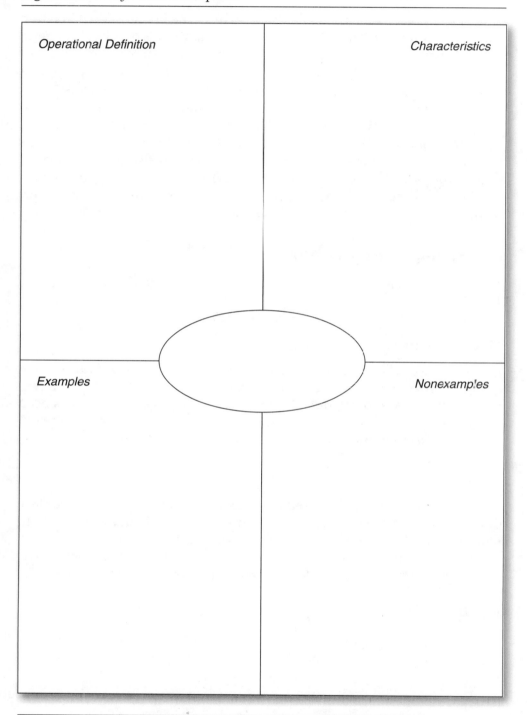

Design and Administration

Begin by using a familiar concept to explain the Frayer Model diagram and demonstrate how to fill it in. Choose a concept or word that is integral to understanding mathematical ideas. Representations and symbols instead of words can also be chosen (for examples, *a/b*, a picture of supplementary angles, or %). Provide students with the concept, term, symbol, or representation you want them to think about, and give them time to complete the diagram. Once the diagram is complete, let the students share their ideas with other students, modifying their diagrams as they accept and assimilate new information. Students can also work in pairs or small groups to create their Frayer model diagrams, using them in a whole-class discussion about the concept and refining them as new information is added to their existing model.

General Implementation Attributes

Ease of Use: High   Cognitive Demand: Medium
Time Demand: Low

Modifications

Frayer Models can also be extended to ask students to provide a visual example or a personal connection. Another alternative is to leave the center bubble blank and provide students with a *Frayer Model* that has been filled in. Ask students to come up with the word, symbol, picture, or concept that goes in to the bubble and explain why they chose it.

Caveats

Frayer Models have been used in content literacy to support vocabulary development and word recognition prior to a reading assignment. In mathematics, their formative purpose should extend beyond vocabulary development and focus on uncovering and promoting conceptual understanding of the terms, symbols, and representations used in mathematics.

Use With Other Disciplines

This FACT can also be used in *science*, social studies, language arts, health, foreign languages, and visual and performing arts.

My Notes

_____

_____

_____

#19. FRIENDLY TALK PROBES

Description

Friendly Talk Probes are two-tiered questions that consist of a selected-response section followed by a justification. The probe is set in a real-life scenario in which friends, family members, or familiar adults talk about a mathematical concept. Students are asked to pick the person they most agree with and explain why. Distracters are based on commonly held ideas from the research on students' misconceptions and common errors. The conversation between the characters draws students into the ideas almost as if they are participating in the conversation (Keeley, Eberle, & Tugel, 2006).

How This FACT Promotes Student Learning

This FACT can be used to engage students in surfacing and examining their preconceptions as well as solidifying concepts and applying understandings in a new context. It promotes engagement with ideas in an accessible way by having friends, family, or other students and adults in familiar roles legitimize the act of putting different ideas forward for scrutiny. Students who can relate an idea they have to one of the characters in the probe are less apt to feel uncomfortable about revealing a "wrong answer."

How This FACT Informs Instruction

Friendly Talk Probes can be used at multiple points prior to or throughout instruction to find out what students are thinking in relation to an important curricular goal. It can be used to engage students in thinking about the concepts they will encounter during their instructional experiences and provide them with an opportunity to share their ideas and explain their thinking. This FACT can also be used as an application of students' learning following the conceptual development phase of instruction. Choose a probe that targets the concept taught and presents ideas in a context different from the students' instructional materials and learning experiences. The responses are useful in determining how well students can transfer their ideas to a new context. Results may signify the need to provide additional activities or to be more explicit about developing the big idea and broader generalizations related to the targeted concept.

Design and Administration

Design or choose probes that use examples of familiar events, processes, or objects that would be realistically discussed by the characters represented. The Appendix includes a source of *Friendly Talk Assessment Probes*. The probe can be administered as a paper-and-pencil task or used orally to stimulate small- or large-group discussion. It can be combined with other FACTs in this chapter such as *Commit and Toss, Four Corners, Sticky Bars,* and *Human Scatter Graphs* to determine the range of ideas held in a class. An example of a *Friendly Talk Probe* is shown in Figure 4.12.

Figure 4.12   *Friendly Talk Probe*

Four friends were studying for their math test. They each had different ideas about finding the mean in a set of data. This is what they said:

Nancy: I think the mean is the number that shows up the most times in our data set.

Alvin: I think you subtract the largest number from the smallest number to find the mean.

Cara: I think the mean has to be one of the numbers in our set of data. It is the one that is in the middle of the data spread.

Truax: I think you find the mean by adding up all the data points and dividing by the number of data points.

Circle the friend you agree with the most. Explain why you agree with that friend and not the others.

General Implementation Attributes

Ease of Use: High   Cognitive Demand: Medium to High
Time Demand: Low

Modifications

To help auditory learners, select students to act out the probe by representing the characters and reading their viewpoints. For visual learners, these probes can be readily turned into *Concept Cartoons* by giving the text to students who demonstrate a talent for drawing or cartooning. Multiple-choice questions included in teachers' instructional materials can be turned into a more engaging question by merely changing the question so that it is set in the context of people talking and changing the letter choices *a, b, c,* and *d* to names of people.

Caveats

Sometimes students will not agree with anyone because they believe there is not enough information or they have an idea that differs from the characters in the probe. Acknowledge this if it occurs and provide an option for these students to add their own statement.

Use With Other Disciplines

This FACT can also be used in *science, social studies, and health.

My Notes

_____

_____

_____

#20. GIVE ME FIVE

Description

Give Me Five is a technique used to promote and publicly share personal reflections that collectively provide feedback from the group. Students are given a prompt and take a minute or two for a "quiet think." Five students then volunteer to publicly share their reflection.

How This FACT Promotes Student Learning

Give Me Five provides students with an opportunity to individually and publicly reflect on their learning during or after a lesson. This FACT encourages students to be thoughtful reflectors and demonstrates teachers' respect and value for students' sharing personal insights into their learning.

How This FACT Informs Instruction

Selecting five students to publicly share their reflection provides a sample collage for the teacher to gain feedback on how students perceived the impact of a lesson on their learning. *Give Me Five* is a simple, quick technique for inviting and valuing public reflection and welcoming feedback from students that will be used to design responsive instruction.

Design and Administration

Provide a reflection prompt that is inviting and open to a variety of responses by all students. Be sure to give time for individuals to quietly reflect, perhaps through a quick write, before asking for five volunteers to share their reflection. Practice the use of wait time if at first students are hesitant to share their thoughts publicly. This FACT can be used at any critical juncture in a lesson or at the end of a lesson or class period as closure. Hold up your fist, showing a finger each time a student shares a reflection until you have completed five fingers. Some examples of reflection prompts follow:

- What was the most significant learning you had during today's lesson?
- How "in the zone" do you feel right now as far as your understanding of functions?
- How did today's lesson help you better understand percentages?
- What was the high point of this week's activities on ratios and proportions?
- How well do you think today's math discussion worked in improving your ability to make and defend conjectures?

General Implementation Attributes

Ease of Use: High   Cognitive Demand: Medium
Time Demand: Low

Modifications

Five is an arbitrary number of students. Depending on time and the number of students in the class, you might consider additional reflections, such as a *Give Me Seven* or *Give Me Ten*. You can also ask for a show of hands indicating how many students had a similar thought each time a student shares his or her reflection.

Caveats

Don't overuse this technique, or it may become a trivial exercise, particularly if the same reflective prompts are used. Be sure to vary the prompts. Make sure the same students are not the ones whose reflections are repeatedly selected to be shared.

Use With Other Disciplines

This FACT can be used in *science*, social studies, health, language arts, foreign languages, and visual and performing arts.

My Notes

#21. HOT SEAT QUESTIONING

Description

Hot Seat Questioning is a FACT used when all students are expected to be ready to respond to mathematical questions at any time. Students are selected to sit in the "hot seat" to respond to questions asked by the teacher while the class provides feedback on the students' responses.

How This FACT Promotes Student Learning

Observations of teachers' questioning techniques reveal that the same few students are frequently called upon to answer questions. Often, these are the students who raise their hands. Students who do not raise their hands "opt out" of not only responding, but also opt out of thinking if they know they are likely not to be called upon. Because any student can be selected at any time to sit in a "hot seat" and respond to a question, this FACT activates thinking among all learners who must be prepared to give a response.

How This FACT Informs Instruction

This FACT helps teachers provide an opportunity for all students to be ready to respond to questions. During the question-response phase, the teacher can assess individual students' conceptual understanding of a mathematical idea or procedure and where they may be having difficulty. Additionally, the teacher can assess the extent to which the class understands the concept or may need further instruction by listening to the feedback given by the class to the student in the hot seat.

Design and Administration

Place anywhere from one to five chairs in an area of the classroom such as the front of the room to serve as the hot seats. Tell students that you are going to ask a question or series of questions and that different students will be asked to sit in the hot seat or seats to respond to the questions. Distribute the question or questions for the whole class to consider first and prepare their own individual responses. Then ask a student or students to sit in the hot seats to share their responses. The class listens to the responses and provides feedback to the students on whether they agree or disagree with the answers presented and why, or on the strategy used to solve the problem. For problem-solving questions, the students in the hot seat may be encouraged to visually demonstrate how they solved the problem.

General Implementation Attributes

Ease of Use: Medium   Cognitive Demand: Medium/High
Time Demand: Medium

Modifications

Hot seats can also be prepared in advance by taping a paper with "You are in the hot seat!" under students' chairs (see Figure 4.13). Students are asked to reach under their chairs or desks to see if they have a note taped to their chair or desk. When they pull it out, they will see the hot seat notice. The teacher then explains the role of the students sitting in those seats. Hot seats can also be determined randomly by labeling the seats and creating a set of cards with one card per seat label. The hot seat is determined by shuffling the set and choosing a card.

Figure 4.13   Hot Seat Notice

You are in the hot seat!

Caveats

Make sure all students have an opportunity to think about and respond to the question before designating the hot seats in order to ensure that all students are engaged in the question.

Use With Other Disciplines

This FACT can also be used in science, social studies, language arts, health, foreign language, and visual and performing arts.

My Notes

_____

_____

_____

#22. HUMAN SCATTER GRAPH

Description

The *Human Scatter Graph* is a quick, visual way for teachers and students to get an immediate classroom snapshot of students' thinking and the level of confidence students have in their ideas. The technique gets the class up and moving as students position themselves on a "floor graph." As students position themselves around the room according to their response to the question and their confidence level, a visual graph of class results is created.

How This FACT Promotes Student Learning

This FACT can be used to encourage metacognition—not only in thinking about the answer but also how confident one is in one's answer. It provides a visual opportunity to see how others in the class think about a particular concept and how confident they are in their thinking. Recognizing that students in the class vary in their answers and confidence levels promotes a safe classroom environment where all ideas are valued. It sends a message that the class will work together to develop their understanding so that everyone can eventually come to an agreement on the best answer to the question and raise their confidence in their own ideas.

How This FACT Informs Instruction

This fact can be used at the beginning of a lesson or sequence of instruction to elicit students' initial ideas and motivate them to want to further explore and discover mathematical ideas. It can be used during the exploration and discovery stage of instruction to determine how well students use mathematical concepts and procedures. Looking about the room to see where clusters of students as well as individuals place themselves gives immediate feedback to the teacher on the different ideas students have and their levels of confidence. *Human Scatter Graphs* can be used to initiate mathematical argument among students who have different ideas by pairing them up with students standing in different areas of the graph. Students who are low on the confidence scale can be asked what it would take to raise the level of confidence in their thinking, sparking discussion and providing opportunities to further discuss their ideas. They can also be matched with students who have the same answer and a higher level of confidence to draw out ideas and ways of thinking that may increase their confidence level.

Design and Administration

Choose selected response questions with at least three and no more than four choices for this FACT. Label the wall (Y-axis) on one side of the room with the choices: for example, A, B, C (and D, if there are four responses). Label the adjacent wall (X-axis) with a range of low confidence to high confidence. Have students position themselves according to where they feel they fall on the graph. Figures 4.14 and 4.15 show examples of a probe used for this strategy and the distribution of students positioned on the graph.

General Implementation Attributes

Ease of Use: Medium   Cognitive Demand: Medium
Time Demand: Low

Figure 4.14   Example Probe Used With *Human Scatter Graph*

What's the Substitute?

When you substitute ½ for x in 4x and simplify the results, what is the correct answer?

A. 4½

B. 2

C. 8

Explain your reasoning:

Source: Rose & Arline (2009). Reprinted with permission.

Figure 4.15   *Human Scatter Graph* for "What's the Substitute?"

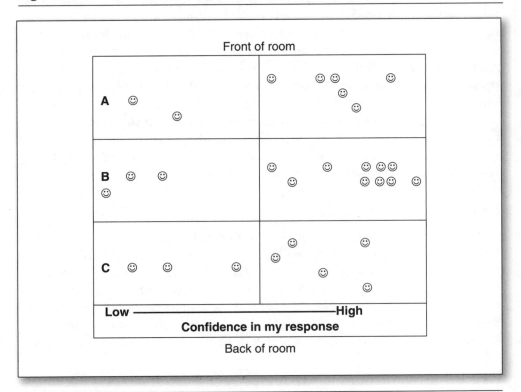

Source: Adapted from Keeley (2008), p. 110. Used with permission.

Modifications

A paper version can be used instead of a human graph. Pass the graph, with axes labeled, around the class and have students put their initials on it according to where their answer falls and their level of confidence, or have students put their initials on a small round sticker and then place the sticker on the graph created on large poster paper. With this method, teachers also have a written record. The graph can then be passed back later after students have had an opportunity to further explore the question. Students then reinitial their positions, drawing a line to connect their initial and later positions, showing the extent to which their confidence level changed or if they changed their response to the question.

Caveats

Students who have difficulty with spatial thinking may need help positioning themselves on the floor graph. Depending on how well your classroom has moved toward a culture that accepts that all ideas matter whether they are right or wrong, you may ask students to commit to an answer on a slip of paper first and have this paper in their hand when they position themselves on the graph. This prevents students from flocking to where they think the students with the right answers are standing.

Use With Other Disciplines

This FACT can also be used in *science*, social studies, language arts, health, foreign language, and visual and performing arts.

My Notes

_____

_____

_____

#23. IS IT FAIR?

Description

Is It Fair? asks students to examine a context in which several mathematical statements are made in response to a problem. Students examine the proposed solution to decide if it is fair (for example, dividing up a quantity so everyone gets an equal portion). If they decide it is unfair, they explain what makes it unfair and how the situation can be made fair. Alternatively, if it is fair, students explain why it is fair. Common misconceptions or mistakes made in mathematics are situated in the context.

How This FACT Informs Instruction

The examples used in the fairness context are based on common errors students make in mathematics. Thus this FACT serves as a diagnostic technique for whether or not students can identify common errors. The information gained from the FACT may be used to revisit mathematical concepts and procedures or inform instruction of a particular mathematical concept or skill.

Design and Administration

Make up a problem using a familiar context in which the proposed solution is either fair or unfair. Provide several statements that describe the situation. Ask students to analyze the statements and decide if the proposed action or decision is fair. If it is fair, students are asked to use mathematics to explain what makes it fair. If it is unfair, students are asked to explain why it is unfair and propose a way to make it fair. Some examples of mathematics topics that can be used in fair or unfair contexts include probability, ratio and proportion, division, graphs and other representations, statistics, percentages, etc. The following is an example of an *Is It Fair?* based on the topic of probability.

> Three friends found a ticket for free admission to the amusement park. Since only one of them could use the free ticket, they decided to flip a coin to see who would get the ticket. Bobby said, "There are three of us, so we'll need to flip two coins. Let's do it like this: I will toss the two coins. If they both come up heads, then David gets the ticket. If they both come up tails, then Trent gets the ticket. If one comes up heads and the other tails, then I get the ticket." Fair or unfair?

General Implementation Attributes

Ease of Use: Medium
Time Demand: Medium

Cognitive Demand: Medium/High

Modifications

Instead of *Is It Fair?* in which students have to decide if the situation is fair or unfair, you can simplify it by changing it to *What's Unfair?* using a situation in which there are one or more fair statements and one unfair statement. Ask students to spot the statement that makes the situation unfair, explain why, and create a new fair statement that is different from the others.

Caveats

If some statements are fair and one is unfair, make sure that the unfair statement is not always the last one stated.

Use With Other Disciplines

This FACT can also be used in science in the context of controlling variables (a fair test) or making decisions based on data.

My Notes

_____

_____

_____

#24. I USED TO THINK . . . BUT NOW I KNOW . . .

Description

I Used to Think . . . But Now I Know . . . asks students to compare, orally or in writing, their ideas at the beginning of a lesson or instructional sequence to the ideas they have after completing the lesson(s). It differs from *K-W-L* (see FACT #27) because both parts of the reflection occur after instruction.

How This FACT Promotes Learning

This FACT is a self-assessment and reflection exercise that helps students recognize whether and how their thinking has changed at the end of a sequence of instruction. It prompts students to recall their ideas at the beginning of the instructional sequence and consider how they changed. Metacognition involves not only the ability to self-regulate learning, recognize the demands of a learning task, and know of one's own learning strengths and weaknesses (Bransford et al., 1999), but also knowing *what* one has learned. *I Used to Think . . . But Now I Know . . .* provides an opportunity for students to self-assess and reflect on their current knowledge and how it may have changed or evolved from their initial ideas. Sharing their reflection with the class provides a public opportunity for all students to recognize how and to what extent individuals' knowledge improves as a result of shared learning experiences.

How This FACT Informs Instruction

This technique enables teachers to hear or read the students' own accounts of how their understanding of mathematics changed for them as a result of their learning experiences. The technique gives the teacher insight into the myriad ways students' thinking changes as a result of instruction and whether students recognize their own prior misunderstandings. The results help teachers determine the effectiveness of their instruction and what parts seemed to have the greatest impact on their students' learning.

Design and Administration

Provide students with a copy of a recording sheet, have them make one similar to the one shown in Figure 4.16, or write down and fill in the sentence: *I used to think _____, but now I know _____*. Provide time for a quiet think and write. Explain to students that they should describe how their ideas changed or how they became more detailed compared to what they knew at the beginning of instruction. Use *Think-Pair-Share, Partner Speaks*, or other pair strategies to have students read and share their reflections with a partner or with the whole class. An example of this FACT is "I used to think <u>multiplication always made larger numbers</u> but now I know <u>it makes smaller numbers when I multiply by a fraction between 0 and 1</u>."

Figure 4.16   Example Recording Sheet

I used to think . . .	But now I know . . .

General Implementation Attributes

Ease of Use: High   Cognitive Demand: Medium
Time Demand: Low

Modifications

The FACT can be extended to include . . . *and This Is How I Learned It* to help students reflect on what part of their learning experiences helped them change or further develop their ideas. This addition provides additional feedback to the teacher on what was effective for learning from the students' viewpoint. Students can be encouraged to provide multiple examples. This FACT can also be used as a whole-class reflection by going around the class and having each student read aloud their *I used to think ____ but now I know ____*.

Caveats

Some students may have difficulty recalling their initial ideas. If a class record of initial ideas exists from other FACTs, it may be helpful to share with the class some of the earlier ideas that were noted. If a probe was used to elicit individuals' preconceptions, students can refer back to that probe after instruction.

Use With Other Disciplines

This FACT can also be used in *science*, social studies, language arts, health, foreign language, and visual and performing arts.

My Notes

_____

_____

_____

#25. JUSTIFIED LIST

Description

A *Justified List* begins with a statement or question about a mathematical concept or procedure. Multiple examples that fit or do not fit the statement or question are listed. Students choose the examples on the list that fit the statement or answer the question and provide a justification explaining their rule or reason for their selections. Figure 4.17 is an example of a justified list used with elementary students learning about triangles.

Figure 4.17   *Justified List* Probe

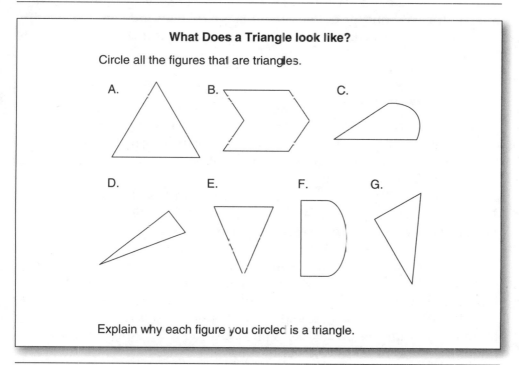

What Does a Triangle look like?

Circle all the figures that are triangles.

A.   B.   C.

D.   E.   F.   G.

Explain why each figure you circled is a triangle.

How This FACT Promotes Student Learning

Justified Lists activate students' thinking about a concept or procedure. *Justified Lists* can be used to elicit preconceptions or solidify ideas during formal concept development. The items on the list can be used to encourage small-group discussion, further promoting student thinking and resolving discrepancies between students' own ideas and those of their peers. *Justified Lists* can also be used for reflection at the end of a unit of instruction. Students examine their original lists, reflecting on how they might respond differently based on new knowledge they have.

How This FACT Informs Instruction

Justified Lists can be used to elicit students' prior ideas about a concept or procedure. It reveals the understandings or misunderstandings students bring to their learning when the concept or procedure is introduced. The FACT helps teachers see whether students can connect a particular concept or procedure to a variety of different examples and often indicates problems students have making generalizations. Listen carefully to the justification students use, because these justifications may point out the need for targeted instructional interventions that will confront students with their existing ideas about the relationship between the items on the list and the targeted concept or procedure. This FACT can also be used as an application to determine the extent to which students are able to transfer the mathematical ideas they developed during the formal concept development stage. It may indicate the need to revise or include additional activities to support transfer of learning to new contexts.

Design and Administration

Design *Justified Lists* that probe a core idea in mathematics and preferably have a cognitive research base that can inform the selection of distracters to put in the list. Mathematics Curriculum Topic Study (see Appendix) includes a process for developing these types of probes. You can also use ready-made *Justified List* probes in the *Uncovering Student Thinking in Mathematics* series (see Appendix). This FACT can be given individually as a written assessment, or it can be given to pairs or small groups to discuss their ideas and come to an agreement as to which examples should be selected from the list. Small groups can share their lists with the whole class for discussion and feedback. If used as an individual written task, consider collecting the probe, analyzing the data to inform the instructional opportunities you will need to design to address examples on the list, and returning the initial list to the student at the end of an instructional unit for reflection. The lists can also be tallied and posted as a class chart so that students can examine the ideas held by the class, signifying the need to work toward developing a class consensus.

General Implementation Attributes

Ease of Use: High   Cognitive Demand: Medium/High
Time Demand: Medium

Modifications

Some students may not recognize a word on the list or may be unfamiliar with a symbol or representation. Have students cross off any examples on the list they do not recognize, and focus only on the familiar items. It may be helpful to provide picture icons where appropriate for younger students or students who are English language learners. The items on the list can also be put on cards and used as a *Card Sort* FACT.

Caveats

Make sure students are familiar with the items on the list. Otherwise, this FACT may end up being a vocabulary exercise or run the risk of being developmentally or contextually inappropriate.

Use With Other Disciplines

This FACT can also be used in *science*, social studies, language arts, health, foreign language, and visual and performing arts.

My Notes

_____

_____

_____

#26. JUSTIFIED TRUE-OR-FALSE STATEMENTS

Description

Justified True-or-False Statements provide a set of statements to be examined by students. The students draw upon mathematical concepts and procedures to analyze their validity. Students describe the reasoning they used to decide whether each statement is true or false.

How This FACT Promotes Student Learning

Justified True-or-False Statements provide individuals or small groups of students an opportunity to activate their thinking about a particular mathematical concept or procedure. Furthermore, this FACT supports the important mathematical skills of proof and conjecture—demonstrating that a statement is true in all cases (proof) or believed to be true (conjecture). Supporting or refuting the statements encourages students to use both inductive and deductive reasoning.

How This FACT Informs Instruction

This FACT is used to examine students' existing ideas, including their ability to defend or refute a mathematical statement. It can be used individually or in pairs, small groups, and whole-class discussions at the beginning of a lesson, at different points during a sequence of lessons, or at the end of an instructional unit as a reflection activity. Listen carefully as students discuss their own ideas and engage in mathematical argumentation with their classmates. Note strengths or weaknesses in their use of deductive and inductive reasoning skills that may need to be further strengthened through targeted instruction. For example, all students should understand that one counterexample proves a conjecture to be false, and older students should understand that finding even multiple examples does not prove the conjecture to be true and move toward forming generalized proofs (Waring, 2000). Identify areas of agreement or disagreement that could be addressed in subsequent lessons and discussions. Careful listening may also reveal areas of uncertainty that indicate the need to ensure adequate time for additional learning opportunities.

Design and Administration

Provide individuals or each group of students with a handout of the set of statements, such as the example on the topic of variables shown in Figure 4.18. This FACT can also be administered orally, posting the list of statements on a chart or overhead for students to discuss in small groups or with the whole class. Students discuss and justify each statement, one at a time, trying to come to an agreement on whether it is true or false and justifying their reasons, noting any instances where they cannot reach consensus.

Figure 4.18 *Justified True-or-False Statements for Variables*

Consider the equation a = 12 + b (when b ≠ 0)	T	F	Why I (we) think so
1) *a* is always greater than *b*			
2) *b* is always greater than *a*			
3) *a* = 12			
4) *a* and *b* could be equal			
5) *a* could not be less than 12			
6) If *b* is odd, then *a* must be even			

General Implementation Attributes

Ease of Use: Medium   Cognitive Demand: Medium/High
Time Demand: Medium

Modifications

For struggling readers, post the statements on a chart and read them aloud with the class. Use no more than three statements for younger children.

Caveats

Avoid using mostly statements that require simple recall. Statements should provoke student thinking, drawing out commonly held mathematical ideas that students might have related to the topic.

Use With Other Disciplines

This FACT can also be used in *science, social studies, language arts, health, foreign language, and visual and performing arts.

My Notes

_____

_____

_____

#27. K-W-L VARIATIONS

Description

K-W-L is a general elicitation technique in which students describe what they **K**now about a topic, **W**ant to know about a topic, and have **L**earned about the topic. There are different variations of *K-W-L*, depending on the students' age and the teacher's purpose.

How This FACT Promotes Student Learning

K-W-L provides an opportunity for students to become engaged with a topic and sets a purpose for learning. It is a metacognitive exercise that requires students to think about what they already know and wonder what they would like to learn. *K-W-L* provides a mechanism for self-assessment and reflection at the end, when students are asked to think about what they learned. The three phases of the *K-W-L* help students see the connections between what they already know, what they would like to learn, and what they actually learned after instruction.

How This FACT Informs Instruction

*K-W-L*s provide information to the teacher about students' prior knowledge at the beginning of a unit of instruction as well as at the end. Teachers can use the *What I know* information to determine familiarity with the concept or procedure and readiness to learn. When ideas that have developed previously are identified, instruction can focus on building new knowledge and experiences from students' starting points. Students' ideas can also be used by the teacher for discussion starters. As students share what they already know, questions are likely to emerge. The *What I want to know* provides an opportunity to design instructional experiences that include students' own ideas about what they would like to learn during the unit of instruction. Finally, the *What I learned* column provides an opportunity to examine the scope and depth of student learning and make adjustments as needed to improve instructional activities and further develop student understanding.

Figure 4.19   *K-W-L*

K: This is what I already KNOW	W: This is what I WANT to find out	L: This is what I LEARNED

Design and Administration

Provide students with a *K-W-L* handout, such as the template in Figure 4.19. Students fill in the first two columns prior to instruction. Collect and save their *K-W-Ls* and return them to use as a reflection at the end of an instructional unit. Students can individually complete a *K-W-L* and then share their responses that are recorded on a class chart and referred to throughout the instructional unit. If *K-W-L* is new to students, the teacher might start off as follows:

> Today we are going to learn about percents. You have a *K-W-L* chart to keep track of your thinking about percents. Take a moment to think about what you already know about percents. Write your ideas down in the *K* column. (Teacher gives students several minutes to write down their ideas.) Now I would like you to share some of the things you already know about percents, and I will record them on our class chart. As I record your ideas, you may have questions that come to mind about something you would like to know more about related to percents. Write down what you would like to know in the *W* column and be ready to share some of your wonderings. When we are done, I will collect your individual charts and return them to you at the end of our lessons so that you can fill in the *L* to share and reflect on what you learned.

General Implementation Attributes

Ease of Use: High   Cognitive Demand: Medium
Time Demand: Medium

Modifications

Other versions include: *K-W-F*: This is what I **K**now, This is what I **W**onder about, This is how I will **F**ind out; *K-T-F*: This is what I **K**now for sure, This is what I **T**hink I know, This is how I **F**ound out; *O-W-L*: This is what I **O**bserved, This is what I **W**onder about, This is what I **L**earned; *P-O-E*: This is what I **P**redict, This is what I **O**bserved, This is how I can **E**xplain it. A fourth column can be added to the standard *K-W-L* making it a *K-W-L-H*. The **H** stands for This Is **H**ow I Learned It.

Caveats

Be careful not to overuse this strategy, because students quickly tire of it if it is used in the same way with every instructional unit. Be aware that the open-ended nature of this FACT is not as effective in pinpointing specific misconceptions, learning gaps, or conceptual difficulties as some of the other probing techniques. The sharing of learning goals or targets before students complete the *K* and *W* columns can help keep students' elicited ideas more focused.

Use With Other Disciplines

This FACT can also be used in *science, social studies, language arts, health, foreign language, and visual and performing arts.

My Notes

_____

_____

_____

#28. LEARNING GOALS INVENTORY (LGI)

Description

An *LGI* is a set of questions that relate to an identified learning goal in a unit of instruction. Students are asked to "inventory" the extent to which they feel they have prior knowledge about the learning goal. They also describe prior learning experiences related to the learning goal.

How This FACT Promotes Student Learning

The *LGI* activates student thinking about a topic of instruction that targets explicitly identified learning goals. It requires them to think about what they already know in relation to the learning goal statement as well as when and how they may have learned about it. It also helps make the target learning goals explicit to students. A key principle of learning is that students must know what the learning target is. Explicitly sharing learning goals with students raises their awareness of the focus of a lesson.

How This FACT Informs Instruction

The *LGI* provides information to teachers on students' perceptions of their existing knowledge in relation to identified learning goals, including state or national standards. It also provides information on when and how students may have had opportunities to learn the ideas related to the goal. This information is particularly helpful when students are coming from other schools or classes within a school where there is not a consistent curriculum. It provides an opportunity for teachers to see which goals may be new to students, which are redundant, and which may provide an opportunity to revisit and build upon previous learning experiences.

Design and Administration

Identify the goals from the instructional unit or the state or national standards targeted in the unit of instruction. Create a question inventory on each goal, such as the one shown in Figure 4.20 for a high school unit on coordinate geometry. Give time for students to fill it out. Post the goals in a visible place in the classroom and refer to them throughout the instructional unit so students will know what the learning targets are. The *LGI* can be given back to students at the end of the instructional unit as a self-assessment and reflection on their learning, noting the difference between their ratings before and after the instructional unit.

Figure 4.20 *Learning Goals Inventory* for a High School Unit on Coordinate Geometry

---

Learning Goal: Specify locations and describe spatial relationships using coordinate geometry and other representational systems (National Council of Teachers of Mathematics, 2000, p. 308).

What do you think this learning goal is about?

List any facts, concepts, representations, or skills you are familiar with related to this learning goal:

List any terminology you know of that relates to this goal:

List any experiences you have had (in or outside school) that may have helped you learn about the ideas in this learning goal:

Source: Adapted from Keeley (2008), p. 132. Used with permission.

General Implementation Attributes

Ease of Use: Medium   Cognitive Demand: Medium
Time Demand: Medium

Modifications

The *LGI* can be used in an oral discussion format with younger students or completed as a whole-class inventory.

Caveats

Learning goals that come from state and national standards are interpreted in a variety of ways by teachers. Likewise, expect the same variation in interpretation from students. How one student may interpret a learning goal may be very different from how another student interprets it.

Use With Other Disciplines

This FACT can also be used in *science*, social studies, language arts, health, foreign language, and visual and performing arts.

My Notes

_____

_____

_____

#29. LOOK BACK

Description

A *Look Back* is an account of what students learned over a given instructional period of time. Students recount specific examples of things they know now that they didn't know before and describe how they learned them (B. Chagrasulis, personal communication, 2005).

How This FACT Promotes Student Learning

This FACT provides students with an opportunity to look back on and summarize their learning. Asking students "how they learned it" helps them think about their own learning and the different ways, as learners, they are able to integrate new mathematical understandings.

How This FACT Informs Instruction

Teachers can use the information from this FACT to examine aspects of an instructional sequence students seemed to get the most out of and determine why. The information can be used to inform the use of various strategies that may work well in other instructional units. *Look Back* also alerts teachers to strategies and activities that seem to be most effective for individual students. The information can be used to differentiate instruction for individual learners, based on their descriptions of what helped them learn.

Design and Administration

This FACT is best used no more than three weeks (or midway) into a sequence of instruction. It is important to model this FACT with students the first time you use it. Use a template such as the one shown in Figure 4.21. An example of a middle school prompt used with this FACT is:

> For the last 2 weeks, we have been studying different types of graphs. Please take 15 minutes to make a list of all the things you learned in the last 2 weeks that you didn't know before or understand fully when we began the unit. Next to each new learning you identified, please describe how you learned it and why that way of learning was effective for you. Your descriptions will be used by me to think about ways I can make your learning more effective and relevant.

Figure 4.21   Template for *Look Back*

What I Learned	How I Learned It

Source: Keeley (2008), p. 134. Used with permission.

General Implementation Attributes

Ease of Use: High   Cognitive Demand: Medium
Time Demand: Medium

Modifications

With younger students, use shorter amounts of time to look back. For example, use the end of the week for them to look back on the week's activities.

Caveats

Be aware that failure to mention some key concepts and procedures taught during the instructional period does not mean that students did not learn them. This FACT reveals what stood out most for students in their learning, not necessarily how much they learned. Some students may have difficulty looking back more than a few days. Provide the daily syllabus, sections used in the curriculum materials, or outline of the unit to help them retrace the instructional sequence.

Use With Other Disciplines

This FACT can also be used in *science, social studies, language arts, health, foreign language, and visual and performing arts.

My Notes

_____

_____

_____

#30. MATCHING CARDS

Description

Matching Cards involves finding pairs of cards that share the same relationship or attribute (for example, ¾ and 75%). This strategy works well for pairing problems and solutions, shapes and their attributes, terms and definitions, equations and the value of the variable, equivalence relationships, and words and representations.

How This FACT Promotes Student Learning

To demonstrate number sense, students decompose numbers, use particular numbers as referents, and solve problems using the relationships among operations and knowledge about the base 10 system

(National Council of Teachers of Mathematics, 2000). *Matching Cards* engages students in actively using their number sense to seek equivalent forms of numbers, expressions, and equations. When used in pairs or small groups, the FACT provides an engaging way for students to surface and share their thinking.

How This FACT Informs Instruction

This FACT can be used prior to a lesson for teachers to determine a starting point for instruction or to determine whether students have a misconception (for example, matching 4/5 and 2/3 because the difference between the numerator and denominator is 1). Matching cards can also be used to monitor student learning throughout instruction to examine how students are applying newly learned properties of numbers and operations. By having students share strategies in pairs, in groups, or as a whole group, teachers can use the information to plan instruction.

Design and Administration

Design cards that address the topic of instruction. Create several matching pairs according to the topic chosen. In addition to the pairs, include a few cards that do not match any of the other cards. Use the misconception research to create cards that do not match the others but that may be selected by students because of a commonly held misunderstanding. Cut out the cards, mix them up, and provide sets to pairs or small groups of students with the task of finding the pairs that match and explaining why they match. Figure 4.22 is an example of *Matching Cards* that address the topic of *Equivalence*. There are four matching pairs and four nonmatching cards. Students are asked to find matching pairs of equivalent values and explain why they are equivalent.

Figure 4.22 *Matching Cards* for the Topic of Equivalence

2/5	40%
.04	4/100
5^2	25
25%	1/4
2.5	4/1000
2.5%	2.5
10	5/2

General Implementation Attributes

Ease of Use: Medium   Cognitive Demand: Medium/High
Time Demand: Medium

Modifications

Blank cards can be included for students so they can create their own matches for the cards that do not match any of the other cards.

Caveats

Be sure to listen carefully to students' justifications for their match. Students may select the right match, but their reasoning may be faulty.

Use With Other Disciplines

This FACT can also be used in science, social studies, language arts, health, foreign language, and visual and performing arts.

My Notes

_____

_____

_____

#31. MATHEMATICIAN'S IDEAS COMPARISON

Description

Mathematician's Ideas Comparison provides students with an opportunity to compare how they explain a mathematical concept or solve a problem with how a mathematician would solve the problem or explain the concept to someone learning mathematics. Students compare their own ideas to the mathematician's ideas, looking for differences and similarities.

How This FACT Promotes Student Learning

Mathematician's Ideas Comparison is used to help students make connections between their developing or naïve mathematical ideas and mathematically correct ideas. It provides a metacognitive opportunity for students to examine their thinking to see how similar or different their ideas are compared with the way a mathematics expert might explain a concept or procedure. As they examine the expert's explanation or solution, they look for areas in their own work that might be changed to reflect new ideas gained from the information provided by the expert.

How This FACT Informs Instruction

This FACT is used to guide students toward mathematical thinking and understanding of a concept or procedure. As students work individually and in small groups to explain their own ideas, the teacher listens carefully, noting areas of discrepancy between the students' ideas and the correct answer or explanation. The teacher then provides students with a "mathematician's explanation." As students compare their ideas with the expert's ideas, the teacher notes how the students are considering the expert's explanation and using the information to correct, modify, or enhance their own work. If students are struggling to close the gap between their ideas and the mathematician's, this is a signal to the teacher that additional instructional opportunities are necessary to develop conceptual understanding. *Mathematician's Ideas Comparison* can be used after students have had an opportunity to explore mathematical ideas and are ready to move on to formal concept development.

Design and Administration

Choose a question that provides an opportunity for students to access their mathematical knowledge. For example, Figure 4.23 is a classic thought-experiment question that draws upon students' ideas related to proportionality and circumference (Arons, 1977; Leiber, 1942).

Prepare a handout as a mock example of how a mathematician or someone with expert mathematical knowledge might answer the question and explain it to a student. The mathematicians' ideas are the formal, mathematical explanation of the concept or problem written at a level that students should be able to follow and understand. For example, Figure 4.24 is an example of how a mathematics expert might explain the answer to the *String Around the Earth* question to a student in ninth grade.

Ask students to commit to an answer individually and explain their thinking. In small groups, ask students to make a list of the mathematical ideas they used to support their answer. After students have had an

Figure 4.23   Example Question Used for *Mathematician's Ideas Comparison*

String Around the Earth

Imagine that you tied a string around the center of the Earth along the equator. The string lies on top of the ground and the oceans. You then untied the string and added 6 more meters to the string. You pulled the string away from all sides of the Earth equally. What is the largest animal that could crawl under the string?

A. ant

B. mouse

C. cat

D. goat

E. horse

Explain your thinking. Provide an explanation for your answer.

Source: Keeley and Harrington (2010). Used with permission.

opportunity to generate their own mathematical ideas, provide students with the handout that explains how a mathematician would answer the question. Have students discuss in pairs or small groups how close they think their own ideas are to the mathematicians' ideas. Using the chart in Figure 4.25, have students list the ideas they had that were different from the mathematician's ideas, the ideas they had that were similar to the mathematician's ideas, and the ideas the mathematician described that were new to them or that they had not considered when answering the question. Use the students' charts to orchestrate class discussion about the comparison between their mathematical ideas and the way the mathematician explained it, checking for the extent to which students gained new ideas or changed misunderstandings.

Figure 4.24   Mathematician's Explanation of the *String Around the Earth* Problem

The best answer is *(D)* goat. The answer is highly counterintuitive. First, one needs to understand that the ratio of circumference to diameter (π) is true regardless of the size of the clrcle. Pi is a number that represents the change in the circumference of a circle for each unit of change in the diameter. If the circumference increases by 6 meters then the diameter will change by $6/\pi$ meters or by about 2 meters. Therefore the string will extend about a meter above the Earth on all sides. This answer is independent of the size of the circle that you start with (which is why you do not need to know the circumference of the Earth to answer this question).

You probably thought the string would hardly be off the ground at all. After all, you only added 6m, and the string's length was 40,074,000 meters to start with (the circumference of the Earth). It is surprising that the answer is that the string will be about 1 meter off the ground, all the way around the Earth! You probably think this is a very large distance for so little change to the total length of the string!

Another way to look at the problem may make the answer seem more reasonable. The height of 1 meter is in addition to the *radius* of the Earth. Since the Earth's radius is about 6,378,000 meters, the change in height *is* in fact very small.

Let's try it with this calculation (using approximations):

$C = 2\,\pi\,r$

$C = 2\,\pi\,6{,}378{,}000$ m

$C = 40{,}074{,}157$ m

With 6m added to the string, C now $= 40{,}074{,}163$ m

The radius of the new circle: $r = C/2\pi$ which $= 40{,}074{,}163/2\pi$ which $= 6{,}378{,}001$ m

Radius of circle with string around Earth $= 6{,}378{,}000$ m

Radius of circle with string around the Earth plus 6 added meters of string $= 6{,}378{,}001$ m

Difference between the two radii (which is the height above the Earth) $=$ about 1 meter

Try a similar problem using a basketball. Predict how far do you think the string would stretch above a basketball if you wound a string around its circumference and then added 6 additional centimeters of string and pulled it in all directions.

Figure 4.25   Sample Recording Chart for *Mathematician's Ideas Comparison*

Our Ideas	Similar Ideas	Mathematician's Ideas

General Implementation Attributes

Ease of Use: Medium   Cognitive Demand: High
Time Demand: Medium

Modifications

A Venn Diagram, with two overlapping circles—*Our Ideas* and *Mathematician's Ideas*—can be used as a graphic organizer to compare students' ideas with the mathematician's ideas. In the intersection of the two circles, students record their ideas that were similar to the mathematician's ideas. In the *Our Ideas* circle, they record ideas they had that were different from the mathematician's. In the *Mathematician's Ideas* area, they record ideas from the mathematician's explanation that they had not considered. This FACT can also be used with the *Card Sort* strategy. After students have sorted their cards, if you notice discrepancies between the way students sorted their cards and the "best answer" to the card sort, consider giving students some clues from a mathematician's statement and invite them to resort their cards based on the new information.

Caveats

Mathematicians have a sophisticated way of talking about and representing mathematics. Make sure the terminology and explanations provided in the *Mathematician's Ideas* handout are at an appropriate developmental level for the grade level with which you use this FACT. The purpose is to have a mathematics expert explain the concept, procedure, or solution in ways that a student could understand.

Use With Other Disciplines

This FACT is also used in *science* as a *Scientist's Ideas Comparison*.

My Notes

_____

_____

_____

#32. MORE A–MORE B PROBES

Description

More A–More B Probes are comparison tasks designed to reveal whether students use an intuitive rule, described as "More A–More B," to compare quantities (Stavy & Tirosh, 2000). These types of probes can be used in equality situations (in which two things are equal in one quantity but differ in another, such as same volume, different shape) or inequality situations (inverse ratios and proportions or when there is no fixed relationship between A and B).

How This FACT Promotes Student Learning

This FACT can be used to help students examine situations in mathematics as well as in everyday life in which they are presented with two seemingly different quantities and must decide whether they are the same or different. The probe encourages students to consider how they make judgments about quantities and the factors that might affect their judgment (such as visual perception or number value). It promotes critical thinking in mathematics by encouraging students not to rely on the external features of a task but to draw upon concepts that move them beyond mere perception.

How This FACT Informs Instruction

More A–More B Probes help teachers become more aware of a strongly held intuitive rule that, according to researchers Stavy and Tirosh (2000), may be the common core to many of the misconceptions that are reported in the research literature. By becoming aware of this rule and using questions that reveal its use in students' thinking, teachers can select particular teaching methods that will help students overcome the strong effect the rule has on their learning.

Design and Administration

Designing questions for this FACT is similar to doing so for other types of probes in that it involves a two-tier question: (1) a selected-response-type question that is likely to reveal the misconception a teacher is probing for, and (2) an opportunity for the student to justify his or her thinking. The questions are comparison tasks in which students are asked to compare two quantities and decide whether they are the same or different. They can be given as paper-and-pencil tasks or put up as a visual aid for class discussion. The following is an example of an equality situation. The teacher drew a vertical angle with unequal arms.

The students were asked to decide if the pair of angles is equal. The teacher was looking to see whether some students thought one angle was larger because the arms were longer. This would be an example of the use of more A–more B reasoning.

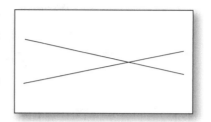

Other types of *More A–More B Probes* include but are not limited to classical Piagetian tasks such as pouring the same amount of water into differently shaped containers, numbers of objects in a row where one row has the same number but the objects are spread out more, area problems where the two shapes are different but have the same area, probability questions where the number of total objects with the same proportion is greater, comparison of fractions with larger denominators, equal proportions with one numerator being much larger than the other, and 0.01 compared to 0.1 versus .10 compared to 0.1. When using a *More A–More B Probe*, make sure students are asked to explain the rule they used to select their answer. Listen carefully for evidence of more A–more B reasoning. If students use this type of reasoning, probe deeper by asking them how they came up with their rule. Ask them to explain where they have seen or used it before.

General Implementation Attributes

Ease of Use: Medium
Time Demand: Medium

Cognitive Demand: Depends on
    question

Modifications

This strategy can be used as a *Card Sort* in which students are given a variety of comparisons and asked to sort them into groups in which the comparison is the same.

Caveats

When using comparison probes such as this one, make sure the correct answer is not always the same. Vary the questions so that sometimes the use of this intuitive rule results in the correct answer being that the elements being compared are different.

Use With Other Disciplines

This FACT can also be used in science.

My Notes

_____

_____

_____

#33. MUDDIEST POINT

Description

Muddiest Point is a commonly used, quick monitoring technique in which students are asked to take a few minutes to jot down what the most difficult or confusing part of a lesson was for them (Angelo & Cross, 1993).

How This FACT Promotes Student Learning

The *Muddiest Point* provides a metacognitive opportunity for students to think about their own learning and what it is that is difficult or easy for them to understand. It is especially helpful when students encounter new information, complicated procedures, or engage in discussions that result in cognitive conflict. This FACT provides a comfortable outlet for students who are reluctant to speak out and let others know when they are having difficulty understanding a concept or procedure.

How This FACT Informs Instruction

The *Muddiest Point* is a feedback and monitoring strategy used to efficiently collect information on what students find most difficult or confusing about a lesson or part of a lesson. It can be used any time during instruction, including on the spur of the moment when teachers detect that students may be experiencing difficulty understanding a concept or using a procedure. The information provides feedback to the teacher that can be used to modify teaching strategies in order to address student difficulties. Teachers can quickly administer, collect, and sort responses to make immediate decisions about instruction for the whole class or to differentiate instruction for individual students. It can also be used at the end of a lesson to assess where students are in understanding the key learning targets of the lesson. The information helps the teacher prepare for strategies or activities that will address students' difficulties in the next lesson.

Design and Administration

At a determined point during a lesson, distribute half sheets of paper or index cards. Ask students to describe the "muddiest point" of the lesson thus far. Clarify what is meant by "muddiest point." For example, a high school algebra teacher using this FACT at the end of a lesson to assess students' content understanding might say:

Today we have been learning about quadratic equations. What has been the muddiest point so far in today's lesson for you? Please take a few minutes to jot down any ideas or parts of the lesson that were difficult for you to understand so I can address them for you tomorrow.

An elementary teacher might use this FACT to determine how well students can use an algorithm: "Today we have been exploring how to subtract two-digit numbers. What is the muddiest point for you so far when you try to subtract the numbers?"

Let students know why you are asking for this information. Collect their responses and decide how the information will inform the rest of the lesson or the following lesson. Be sure to let students know how you plan to use their responses. When they realize that you will seriously consider their feedback to make changes that will benefit them, they will respond thoughtfully and with detail. After reading the responses and taking action, share with students examples of the responses that informed your instructional decisions.

General Implementation Attributes

Ease of Use: High   Cognitive Demand: Low/Medium
Time Demand: Low

Modifications

This strategy can also be used with homework and in-class assignments. It can be combined with a question asking students what could be done to help clear up the "muddy points" for them.

Caveats

This FACT focuses on the negative, rather than the positive. Vary this strategy with *POMS: Points of Most Significance*, to provide opportunities for students to identify the most significant part of a lesson or the parts of the lesson that were best understood.

Use With Other Disciplines

This FACT can also be used in *science, social studies, language arts, health, foreign language, and visual and performing arts.

My Notes

_____

_____

_____

#34. NO-HANDS QUESTIONING

Description

Students typically raise their hands when they wish to respond to a teacher's question. With *No-Hands Questioning* students do not put their hands up to respond to a teacher's question. The teacher poses a question, practices *Wait Time*, and calls on students randomly. This FACT acknowledges that everyone needs to be ready to share his or her ideas. It reinforces the notion that everyone's response is important, not just those of students who show they know the answer by raising their hand (Black et al., 2003).

How This Strategy Promotes Student Learning

No-Hands Questioning is used to stimulate thinking and provide an opportunity for all students to be asked to share their ideas, not just students who raise their hands. Often, when a question is asked, hands will shoot up immediately. As a result, the students who take longer to think about a problem stop thinking once they see that others already have the answer. This FACT can increase students' engagement and motivation to think about their ideas and frame a high-quality response, since everyone in the class has an equal chance of being called upon to respond.

How This Strategy Informs Instruction

This FACT, combined with *Wait Time*, is a way for teachers to encourage all students to be active participants in the learning process. Many students have been habituated to raise their hands. *No-Hands Questioning* provides an opportunity for teachers to hear from a wide range of students in the class, not just those who raise their hands or opt out by not raising their hand. It is particularly useful when you need to learn what certain students in the class who typically do not raise their hands are thinking.

Design and Administration

Prepare a set of high-quality questions ahead of time (see Appendix for source material on developing high-quality questions). Practice *Wait Time* both before and after posing a question. Call on a student by name before posing the full question and then extend the question further to probe for his or her ideas, giving the student additional time to think. The manner in which questions are asked by the teacher when a student is called upon indicates to students that the teacher is interested in their thinking. The following example shows how questions can be framed using this FACT:

Teacher: "What do you think would happen to the area of this square if I doubled the length of the sides?"

Teacher pauses for wait time.

Teacher: "Jana, what do you think?"

Jana: "Well, I think the area would be twice as large because it's multiplied by 2."

Teacher pauses for wait time after Jana's response.

Teacher: "What do others think about Jana's idea?"

Teacher pauses for wait time.

Teacher: "Tyrone, what do you think?"

Tyrone: "I think it would be more than double because if you started with a side that was 3 centimeters, the area would be 9, but if you doubled 3 to make 6, the area would be 36. That's more than doubling 9."

Teacher pauses for wait time.

Teacher: "Would someone like to add to Tyrone's idea or share a different thought?"

Teacher pauses.

Teacher: "Petra, what are you thinking about right now?"

Share the reason for using this FACT with students so they understand that it is intended to help them think, provide an opportunity for any student to be heard, and share various ideas that different students may have. Make sure students know that every idea is valued, not just the right answer, so all students feel they have something to share in response to the question. Encourage students to challenge statements or build upon each others' ideas.

General Implementation Attributes

Ease of Use: High

Time Demand: Low

Cognitive Demand: Depends on the question

Modifications

You may choose to use random selection techniques such as cards with students' names on them or the *Hot Seat Questioning* or *Popsicle Stick Questioning* FACT to select specific students you want to hear from. A modified version of *No-Hands Questioning* combined with *Wait Time* is to have students put their hands up when they have an idea or comment to share. The teacher nods to the individual student when a hand goes up. The nod is the signal to then put the hand down. Once a significant number of hands have gone up and then down, call on selected students.

Caveats

Avoid the use of recall questions, as they tend to result in more "I don't know" responses and provide little information on conceptual understanding.

Use With Other Disciplines

This FACT can also be used in *science*, social studies, language arts, health, foreign language, and visual and performing arts.

My Notes

_____

_____

_____

#35. ODD ONE OUT

Description

Odd One Out combines seemingly similar items and challenges students to choose which item in the group does not belong (Naylor et al., 2004). Students are asked to justify their reason for selecting the number, symbol, representation, or mathematical term that does not fit with the others.

How This Strategy Promotes Student Learning

Odd One Out provides an opportunity for students to access mathematical knowledge to analyze relationships between items in a group. By thinking about the similarities and differences, students are encouraged to use their reasoning skills in a challenging and engaging way. The FACT can be used to stimulate small-group discussion after students have had an opportunity to think through their own ideas. As students discuss their ideas in a group, they may modify their thinking or come up with ways to prove or disprove their ideas.

How This Strategy Informs Instruction

Odd One Out can be used at the beginning of instruction to find out what students already know about a mathematics topic. It can also be used during the development of conceptual understanding to examine the reasoning students use in comparing and contrasting the items on the list. Teachers can use this FACT to examine how their students make connections among concepts. The information is helpful in considering instructional experiences that can challenge students' misunderstandings.

Design and Administration

Select items that lend themselves to a grouping where one item justifiably does not fit with the others. Be sure to choose items and a relationship that is not immediately obvious in order to promote deeper thinking. Provide the list as a handout, overhead projection, chart, or set of cards. Alert students to what the topic of the *Odd One Out* is before they examine the items. Have students record their own answers and thinking before discussing their ideas with a partner or in small groups. Allow students enough time to discuss the various possibilities before homing in on "the odd one out." Figure 4.26 shows an example of an *Odd One Out* designed for middle school students learning about fractions.

Figure 4.26   Fractions Example for *Odd One Out*

Which is the "odd one out"? Circle the fraction in each set that does not belong				Explanation
3/4	15/20	8/9	33/44	
2/3	2/5	3/8	7/15	
2/7	8/9	4/10	1/5	
1/2	1/3	1/4	1/5	

General Implementation Attributes

Ease of Use: High   Cognitive Demand: Medium/High
Time Demand: Medium

Modifications

With younger children, provide three examples on cards and ask them to pick the card that does not belong.

Caveats

Make sure students are familiar with the words or representations used before they are asked to examine the relationship between them. Be aware that some students may choose a different odd one out, and correctly note relationships that you did not have in mind when you made up the examples and selected the odd one out.

Use With Other Disciplines

This FACT can also be used in *science*, social studies, language arts, health, foreign language, and visual and performing arts.

My Notes

_____

_____

_____

#36. OPPOSING VIEWS PROBES

Description

Opposing Views Probes present two or more characters with conflicting mathematical ideas. Students are asked to pick the person whom they most agree with and explain why.

How This Strategy Promotes Student Learning

Opposing Views provides an opportunity for students to access their mathematical knowledge to compare two or more different ways to think about a mathematical problem or concept. This FACT can be used to stimulate small-group discussion after students have had an opportunity to think through their own ideas and decide whose viewpoint most closely matches their own. As students discuss and defend their viewpoints in small groups, they are encouraged to carefully listen and consider others' viewpoints. As a result they may modify their thinking or switch their view based on convincing arguments.

How This Strategy Informs Instruction

Opposing Views can be used at the beginning of instruction to find out what students already know about a mathematics topic. It can also be used during the development of conceptual understanding to examine the reasoning students use in comparing and contrasting opposing views. Teachers can use this FACT to examine not only their students' conceptual knowledge but also their ability to make convincing arguments that support their mathematical view. This information can be used to design experiences that will provide students with the opportunity to practice strategies that will help strengthen their mathematical arguments.

Design and Administration

Choose *Opposing Views* that reflect commonly held misconceptions or procedural errors. *Mathematics Curriculum Topic Study* (Keeley & Rose, 2006) is an excellent resource for connecting common misconceptions to a mathematical topic. Use a cartoon design such as the example in Figure 4.27 or use a *Friendly Talk Probe* format. After students select the person whose view most closely matches their own, they are asked to provide a justification to explain their thinking. This probe can be administered as a paper-and-pencil assessment or used as a discussion prompt combined with other FACTs to stimulate mathematical discussion.

Figure 4.27   Example of *Opposing View Probe* on Multiplication

Source: Rose, Minton, & Arline (2007), p. 75. Used with permission.

General Implementation Attributes

Ease of Use: High   Cognitive Demand: Medium/High
Time Demand: Medium

Modifications

With younger children, it is best to use no more than two views. Consider adding visual cues for English language learners.

Caveats

As a result of learning some test-taking strategies, some students will not select answers that contain the words *always* or *never*. Vary the use of the probe so that the correct answer sometimes includes these qualifiers.

Use With Other Disciplines

This FACT can also be used in science, social studies, language arts, health, foreign language, and visual and performing arts.

My Notes

_____

_____

_____

#37. OVERGENERALIZATION PROBES

Description

Sometimes students learn an algorithm, rule, or shortcut and then extend this information to another context in an incorrect way (Rose & Arline, 2009). *Overgeneralization Probes* are two-tiered selected response questions that elicit these overgeneralizations.

How This FACT Promotes Student Learning

Overgeneralization Probes activate student thinking about a particular algorithm, rule, procedure, definition, or concept they learned about in prior instruction. The probe encourages them to think about different contexts in which they can apply their mathematical ideas.

How This FACT Informs Instruction

Overgeneralization Probes help teachers identify areas where students make incorrect generalizations that often remain hidden unless the teacher uses specific strategies to surface them. Once these overgeneralizations are identified, teachers can select appropriate strategies to help students understand when a rule, definition, algorithm, symbol, or other mathematical idea or representation applies or does not apply in a given context.

Design and Administration

Overgeneralization Probes are designed much like a *Justified List*. Students are given a variety of examples that have some similarity to the targeted mathematical concept or idea and are asked to select the examples that match a given situation, word, or concept. The distracters selected should have the potential to reveal a lack of conceptual understanding. Students are asked to provide a justification for the examples they selected. Figure 4.28 is an example of an *Overgeneralization Probe*. In this probe literal symbols are used to represent an unknown number (variable). The literal symbols in E and F are considered variables in mathematics. While other literal symbols (B, C, and D) may indicate abbreviations for units of measurement, an operation sign ($\times$), or positions or points on a geometric figure.

Figure 4.28　Example *Overgeneralization* Probe

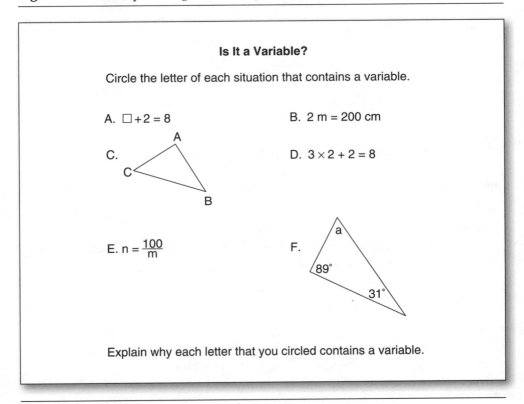

Is It a Variable?

Circle the letter of each situation that contains a variable.

A. □ + 2 = 8

B. 2 m = 200 cm

C.

D. 3 × 2 + 2 = 8

E. $n = \dfrac{100}{m}$

F.

Explain why each letter that you circled contains a variable.

Source: Rose & Arline (2009), p. 200. Used with permission.

General Implementation Attributes

Ease of Use: Medium
Time Demand: Medium

Cognitive Demand: Medium/High

Modifications

This type of probe can also be used as a *Card Sort.*

Caveats

Be sure to provide a follow-up experience so that students recognize the incorrect application of the targeted mathematical idea and can work through their misunderstandings.

Use With Other Disciplines

This FACT can also be used in science, social studies, language arts, health, and visual and performing arts.

My Notes

_____

_____

_____

#38. PARTNER SPEAKS

Description

Partner Speaks provides students with an opportunity to talk through a concept or problem solution with another student and receive feedback before sharing with a larger group. When ideas are shared with the larger group, pairs speak from the perspective of their partner's ideas. This encourages careful listening between student pairs and encourages students to summarize their partner's' thinking so that others can understand.

How This Strategy Promotes Student Learning

Having a partner to talk with allows students to think through and articulate their ideas to others for feedback before sharing with a larger group. It helps students develop careful listening and paraphrasing skills since the strategy requires them to share their partner's thinking, not their own. *Partner Speaks* provides an opportunity for shy, less confident students who may not be comfortable sharing their own ideas in a large group to let their ideas be heard through someone else. It also teaches overconfident, dominating students to honor and accept the ideas of others rather than focusing solely on their own ideas. *Partner Speaks* can be used to promote deeper engagement with an idea, especially when there is a need to have students think through a new idea, difficult question, or novel context.

How This Strategy Informs Instruction

This FACT can be used during any point in a lesson when social engagement enhances the development and sharing of ideas. As teachers listen to the interaction, they learn more about student thinking in preparation for the next steps in a lesson or sequence of instruction.

Design and Administration

Have students turn to their "elbow partner" and provide time for them to take turns discussing a concept or problem and giving feedback on each other's ideas. When using this strategy for the first time, it may be helpful to model for students what it looks and sounds like when two people are engaged in dialogue (one person speaks while the other listens and vice versa, with the purpose of deepening thinking) and when it is appropriate to give feedback (after students have had a chance to articulate their thinking). Each pair then tries to summarize what their partner's ideas were and what feedback was helpful. Encourage students to make eye contact and think about what their partner is saying as they respectfully listen without interrupting. The following is an example of how a teacher might describe this FACT to learn more about algorithms students use to add three-digit numbers.

> Today we are going to explore different ways to add three-digit numbers together. What different kinds of strategies can you use to add 346 + 525? Turn to your partner and take turns discussing your strategies. Be sure to listen carefully, without interrupting, as your partner shares his or her thinking. When you describe your own thinking, be sure to explain to your partner the reasons for your ideas. When you are finished taking turns, each of you will need to be prepared to share one way your partner added these numbers with the rest of the class. You will not be talking about your own method but rather the method your partner used. Thus it is very important for you to be a good listener and not interrupt your partner's thoughts. When your partner finishes speaking or seeks your help, you may provide feedback to help your partner with his or her thinking.

General Implementation Attributes

Ease of Use: High   Cognitive Demand: High
Time Demand: Medium

Modifications

Combine this strategy with various methods for mixing up students and assigning partners so that students are not always talking with the same person. This strategy can also be used in triads if necessary.

Caveats

In some classes, gender and friendship issues may hinder the use of *Partner Speaks*. It is recommended that teachers establish norms for partner discussions. Students should also be reminded not to pass judgment on their partner's ideas when they report to the class. Provide time for the whole class to give feedback on the different ideas that emerge.

Use With Other Disciplines

This FACT can also be used in *science*, social studies, language arts, health, foreign language, and visual and performing arts.

My Notes

_____

_____

_____

#39. PASS THE PROBLEM

Description

Pass the Problem provides an opportunity for students to collaborate in activating their own ideas and examining other students' thinking. Students begin by working together in pairs to respond to a problem, partially completing a solution to the problem. When the time is up, they exchange their partially completed solution with another pair to finish—modifying, adding to, or changing it as the pair deems necessary.

How This FACT Promotes Student Learning

The interactive nature of the pair discussion provides an opportunity for students to think about what they know and come to a consensus of thinking with their partner. After the partially finished solution is passed to a new pair of students, the new pair must examine the solution strategy of their peers and decide whether they agree with the approach to solving the problem. If so, the pair finishes solving the problem by completing what was already started by the other pair. If their strategy differs, they may modify or change the response the other pair started and complete it for them, but they must explain why they chose not to use the other pair's strategy. Pairs then get together to give feedback to each other on why they did or did not change the strategy. They also provide feedback on how well they felt the record of the other pair's thinking helped them pick up where the original pair's solution left off. This FACT also helps students recognize the importance of showing your work so that others can follow your thinking.

How This FACT Informs Instruction

As teachers listen carefully to students discuss their ideas in response to the problem, they gather evidence on the nature and depth of students' understanding of the concepts and procedures related to the problem. The information may surface disagreements students have about what the problem is asking for or the solution strategy used, furthering the need to design additional opportunities that will address the type of problem students are working on. The student responses can also be collected and examined to see the range of students' thinking about the problem and the strategies they used, indicating the need for differentiation with certain groups of students.

Design and Administration

Choose a problem that requires students to analyze the context in order to determine what it is the problem asks for and what their solution strategy is, preferably one that involves multiple steps. Arrange students in pairs. Provide students with the problem. Give pairs 3 to 5 minutes to discuss the problem and collaboratively begin working on the solution. Make sure students know they need to show their work and make their thinking visible so that another pair can follow their strategy but not so much that it doesn't leave room for the other pair to complete it. Then have pairs swap their partially completed problems with another pair. The pairs then continue to pick up from where the other pair left off. Encourage pupils to cross off parts they don't agree with and modify or exchange the crossed-off part with their own ideas or strategy or continue by adding their own ideas to enhance and complete the solution. When both pairs are finished, they share the completed responses with each other, defending their reasons for any changes they made and providing feedback on each other's thinking and chosen strategy. The teacher may ask pairs to share some examples, providing feedback from the teacher and/or the class on the various solutions and ways of recording their solutions so others can follow.

General Implementation Attributes

Ease of Use: Medium   Cognitive Demand: High
Time Demand: Medium

Modifications

This FACT can also be used with individuals. An individual student starts the response and then exchanges with another student for completion and sharing. It can also be a written exchange between two different classes solving the same problem.

Caveats

Make sure time is provided to debrief the problem and engage students in a class discussion about the solution.

Use With Other Disciplines

This FACT can also be used in *science* to examine approaches to a scientific problem.

My Notes

_____

_____

_____

#40. P-E-O PROBES (PREDICT, EXPLAIN, OBSERVE)

Description

The P-E-O strategy was developed by White and Gunstone (1992) to uncover individual students' predictions and their reasons for making their prediction about a specific event. In mathematics, _P-E-O Probes_ present a situation in which students are asked to make a prediction or select a prediction from a set of responses that best matches their own thinking. Students must explain the reasoning that supports their prediction. The probe is followed by an opportunity for students to test their prediction, observe and analyze the results, and modify their explanation as needed.

How This FACT Promotes Student Learning

P-E-O Probes draw out students' ideas and explanations related to mathematical ideas that can lead to an investigation where students have an opportunity to test their ideas. This FACT activates student thinking about mathematical ideas and provides an opportunity to discuss their thinking and defend their reasoning. The probe provides an entry point into a mathematical investigation that engages students in wanting to know if their prediction is correct. When their observation does not match their prediction, it creates a dissonance that leads to further investigation or discussion to resolve the conflict between the ideas that led to their prediction and the explanation that supports the actual outcome.

How This FACT Informs Instruction

P-E-O Probes provide a way for teachers to gather data on students' common misunderstandings in mathematics. For example, in the Gumballs in a Jar probe shown in Figure 4.29, some students may predict that there is a better chance of getting a black gumball in Jar B. This response comes from a common misunderstanding of probability in which the students focus on the absolute size of the sample instead of the relative size of the sample when comparing the likelihood of events. _P-E-O Probes_ are best used as an elicitation and exploration into testing students' ideas. This FACT can be used individually as a written assessment or given to pairs and small groups to discuss their ideas and come to agreement on a prediction. They can then test their prediction using a hands-on activity,

Figure 4.29   Example *P-E-O Probe*

Gumballs in a Jar

Two jars hold black and white gumballs.
Jar A: 3 black and 2 white
Jar B: 6 black and 4 white

Jar A   Jar B

Which statement best describes the chance of getting a *black* gumball?

A. There is a better chance of getting a black gumball from Jar A.

B. There is a better chance of getting a black gumball from Jar B.

C. The chance of getting a black gumball is the same
for both Jar A and Jar B.

Explain your reason for the statement you selected.

Source: Rose, Minton, & Arline (2007), p. 122. Used with permission.

manipulatives, or an interactive technology-based simulation such as the one shown in Figure 4.30. Teachers examine or listen carefully to the students' justification for their predictions and monitor students' explanations after they test their predictions, especially if they find that their results do not match their original prediction. This is an opportunity to guide students toward reconciling what they believed would happen and what the actual result was. Teachers can use this opportunity to help students think through, discuss, and get feedback on their revised explanations in order to accommodate the change in their thinking that resulted from their investigation. For example, when students test their ideas with similar numbers of black and white objects, that experience provides an ideal time to revisit part-whole relationships and develop conceptual understanding of how probability is used to predict outcomes. The discussion might also reveal instances where students make a correct prediction but their explanation reveals a lack of conceptual understanding of the mathematics. For example, in Figure 4.29 some students might select the correct response *C* but reveal incorrect reasoning such as "It's the same because you can't know for sure what would happen."

Figure 4.30 Example P-E-O Tool for Observation

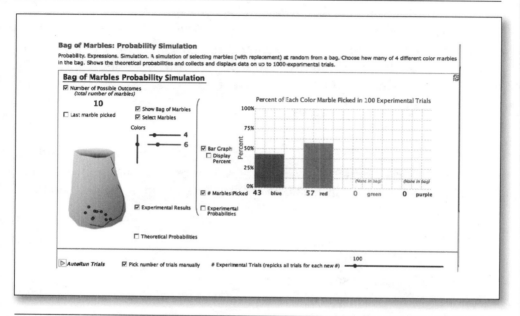

Source: Educational Development Center in Maine (2010); http://res4me.edc.org/ggb/BagOfMarbles. Used with permission.

Design and Administration

Design *P-E-O Probes* to target important learning goals in mathematics that can be tested using simple materials or technology-based simulations. You can also use ready-made probes that have been extensively field-tested. A source for these probes is given in the Appendix. Encourage students to record their own prediction and explanation before discussing their ideas in small groups. After students have had an opportunity to discuss their predictions and modify their ideas as needed, have small groups engage in a mathematical investigation using manipulatives or materials similar to the ones in the probe to test their predictions. After they observe the result, be sure to provide time for students to revisit and revise their explanation, extending the probe to become *P-E-O-E*, in which students must now revise their explanation based on the results of their investigation. Engage the whole class in a discussion to help students accommodate the result and solidify their conceptual understanding of the mathematics that led to the correct prediction.

General Implementation Attributes

Ease of Use: Medium   Cognitive Demand: Medium/High
Time Demand: Medium/High

Modifications

After students have committed to an outcome and discussed their ideas with others, teachers can use the probe scenario as a whole-class demonstration if materials or time are limited. The results of the demonstration can be used in orchestrating discourse to help students revise their original explanation and further develop their conceptual understanding.

Caveats

To use this FACT effectively, make sure you provide adequate time for students to explain their thinking before testing their prediction and observing the result.

Use With Other Disciplines

This FACT is also used in *science.

My Notes

_____

_____

_____

#41. PEER-TO-PEER FOCUSED FEEDBACK

Description

To support both self- and peer-assessment, the teacher must provide structure and support that enables students learn to reflect on their own work and that of their peers, allowing them to provide meaningful and constructive feedback (Council of Chief State School Officers, 2008, p. 5). *Peer-to-Peer Focused Feedback* is a technique used to focus peer-to-peer assessment on providing feedback that can be used to move thinking forward. The FACT is designed to help students address for their peers three important questions (Hattie & Timperley, 2007; Sadler, 1989):

1. What are the goals?

2. What progress is being made toward the goals?

3. What do I need to do next to reach the goals?

How This FACT Promotes Student Learning

Receiving feedback and being given an opportunity to respond to it is an important and rich activity for the learner. The feedback clarifies the learning goal as well as where the student has met or has not met the goal. If the student has not met the goal fully, the feedback provides guidance on next steps to better meet the goal. Research shows that those who provide feedback benefit just as much as those who receive the feedback because the givers of the feedback are forced to internalize learning intentions and success criteria in the context of someone else's work, which is less emotionally charged than examining one's own work (Wiliam & Thompson, 2006, p. 6).

How This Fact Informs Instruction

Teachers who use this strategy support a classroom culture in which peer and self-assessment are considered key to the formative assessment process. *Peer-to-Peer Focused Feedback* provides insight on two levels: (1) the ability of a student to identify attributes related to the criteria for success in others' work and (2) the ability for students to use feedback to make changes to their own work.

Design and Administration

Use with assignments that provide an opportunity for students to demonstrate their conceptual understanding, including solving multistep problems and explaining solution steps, making and justifying conjectures, and providing examples and nonexamples. Establish the criteria for success prior to having students complete the task. Have each student complete Question 1 on the Focusing Feedback template in Figure 4.31. After the task is completed, pair students to provide each other feedback by having each student answer Question 2 and Question 3 about the other student's work. Provide time for students to review the peer feedback and to make revisions.

General Implementation Attributes

Ease of Use: High   Cognitive Demand: High
Time Demand: High

Modifications

This FACT can also be used by the teacher to provide feedback to students or by students to self-assess their own work.

Caveats

For this FACT to be used successfully, teachers must first model the process. Model the process of providing feedback with students by using

Figure 4.31 *Peer-to-Peer Focused Feedback*

Peer-to-Peer Focused Feedback   Name:_____

1. What are the criteria for success?

Peer Reviewer:_____

2. Which of the criteria have been met? List specific examples in my work that showed you I have met the criteria.

3. Which of the criteria haven't been met? Provide suggestions that may help me when I revise my work.

mock student work or student work from previous years, if available. Because this strategy reinforces the notions that the teacher wants students to improve their work and that their improvement is being monitored by the teacher, time should be provided in class for students to read and react to the peer comments. Whenever possible, provide at least some time in class for students to begin work with clear direction for them to continue on their own.

Use With Other Disciplines

This FACT can also be used in science, social studies, language arts, health, foreign language, and visual and performing arts.

My Notes

_____

_____

_____

#42. A PICTURE TELLS A THOUSAND WORDS

Description

In this FACT, students are digitally photographed during a mathematical investigation using manipulatives or other materials. Students are given the photograph and asked to describe what they were doing in the picture (Carlson et al., 2003). Students write about the activity under the photograph, describing what they were doing and what they learned as a result.

How This FACT Promotes Student Learning

Students enjoy seeing themselves in photographs. There is a high level of engagement and an intrinsic desire to want to explain what is happening in a picture when the student is part of it. Asking students to annotate a photograph that shows them engaged in a mathematics activity or investigation helps them activate their thinking about the mathematics, connect important concepts and procedures to the experience shown in the picture, and reflect on their learning. This FACT can motivate reluctant writers to write more vivid, detailed accounts of their mathematics learning because the photograph personalizes it for them.

How This FACT Informs Instruction

Periodically taking digital photographs of the class during mathematics investigations and other activities involving manipulatives and other objects provides the teacher and the class with a documented way to track how students' ideas and skills are developing through mathematical inquiry using a variety of materials. The images can be used to spark student discussions, explore new ideas, and probe their thinking as it relates to the moment the photograph was snapped. By asking students to annotate the photos with descriptions of what they were doing, why they were doing it, and what they were learning at that moment, teachers can better understand what students are gaining from the instructional activity and adjust it as needed. If students can't describe what they were learning, then this is a signal to the teacher that the purpose of the activity was not clear. It also helps the teacher see how students' conceptual understanding evolves throughout an investigation and what might be done differently to help students move forward in the investigation. The photographs can also be used to spark whole-class discussions that provide an opportunity to probe deeper into students' ideas, thinking processes, and problem-solving strategies. At the end of a unit, the photographs can be posted on a reflection wall and used as a class reflection to retrace the students' thinking and learning.

Design and Administration

Digital cameras make it quick and easy to take and print a picture. This FACT can be used at any time during students' mathematical investigations.

It is particularly effective when students are excited about a discovery, experience something unexpected, or have an "aha" moment during the activity. Choose situations where students can relate to and remember what happened in the photograph. Encourage students to call you over to take a picture when they think it is important to share something that happened or show the result of a manipulation. After taking photographs, download and copy them onto a page that allows enough space on the paper for students to describe their "mathematical moment." Distribute the photograph to students for reflection as soon as possible after taking the photograph. Encourage students to write a detailed description of what they were doing, thinking, and learning about when the photograph was taken. In addition, the teacher can add feedback notes to comment on the students' pictures and annotations. Posting the annotated photos further reinforces the importance of sharing students' experiences and thinking.

The reflective, annotated writing can be assigned to individual students or as a group reflection by the students shown in the photograph. The group reflection provides an additional opportunity for students to discuss and share their thinking about what they were doing and learning during an activity. A collection of class photographs with annotations can be displayed as a visual record of students' learning during inquiry for others to see, read, and provide feedback and reflect upon.

General Implementation Attributes

Ease of Use: Depends on availability   Cognitive Demand: Medium
    of camera and printer
Time Demand: Low

Modifications

Younger students may dictate their descriptions to the teacher to be added as annotations on the photographs. If computers are available, students can annotate their photographs digitally and share them on a common web space. This FACT can also be used with videos. Students can voice-over short videos taken with Flip-Cams or other digital recording devices.

Caveats

It may not be possible to photograph every student during every activity. Make sure over the course of a unit that all students have an opportunity to see and describe themselves in a photograph. Try not to take more than one day to return the photographs for annotation. Follow school policies for using digital images of students.

Use With Other Disciplines

This FACT is also used in *science.*

My Notes

_____

_____

_____

#43. POMS: POINT OF MOST SIGNIFICANCE

Description

POMS is the opposite of the *Muddiest Point*. In this quick technique students are asked to identify the most significant learning or idea they gained from a lesson.

How This FACT Promotes Student Learning

POMS is a metacognitive strategy used to help students connect with the important goals of a lesson. Students reflect back on the lesson and identify the key points that contributed to their learning.

How This FACT Informs Instruction

POMS is used at the end of a lesson to gather information on what students feel were the most significant points made during a lesson. Teachers can quickly administer, collect, and sort responses to make judgments about how well the key ideas of the lesson were perceived as important by the students. If the *POMS* of the students differ from the important points the lesson was intended to develop, the teacher can use this information to clarify and add more emphasis to those key points.

Design and Administration

At the end of a lesson, ask students to describe orally or in writing the most significant point made during the lesson that contributed to their learning. For example, a lesson on linear measurement might conclude with, "Today we investigated and discussed different ways to measure dimensions, such as lengths, heights, and widths. What point made during today's lesson best helped you understand ways to measure the dimensions of different-shaped objects?" Collect and analyze students' responses to decide if the lesson met its goal or needs to be modified. Be sure to let students know how you used their responses. When they understand that the information is seriously considered by you to make changes that will benefit them, they will respond thoughtfully and in detail.

General Implementation Attributes

Ease of Use: High   Cognitive Demand: Low
Time Demand: Low

Modifications

POMS can be changed to *Part of Most Significance* and used as a reflection on the most effective part of a lesson, rather than the key points that contributed to their learning.

Caveats

Focusing only on the most significant point of the lesson may result in overlooking areas where students are experiencing conceptual difficulties. Vary this strategy with *Muddiest Point* in order to provide opportunities for students to express what was difficult for them as well.

Use With Other Disciplines

This FACT can also be used in *science*, social studies, language arts, health, foreign language, and visual and performing arts.

My Notes

_____

_____

_____

#44. POPSICLE STICK QUESTIONING

Description

Popsicle Stick Questioning is a technique used to selectively choose students for *No Hands Questioning*. The purpose of this technique is to ensure that certain students, identified in advance by the teacher, are called on during "random" class questioning. Names are written on Popsicle sticks and placed in a cup. An inner cup, placed inside the outer cup, holds the Popsicle sticks with the names of students the teacher wants to be sure to call on. The names can be pulled out from the inner cup when needed while giving the appearance that students are all randomly selected when called upon to respond to a question (Wiliam, 2005).

How This FACT Promotes Student Learning

This is a type of *No Hands Questioning* strategy that encourages all students to think and be prepared to answer questions when randomly called on. Since hands are not raised, students who do not raise their hands cannot opt out of the questions; therefore, students tend to engage more in their own thinking to prepare for the chance of being called on for a response. All students think they have an equal chance of being called on. However, this selection strategy ensures that students who need to be heard from will have an opportunity to formulate and express their ideas.

How This FACT Informs Instruction

There are times when it is important for the teacher to gather specific information about individual students in a class. This FACT provides a way for teachers to ensure that certain students are called on to share their thinking without their feeling as if they had been singled out. The teacher can use the information to examine how individual students are progressing in their learning and select differentiated strategies as needed to improve their learning.

Design and Administration

Write all students' names on the Popsicle sticks and place them in an opaque cup such as a coffee mug. Place another smaller cup inside the larger cup. The names of a few preselected students the teacher wants to be sure to call on are placed in the inner cup, which is visible only to the teacher. The other Popsicle sticks are placed outside of the inner cup. When the teacher feels a need to call on a particular student, his or her name is drawn from the inner cup. The following describes how a teacher might use this FACT:

> Mrs. Johnston was questioning students about their ideas related to transformations. She noticed that three of her students were struggling through the previous day's activity. She decided she needed to call on them during the class discussion so they would make their thinking visible to the class and receive feedback to help understand the different types of transformations. In order to ensure that they would be selected during the "random" Popsicle stick draw, she placed their Popsicle sticks in the inner cup, where she could easily draw them out as needed during the class discussion.

General Implementation Attributes

Ease of Use: High
Time Demand: Low

Cognitive Demand: Depends on the
question asked

Modifications

Use different-colored inks for particular subgroups of students. Write some students' names down more than once to increase their probability of being selected. For teachers who teach multiple classes throughout the day in the same classroom, seats can be labeled with the labels written on the Popsicle sticks.

Caveats

Don't allow students to see the inner cup!

Use With Other Disciplines

This FACT can also be used in *science*, social studies, language arts, health, foreign language, and visual and performing arts.

My Notes

_____

_____

_____

#45. PVF: PAIRED VERBAL FLUENCY

Description

PVF is a technique used to activate thinking about a topic. It is used between partners to elicit prior knowledge, review a lesson, or reflect on learning at the end of a lesson or conclusion of an instructional sequence. Partners take turns in timed rounds talking about an assigned topic without interruption. While one person talks, the other listens without speaking until the allotted time has elapsed and partners switch roles (Lipton & Wellman, 1998).

How This FACT Promotes Student Learning

The purpose of *PVF* is to activate reflective thinking. This FACT stimulates students to dig deeper into what they have learned and make sense of it as they talk without stopping for a specified interval of time. Active listening by the partner stimulates their own thinking about the topic as they build upon their partners' thoughts when it is their turn. The structured protocol provides a vehicle for students to be metacognitive in a verbally active way. In a very short period of time, students can surface a significant amount of information, beliefs, questions, and understandings from their instructional experiences.

How This FACT Informs Instruction

After students have engaged in *PVF*, they may have identified unresolved difficulties to bring to the attention of the teacher. These difficulties are then addressed by the teacher to further develop conceptual or procedural understanding through class discussion or additional learning experiences. Watching nonverbal behaviors also indicates the students' level of engagement, which may be useful to teachers in assessing their interest in sharing their ideas about the topic.

Design and Administration

PVF can be used prior to instruction to activate thinking, as a review of a lesson, or for reflection purposes at the end of a sequence of instruction. It also works well as a prelude to whole-class discussion. Some ways to use *PVF* include having students talk about a topic to be introduced by sharing what they already know about it, having students discuss results of a mathematical investigation, or having students reflect at the end of a mathematics unit by talking about their key learnings. Start by asking students to find an "eye contact partner" by standing up and making eye contact with someone who is not sitting near them. The partners move together and wait for the teacher's instructions. Ask each pair to decide who will be partner A and who will be partner B. (Usually, the student who wants to go last chooses partner B, so you may want to announce that partner B will go first!) Give the class a discussion prompt or topic to discuss. For example, the teacher might say,

> For the past 3 weeks, we have been learning about number properties. I would like you to talk about what you now know about various properties. What were the most important things you have learned, and why are they important to you? If there are areas you are still struggling with, talk them through for your partner to address when it is his or her turn.

Announce that when you give the signal, one partner will talk for exactly one minute while the other partner only listens (emphasize that the other partner may not speak at all until it is his or her turn). Encourage the listeners to note areas in their partners' talk that they can build upon or provide feedback about. Call out "Go" and time the *PVF* talk for exactly one minute. After one minute has lapsed call out "Switch"; partners should trade roles and repeat. At the next switch, the first partner talks for 30 seconds, followed by another switch, after which the other partner talks for 30 seconds. End the activity by having students thank their partners and go back to their seats. Ask for a few volunteers to share insights from their partners or to comment on any learning issues they discussed that may need to be resolved.

General Implementation Attributes

Ease of Use: High
Time Demand: Low

Cognitive Demand: High

Modifications

The time intervals can be changed to other configurations, such as 1 minute, 40 seconds, 20 seconds; 60 seconds, 30 seconds, 10 seconds (for a closing statement), or other configurations the teacher or students select.

Caveats

This strategy may be difficult for English language learners or students who have difficulty concentrating or hearing. There is a high level of noise in the classroom when many students are talking at the same time. Have them spread out so they may better hear their partners. Refraining from speaking while one is in the listener role can be difficult. Students should be reminded to only listen until it is their turn to speak.

Use With Other Disciplines

This FACT can also be used in *science*, social studies, language arts, health, foreign language, and visual and performing arts.

My Notes

_____

_____

_____

#46. QUESTION GENERATING

Description

Question Generating is a technique that switches roles from the teacher as the generator of questions to the student as the question generator. The ability to formulate good questions about a topic can indicate the extent to which a student understands ideas that underlie the topic.

How This FACT Promotes Student Learning

Students typically think that asking questions is easy and answering them is difficult (Naylor et al., 2004, p. 120). When they are put in a position to develop thinking questions that go beyond recall, they realize they have to draw on their own understanding of the topic. Generating good questions in mathematics requires more than superficial knowledge of the topic. It requires students to delve deeper into their existing knowledge base. As they formulate "thinking questions," they practice metacognition by recognizing the level of understanding needed not only to form the question but to respond to it as well.

How This FACT Informs Instruction

Question Generating can be used at the beginning of instruction in a topic to find out what students already know about the topic or throughout a unit of instruction. The number of questions students come up with, the quality of the questions (recall versus thinking questions), and the sophistication of the ideas embedded in the question reveal information about students' knowledge. As students learn to distinguish productive questions from nonproductive ones, their higher-level questions reveal interesting insights into their thinking about the content. Teachers can also have students exchange or answer their own questions, revealing further information about students' ideas related to the topic. Selected student-generated questions can be saved and used at the end of a unit of instruction for self-assessment, reflection, or summative assessment.

Design and Administration

Provide a stimulus such as an object, picture, statement, or problem around which students can generate their questions. For example, in a unit on triangles, the teacher might show three different types of triangles and ask the students to think of some good questions to ask about the triangles. To help students develop good questions, the teacher can provide a list of question stems or post a chart of question stems to refer to in the classroom. Figure 4.32 shows examples of *Question Generating* stems.

Figure 4.32   Sample *Question-Generating Stems*

Question-Generating Stems

Why does ___?
Why do you think ___?
Does anyone have a different way to explain ___?
How can you prove ___?
Is ___ always true?
How would you use ___?
What could be the reason for___?
What would happen if ___?
How does this relate to ___?
What facts support ___?
Does ____ when ___ ?
How could we find out if ____?
What examples show ___?
What other way could you ___?
What would happen to the pattern if ___?
What kind of pattern does ____ show?
What rule explains ____?
What would best ___?

Source: Adapted from Keeley (2008). Used with permission.

General Implementation Attributes

Ease of Use: Medium
Time Demand: Medium

Cognitive Demand: High for
   higher-level questions

Modifications

If individual students have difficulty generating questions, provide an opportunity for students to develop questions in small groups. Questions can also be developed as a whole-class activity.

Caveats

Some students, particularly younger students, may lack the prior knowledge to answer some *how* or *why* questions. These questions could be better phrased with stems such as "Why do you think . . .?" rather than "Why does . . . ?"

Use With Other Disciplines

This FACT can also be used in *science*, social studies, language arts, health, foreign language, and visual and performing arts.

My Notes

_____

_____

_____

#47. RESPONSE CARDS

Description

Response Cards are a quick way to check for students' conceptual and procedural knowledge. This FACT involves students holding up cards that indicate their answer. The cards can be from a set prepared by the teacher or blank cards the students write on and then hold up.

How This FACT Promotes Student Learning

Response Cards activate thinking and engage all learners in the lesson because everyone responds, not just those who raise their hands. It is a technique that can be used to support a classroom culture in which all ideas are valued, not just the right answers. When the cards are held up in front of the students at chest height facing the teacher, they provide a way to privately share their answers; because most students are facing the teacher, it will primarily be the teacher who sees the different responses.

How This FACT Informs Instruction

Response Cards help teachers quickly determine levels of understanding and proficiency in the class after a concept or procedure has been taught. The teacher uses the information to plan whole-class instruction or form small groups for reteaching or enrichment. The cards can also be used to engage students in mathematical discussions by grouping together students with different responses and encouraging students to defend their responses.

Design and Administration

Response Cards can be used in a variety of ways. They can be sets of A, B, C, D, and E responses used to select answers to an assessment probe or other selected-response question. They can be *T* or *F* for true-or-false statements. They can be used to indicate confidence levels (low, medium, high). They can be made up of the numbers 0 through 9 and used individually or in combination. They can also be made up of symbols or shapes. After deciding what topic the cards will be used for, develop and distribute the cards to students. Explain how they will be used, and model the procedure with a practice question. Students can respond at their seats or stand facing the teacher with cards held at their chests so only the teacher can see their answers. Responses can be sorted by having students use the *Four Corners* strategy to discuss the reasons for their answers in small groups. Teachers can also select different students to come to the front of the room and share the reasons for their responses, eliciting feedback from other students or the teacher as they share their reasoning.

General Implementation Attributes

Ease of Use: Medium   Cognitive Demand: Depends on
Time Demand: Low   the question

Modifications

Response Cards can be left blank for students to write an answer on and hold up. This technique can also be used with small whiteboards.

Caveats

Make sure students respond individually before seeing what cards other students hold up. Establish the rule that they can't switch cards once they hold them up (except after discussion, when their ideas may change).

Use With Other Disciplines

This FACT can also be used in science, social studies, language arts, foreign languages, health, and visual and performing arts.

My Notes

_____

_____

_____

#48. SAME A–SAME B PROBES

Description

Same A–Same B Probes are questions that reveal the use of the intuitive rule "Same A–Same B" (Stavy & Tirosh, 2000). The probe involves comparing quantities when direct perceptual cues are not available to determine whether or not they are equal.

How This FACT Promotes Learning

One of the goals of mathematics education is to encourage students' critical thinking. *Same A–Same B Probes* often result in responses where students rely on external, irrelevant features to compare problems, figures, or quantities. These probes encourage students not to rely on external features but to critically examine the task and their responses to it. It encourages questions such as (Stavy & Tirosh, 2000): Is my response valid for different types of numbers? Is my response valid under all conditions? Does this fit with other things I know?

How This FACT Informs Instruction

Research shows that this rule is widely used in mathematics and science. By being aware of when students use this rule, teachers can take students' reasoning into consideration when they plan instruction.

Design and Administration

Same A–Same B Probes are designed to ask students to compare quantities in situations in which two things differ in one quantity but are the same in another. For example, in Figure 4.33, students are asked to compare the volume of a cylinder constructed from a sheet of paper with given dimensions but changing which side of the paper forms the height of the cylinder. Students often incorrectly apply the Same A–Same B rule because it is the same piece of paper without considering the change to the area when the measures of the base and the height of the cylinder are switched.

General Implementation Attributes

Ease of Use: Medium
Time Demand: Low

Cognitive Demand: Depends on
    the question

Figure 4.33   Same A–Same B Example

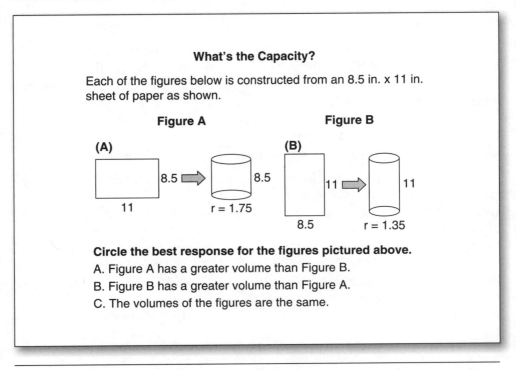

What's the Capacity?

Each of the figures below is constructed from an 8.5 in. x 11 in. sheet of paper as shown.

Figure A   **Figure B**

Circle the best response for the figures pictured above.
A. Figure A has a greater volume than Figure B.
B. Figure B has a greater volume than Figure A.
C. The volumes of the figures are the same.

Source: Rose & Arline (2009), p. 122. Used with permission.

Modifications

A *Same A–Same B Probe* can be used as a *P-E-O Probe* when the concept can be followed with a hands-on investigation or observable demonstration. Students can also generate their own examples and nonexamples for the rule Same A–Same B.

Caveats

When using comparison probes such as this one, make sure it is clear to the student what is being compared. For example, in Figure 4.33 the volume of the cylinders is being compared, not the dimensions of the paper of which the cylinder is made.

Use With Other Disciplines

This FACT can also be used in science.

My Notes

_____

_____

_____

#49: SEQUENCING CARDS

Description

Sequencing Cards involves taking a set of statements, procedures, pictures, or ideas about a mathematical concept or procedure and putting them together in a logical order. Students reveal their thinking as they describe why the cards are placed in a particular order.

How This FACT Promotes Learning

As students examine the cards and discuss their ideas about a possible sequence, they must clarify their mathematical ideas and identify areas of uncertainty. In the process of placing the cards in a sequence, students must defend their ideas and provide a logical argument for why the sequence is correct.

How This FACT Informs Instruction

When used at the beginning of a lesson, *Sequencing Cards* provides an opportunity for the teacher to identify prior knowledge students have about a concept or mathematical skill. It helps the teacher pinpoint areas to target during the lesson in response to what the learners know. Used after instruction, it helps teachers see how well students can apply their mathematical ideas.

Design and Administration

Choose a mathematical topic that can be sequenced. Decide on a series of statements, pictures, algorithmic or problem-solving steps. Place these on cards and distribute the cards to small groups of students. Students must decide on a logical sequence in which to place the cards and justify their reasons for the sequence. As students place their cards in a sequence, circulate among groups, asking probing questions to reveal their mathematical thinking. Students can also be invited to share their sequences with the class, inviting feedback by their peers. Some examples that might be used for sequencing include different ways of representing numbers placed from smallest to largest, steps in using a protractor to make an angle, steps in creating a graph given a set of data, probability examples placed in order of highest to lowest probability, steps in solving a word problem, and Fibonacci sequences and other interesting number patterns.

General Implementation Attributes

Ease of Use: Medium   Cognitive Demand: Medium/High
Time Demand: Medium

Modifications

Once students have sequenced their cards, they can be glued on paper and collected by the teacher for analysis. When used as an elicitation, they can be returned after students have completed instruction in the topic, and students can be invited to modify or change their sequence based on what they learned after instruction. You can also insert a blank card in the set and ask students to provide the missing card for the sequence or extend the sequence with the additional card.

Caveats

Choose a format, number of cards, and topic for sequencing that matches the developmental level of your students. Choose more concrete examples, including ones with pictures, for younger children.

Use With Other Disciplines

This FACT can also be used in *science, social studies, language arts, health, foreign language, and visual and performing arts.

My Notes

_____

_____

_____

#50. STICKY BARS

Description

Sticky Bars help students recognize that there is often a range of ideas among their classmates about a mathematics concept or a solution to a problem. *Sticky Bars* are the low-tech version of personal response systems (clickers). Students are presented with a selected response question. The answer is anonymously recorded on a Post-it note and passed in to the teacher. The teacher or a student arranges the sticky notes on the wall or whiteboard as a bar graph representing the different student responses.

How This FACT Promotes Student Learning

Sticky Bars makes students' ideas public. It visually shows that not everyone in the class responds the same way to a question. It helps students understand and accept that ideas may differ and that mathematics learning involves the process of working together to develop a common understanding. Additionally, it promotes students' desire to know how their thinking compares to that of their peers.

How This FACT Informs Instruction

Sticky Bars can be used as an elicitation to publicly share students' ideas before instruction. The graph can be left on the wall and revisited at any time during instruction to identify the extent to which students have changed their original answer as a result of their learning experiences or interactions in group mathematics talk. *Sticky Bars* provide a quick way to identify the range of ideas held by the class, including the percentage of students who may hold misconceptions or make common errors. The teacher can use this information to plan targeted learning experiences.

Design and Administration

Develop a selected response question that elicits a variety of student responses. *Always, Sometimes, Never Probes; Example, Nonexample Probes; Friendly Talk Probes; More A–More B Probes; Overgeneralization Probes; P-E-O Probes;* and *Same A–Same B Probes* described in this book can be used with this FACT. Additionally, a source of excellent probes for this FACT can be obtained through the source material described in the Appendix at the back of this book. Remind students to record their own answers, regardless of whether they think they might be right or wrong. Keep the Post-it notes anonymous. Collect and quickly sort them into like responses (with the help of a student assistant if needed). Create a bar graph by placing each similar response atop the other. Figure 4.34 shows what a *Sticky Bar* wall graph looks like. Provide time for students to discuss the data and what they think the class needs to do in order to come to a consensus on the best answer.

Figure 4.34 *Sticky Bars*

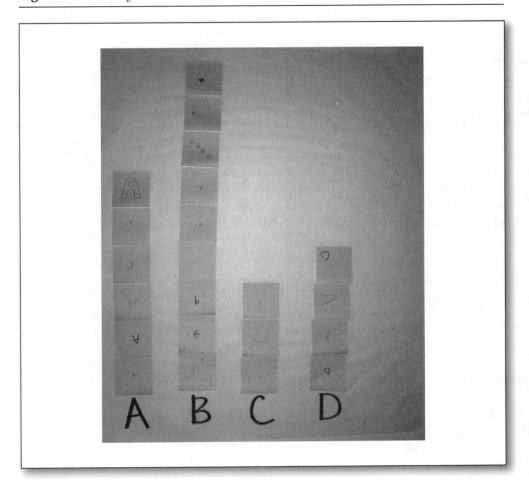

General Implementation Attributes

Ease of Use: High   Cognitive Demand: Depends
Time Demand: Low   on the question used

Modifications

For teachers with more than one class, consider using a different color for each class and making a combined histogram of responses from all classes. Compare differences or similarities across classes. As a reflection activity, compare the first *Sticky Bars* with a mid- and post-instruction version using a different-colored sticky note and placing them alongside the previous results for comparison. Teachers with technology-based response systems, or clickers, can have students use the devices to input responses instead of using sticky notes.

Caveats

Sticky Bars work best with questions that are followed up with instructional experiences in which students are challenged to change their ideas as they gain additional knowledge and information.

Use With Other Disciplines

This FACT can also be used in *science*, social studies, language arts, health, foreign language, and visual and performing arts.

My Notes

_____

_____

_____

#51. STRATEGY HARVEST

Description

In this strategy, students complete a problem-solving task and then circulate among their peers to find students who used a strategy different from theirs to solve the problem. Students record the other strategies and describe how the strategy differs from the one they used. During the process, students give feedback to each other on their strategy.

How This FACT Promotes Student Learning

A *Strategy Harvest* provides an opportunity for students to examine others' processes and compare them to their own. While examining others' processes, students build upon them or add new processes of their own. "Thinking cannot be articulated unless students reflect on the problem and the strategies used to solve it; articulation, in turn, increases reflection, which leads to understanding" (Fennema & Romberg, 1999, p. 188). Often in whole-group sharing situations, not all students have a chance to share, ask questions, and provide feedback, due to either time constraints or comfort level. The *Strategy Harvest* FACT allows all students to share their own particular strategy and to ask questions and give feedback to other students prior to the whole-class discussion.

How This FACT Informs Instruction

Strategy Harvest elicits different processes students use to solve a problem. As students are sharing, the teacher can gather information on the range of processes used in order to determine those to be shared with the whole class. Used prior to instruction, Strategy Harvest enables the teacher to use the information to plan lessons that move students toward a particular strategy or process. Used during the concept development stage, teachers can use the FACT to gather information to determine students' ability to apply new learning within a problem context.

Design and Administration

Provide students with a *Strategy Harvest* handout, such as the template in Figure 4.35, and review the problem to be solved. Allow students time to individually complete the problem, using the first section to record their processes and solutions. Determine the amount of time and number of strategies to "harvest" based on the complexity of the problem. Start by asking the students to find an "eye contact" partner by standing up and making eye contact with someone who is not sitting near them. Ask each pair to choose who will be Partner A and who will be Partner B. Partner A then explains his or her strategy while Partner B asks questions and provides feedback; once that is finished, the roles are reversed. Continue the process with two to three additional "eye contact" partners. At the end of the *Strategy Harvest*, ask for a few volunteers to share a particular type of strategy learned from a partner.

General Implementation Attributes

Ease of Use: Medium   Cognitive Demand: High
Time Demand: Medium

Modifications

Students can work in pairs on the problem and form groups of four to share strategies. The time interval and number of partners can be changed to reflect the complexity of the problem. For less complex problems, a more random approach can be used, with students moving quickly from partner to partner in order to find strategies that differed from their own in at least one way.

Figure 4.35 Example *Strategy Harvest* Sheet

My Strategy	_____'s Strategy
_____'s Strategy	_____'s Strategy

Caveats

This strategy may be difficult for English language learners or students who have a hard time concentrating or hearing. There is a high level of noise in the classroom when many students are talking at the same time. Have them spread out so they may better hear their partners.

Use With Other Disciplines

This FACT can also be used in science to share ways students might investigate a problem.

My Notes

_____

_____

_____

#52. STRATEGY PROBE

Description

In this strategy, students complete a problem-solving task and then review written examples of how other students correctly solved the task. Students are asked to circle the solution process that best matches their own and to make sense of the other solutions provided. Figure 4.36 shows an example of a *Strategy Probe*.

Figure 4.36   *Strategy Probe*

What's your Subtraction Strategy?

Sam, Julie, Pete, and Lisa each subtracted **284 from 672**. Circle the method that most closely how you would solve the problem.

	Do the other three methods make sense mathematically? Why or why not?

Sam's Method
 	
(A)   672
    −284
    +400
    −10
    −2
    388	

Lisa's Method
 	
(B) 672 − 284
    672 − 200 = 472
    472 − 80 = 392
    392 − 4 = 388	

Pete's Method
 	
(D) 672 − 284
    ↓ +6   ↓ +6
    678 − 290
    ↓ +10 ↓ +10
    688 − 300 = 388	

Julie's Method
 	
(C) $6\overset{5}{\cancel{7}}{}^{1}2$
    −284
    388	

Source: Rose & Arline (2009), p. 84. Used with permission.

How This FACT Promotes Student Learning

Comparing and contrasting solution methods promotes greater understanding (Rittle-Johnson & Star, 2007). *Strategy Probes* draw out students' ideas regarding different methods by providing students with predetermined solutions targeting the strategies, concepts, and procedures important to the goals of the unit of instruction.

How This FACT Informs Instruction

By first engaging students in solving the task on their own, teachers gather important information regarding choices of strategies. By then providing solution strategies ranging from those using concrete to those using more abstract methods, teachers can determine how to bridge gaps in understanding and use of methods. For example, the result of using the *What's Your Subtraction Strategy* probe (Figure 4.36) may be that the teacher decides to focus a lesson on subtraction as a constant difference after noticing the majority of the students were unable to make sense of Pete's method.

Design and Administration

If used prior to a lesson, select tasks and solution methods that focus on specific concepts and procedures students will encounter in the mathematics lesson. If used after introducing the concept or procedure, select examples that address the concepts and procedures students have had opportunities to develop. Write out the solutions using a format that students are familiar with.

General Implementation Attributes

Ease of Use: High   Cognitive Demand: High
Time Demand: Medium

Modifications

Use actual student work collected from previous years, other classes, or during the unit of instruction. Use the fictitious or actual work as a *Card Sort*, having students sort the cards into two piles, one for methods they could use and explain and the other for methods they need to know more about before being able to use and explain. Have the students create their own *Strategy Probes*, demonstrating that they can generate multiple solution methods. If a *Strategy Probe* is used prior to instruction, revisit it again at the end of a lesson with a reflection FACT such as *I Used to Think . . . But Now I Know . . .* or a *K-W-L* variation.

Caveats

Students who have not been given previous opportunities to compare and explain others' strategies may struggle with this FACT. If so, adapt the instructions to allow students to explain at least one other solution strategy or use the *Card Sort* strategy by having students work in pairs to support each others' learning.

Use With Other Disciplines

This FACT can also be used in science.

My Notes

_____

_____

_____

#53. STUDENT EVALUATION OF LEARNING GAINS

Description

The *Student Evaluation of Learning Gains* is a teacher-designed instrument used to gather feedback on students' perceptions of how well a unit of instruction helped them learn. It consists of statements, on a 5-point scale, about the "degree of gain" in areas such as skills, content knowledge, attitudes, and dispositions toward mathematics.

How This FACT Promotes Student Learning

Use of a student evaluation instrument provides an opportunity for students to reflect upon their own learning processes and to become aware of what they think enables or impedes their learning. It provides an opportunity for students to self-assess the extent to which they feel that they gained new knowledge, skills, attitudes, or dispositions. It increases engagement in learning and student motivation when students see that their teachers take the feedback seriously to improve their teaching for the benefit of their students.

How This FACT Informs Instruction

A formal student evaluation instrument of a unit of instruction can spotlight teaching strategies and components of an instructional unit that are seen by students as best supporting student learning and those that need improvement. The FACT provides an opportunity for teachers to analyze their instruction through the eyes of their students. The feedback allows teachers to effectively adjust their teaching strategies and activities to better meet student learning needs.

Design and Administration

Translate your instructional unit into evaluation statements that reflect the content, instructional strategies, and activities that occurred during the sequence of instruction. Use the example in Figure 4.37 as a guide. For middle and high school students, see the Appendix for a link to a website that will help you create an online survey or use a web-based survey program your school may have available. For each item, keep in mind that you are trying to get feedback on students' personal learning gains for each component of the instructional unit that you deem important. Check the questions to ensure that they are clear and unambiguous, and do not ask about more than one thing at a time. Explain to students how to fill out the form and when it is due. You might consider giving it as a homework assignment in order to provide enough time for students to thoughtfully complete it. Emphasize the importance and usefulness of the feedback the students provide for you and the seriousness with which their responses and comments are taken. After responses are analyzed, consider sharing with students what you learned from their comments and how they will be used to inform their instructional experiences as well as with future classes.

General Implementation Attributes

Ease of Use: Medium   Cognitive Demand: Medium
Time Demand: Medium

Modifications

The evaluation form may also be used partway through a unit of instruction to make midcourse corrections to the instructional methods or activities used. You may consider other data to be correlated with learning gains such as gender, grade (such as multigrade classes in high school), class (if not self-contained), and so on.

Caveats

To ensure meaningful results, student responses should be anonymous. Beware of changing the emphasis of the instrument on student "gains" to other purposes such as asking students what they "liked" about the unit. The purpose of this FACT should stay focused on student achievement by emphasizing what students perceive as a gain in their learning.

Figure 4.37   *Student Evaluation of Learning Gains* for a Fourth-Grade Unit on Data Analysis

Check off how well each of the following helped you learn during the Representing Our Data unit	Not Useful at All	Somewhat Useful	Useful	Very Useful!
1. The *How Many of Each* activity				
2. The *What Happens If* investigation				
3. The *Comparing Graphs* activity				
4. Working in pairs				
5. Working in small groups				
6. The class discussions				
7. Working on my project				
8. The class project presentations				
9. The Word Wall				
10. Asking questions in class				
11. Listening to others ask questions				
12. The homework assignments				
13. The computer applets				
14. Reading graphs from newspapers				
15. The *Human Scatter Graph* activity and discussion				

Please share any ideas you have that could help me improve the way I teach this unit:

Use With Other Disciplines

This FACT can also be used in *science*, social studies, language arts, health, foreign language, and visual and performing arts.

My Notes

_____

_____

_____

#54. STUDENT INTERVIEWS

Description

In this strategy, the teacher interviews students individually or in small groups of two or three students by asking a small number of predetermined questions relating to concepts, skills, and procedures foundational to the grade-level learning goals. For each response, whether correct or incorrect, students are asked to explain their reasoning or solution method. Figure 4.38 shows an example of question prompts to use in an elementary grades student interview.

Figure 4.38   Sample Interview Prompts for Elementary Mathematics

About how much do you think the answer to [insert computation] would be? How did you think about this?

What do you call these shapes? How are they different from each other?

How would you solve this problem [insert problem]? Why did you do it that way?

Can you use these blocks to build a ___? Why did you build it that way?

What is another way you could solve this? Tell me why you could solve it this way.

How many _____ do you think can fit in this? Tell me how you thought about this.

What would the next three numbers be [insert sequence]? How did you think about this?

Which is bigger? How did you decide?

Are these the same number? How did you decide if they are the same or different?

What does this symbol mean to you?

How did you do that?

Tell me more about that.

Can you draw it for me?

Can you show me how you did that?

How This FACT Promotes Student Learning

The depth of a misunderstanding is often uncovered only with follow-up questions pertaining specifically to a student's solution or strategy. A one-on-one or small-group interview provides students with an opportunity to communicate mathematically in a setting where they have the sole attention of their teacher, creating an opportunity that is more likely to uncover areas of misunderstanding or difficulty. In addition, putting mathematical knowledge into words is an important literacy skill in mathematics. The FACT helps students put ideas into words and explain their thinking, a critical skill in mathematics and language.

How This FACT Informs Instruction

One-on-one or small-group interviews often reveal valuable information that is not available when teachers rely solely on students' written work (Burns, 2010). Interviewing provides insight into a student's level of understanding and ability to put mathematical ideas into words and representations. The FACT also allows teachers to gather information about the range of learning needs within a class of students.

Design and Administration

"Good interviewing requires careful preparation in advance, keeping in mind purposes, method of selection, environment, questions and follow-up probes, and uses" (Stepans et al., 2005, p. 277). Select a topic that is going to be taught in a future unit of instruction. Align the interview questions to the learning goals of the unit, and be sure to include questions that target concepts and procedures that are foundational to developing the key mathematical ideas within the goals. Use the general prompts in Figure 4.38 to help you frame specific questions. Prepare in advance a recording instrument in order to capture student thinking easily. Create picture cards, or have manipulatives on hand to use during the interview. Decide on the learning task other students will be engaged in so that you are able to focus on student responses during the interview.

General Implementation Attributes

Ease of Use: High
Time Demand: High

Cognitive Demand: Depends
on questions asked

Modifications

Rather than interview each student for each topic, teachers can select a sample of students to interview, making sure all students are included over time.

Caveats

Teachers often find it difficult to hold back from turning an interview into a teachable moment. Refrain from correcting or teaching during an interview.

Use With Other Disciplines

This FACT can also be used in *science* with *Informal Student Interviews*.

My Notes

_____

_____

_____

#55. TERMINOLOGY INVENTORY PROBE (TIP)

Description

TIPs are short, simple questionnaires that determine students' familiarity with mathematics terminology. Students select a response based on their level of familiarity with the mathematical term. If students claim to be familiar with the term, then they are asked to provide a description to reveal the extent of their conceptual understanding.

How This FACT Promotes Student Learning

This FACT provides a metacognitive opportunity for students to determine how familiar they are with the mathematics terminology used in an instructional unit. Students may recall a mathematical term but realize they have little or no understanding of its meaning. Conversely, some students may realize they not only recall a term from prior experiences but understand it well enough to explain it to another student.

How This FACT Informs Instruction

TIPs are used at the beginning of a sequence of lessons to determine how familiar students are with the mathematics terminology they will encounter in the topic they will study. The results are used to consider ways to effectively introduce terminology into an instructional unit so that students can attach conceptual meaning to a mathematics term.

Design and Administration

Select no more than 12 words from the key mathematics terminology that students will encounter, learn, and use during the topic of instruction. Figure 4.39 shows an example of a *TIP* for a high school trigonometry unit. Leave plenty of space for students to describe the term if they are familiar with it, using formal or operational definitions, descriptions, or examples. Collect and save student responses if you are planning to administer the

TIP again as a post-assessment, providing an opportunity for students to reflect on their pre- and post-familiarity with mathematics terminology and conceptual understanding of the words used during the unit of instruction.

Figure 4.39   *TIP* for a Trigonometry Unit

Opposite	Adjacent	Hypotenuse
☐ I have never heard of this. ☐ I have heard of this but I'm not sure what it means. ☐ I have some idea what it means. ☐ I clearly know what it means and can describe it:	☐ I have never heard of this. ☐ I have heard of this but I'm not sure what it means. ☐ I have some idea what it means. ☐ I clearly know what it means and can describe it:	☐ I have never heard of this. ☐ I have heard of this but I'm not sure what it means. ☐ I have some idea what it means. ☐ I clearly know what it means and can describe it:
Coordinate Plane	**Right Triangles**	**Indirect Measurement**
☐ I have never heard of this. ☐ I have heard of this but I'm not sure what it means. ☐ I have some idea what it means. ☐ I clearly know what it means and can describe it:	☐ I have never heard of this. ☐ I have heard of this but I'm not sure what it means. ☐ I have some idea what it means. ☐ I clearly know what it means and can describe it:	☐ I have never heard of this. ☐ I have heard of this but I'm not sure what it means. ☐ I have some idea what it means. ☐ I clearly know what it means and can describe it:
Tangent	**Cosine**	**Sine**
☐ I have never heard of this. ☐ I have heard of this but I'm not sure what it means. ☐ I have some idea what it means. ☐ I clearly know what it means and can describe it:	☐ I have never heard of this. ☐ I have heard of this but I'm not sure what it means. ☐ I have some idea what it means. ☐ I clearly know what it means and can describe it:	☐ I have never heard of this. ☐ I have heard of this but I'm not sure what it means. ☐ I have some idea what it means. ☐ I clearly know what it means and can describe it:

General Implementation Attributes

Ease of Use: Medium   Cognitive Demand: Medium
Time Demand: Medium

Modifications

For the third selected response (□ *I have some idea what it means*) consider leaving a blank space to have students describe their preconceived ideas about the term. With younger students, consider using only a few key mathematics terms, providing an opportunity for them to explain their understanding of the word orally or in drawings.

Caveats

Be aware that students can memorize definitions without conceptual understanding. *TIPs* are used to gauge familiarity with terminology, not assess for deep conceptual understanding.

Use With Other Disciplines

This FACT can also be used with other types of terminology encountered in *science, social studies, language arts, health, foreign language, and visual and performing arts.

My Notes

_____

_____

_____

#56. TEN-TWO

Description

Ten-Two is a reflection strategy originally developed by Dr. Mary Budd Rowe (Rowe, 1974). Dr. Rowe stated that for every 10 minutes of instruction, there should be 2 minutes of debriefing or sharing of notes by students. After 10 minutes of instruction, students work individually or in teams to summarize, fill in gaps, and help each other clarify concepts.

How This FACT Promotes Student Learning

Ten-Two provides a metacognitive opportunity for students to frequently summarize and reflect on their learning. It is particularly beneficial when large amounts of information, difficult and abstract ideas, or new information is presented either by the teacher or through guest lecture, video, audio, or other media.

How This FACT Informs Instruction

Ten-Two is primarily used as a metacognitive instructional technique. Linking it to formative assessment for the purpose of informing instruction, the teacher asks if the students are ready to move on after they have had an opportunity to summarize; or, by circulating through the room and examining students' summary notes or discussions with a partner, the teacher may discover that students are struggling with the information and are not ready to proceed further without help from the teacher. Student feedback on use of this strategy may reinforce the critical need to build in short periods of reflection time throughout any lesson.

Design and Administration

Explain the purpose of the *Ten-Two* to the students. After 10 minutes of instruction, give students 2 minutes of time to quietly think, summarize, look at their notes, jot down key points or learnings, or discuss what they have learned so far with a partner. Combine this FACT with *Fist to Five* to gather feedback on whether students feel they are ready to proceed or need time to discuss their ideas with the class. Resume instruction and repeat again after 10 minutes if needed. Debrief the usefulness of this FACT with students the first time it is used to get their feedback on whether it was helpful to them.

General Implementation Attributes

Ease of Use: High   Cognitive Demand: Medium/High
Time Demand: Low

Modifications

Use any time interval—Five-One, Seven-Two, Ten-Three, Fifteen-Five—as long as it provides adequate time for instruction and reflection.

Caveats

Break for summarizing only when the flow of the lesson is not compromised. Breaking at 10-minute intervals without considering how the concepts are unfolding may contribute to incoherence. It is also important to recognize the difference between recall and conceptual understanding. Often the latter takes much longer to develop, although recall can provide a starting point from which to build students' own ideas.

Use With Other Disciplines

This FACT can also be used in *science*, social studies, language arts, health, foreign language, and visual and performing arts.

My Notes

_____

_____

_____

#57. THINKING LOG

Description

Thinking Logs are a type of writing journal used during problem solving or other conceptual activities in which students react to a series of sentence stems as thinking starters. The purpose is to prompt metacognition during students' mathematical inquiry and concept development learning experiences (Flick & Tomlinson, 2006).

How This FACT Promotes Student Learning

Thinking Logs promote metacognition and help students see how their prior knowledge and classroom experiences relate to their mathematics problems and the development of conceptual and procedural knowledge. Using this FACT helps students become more aware of their own learning and what they can do to self-direct it.

How This Fact Informs Instruction

Thinking Logs help the teacher identify areas where the students are aware of their own learning successes or challenges. The information can be used to provide interventions for individual or groups of students as well as match students with peers who may provide learning support. *Thinking Logs* may also indicate instances where the class as a whole is having difficulty with a problem-solving activity or other type of learning experience. It then serves as a signal to the teacher to modify or redirect the experience to meet the learning needs of the class.

Design and Administration

Thinking Logs can be constructed for an individual unit of instruction from five or six sheets of paper folded and stapled down the center. Students personalize the cover of their *Thinking Log.* Inside the cover of the *Thinking Log,* print, paste, or attach a sticker with the thinking stems you would like students to use. Examples of thinking stems are shown in Figure 4.40.

Figure 4.40   *Thinking Log* Stems

I was successful in . . .
I got stuck . . .
I figured out . . .
I got confused when . . . so I . . .
I didn't expect . . .
I think I need to redo . . .
I need to rethink . . .
I first thought . . . but now I realize . . .
I'm not sure . . .
What puzzled me the most was . . .
I was really surprised when . . .
I will understand this better if I . . .
I stopped . . . because . . .
I think tomorrow I would like to try . . .
The hardest part of this was . . .
I figured it out because . . .
Right now I am thinking about . . .
I wish I could . . .
I really feel good about the way . . .

Composition or spiral notebooks can also be used for *Thinking Logs* that are maintained throughout the year rather than for individual units. Use impromptu moments during a learning experience or at the end of a lesson to have students record in their *Thinking Logs.* Students choose the thinking stem that would best describe their thinking at that moment. Provide a few minutes for students to write down their thoughts using the stem. If the purpose of using the *Thinking Log* is to promote student metacognition, there is no need to collect the logs. However, there are times when it is helpful to collect the logs and analyze them to gather information to inform instruction as well as provide constructive feed-back to the student.

General Implementation Attributes

Ease of Use: Medium   Cognitive Demand: Medium
Time Demand: Medium

Modifications

As students become used to using the *Thinking Logs,* ask them to gener-ate additional prompts to add to the list of thinking stems. With younger students, it may be helpful to begin by choosing a common thinking stem that everyone responds to, giving examples of how to fill in the stem the first time it is used.

Caveats

If *Thinking Logs* are collected by the teacher for analysis, be sure to let students know the reason you are reading their responses is to help you adjust instruction to meet their needs. Otherwise students may feel their entries are being read to pass judgment on their abilities or performance, which might change the reflective nature of their entries.

Use With Other Disciplines

This FACT can also be used in *science,* social studies, language arts, health, foreign language, and visual and performing arts.

My Notes

_____

_____

_____

#58. THINK-ALOUDS

Description

Think-Alouds are used to model comprehension processes such as mak-ing predictions, creating images, linking information in text with prior knowledge, monitoring comprehension, and solving problems (Gunning,

1997). The teacher models the process he or she used to solve a problem by thinking aloud through each step from reading the problem to thinking about a strategy to use to work through the steps and checking the reasonableness of the results. Students in turn model *Think-Alouds* with partners.

How This FACT Promotes Student Learning

Students do not necessarily talk about mathematics naturally; teachers need to help them learn how to do so (Cobb, Wood, & Yackel, 1991). When modeled, the *Think-Aloud* FACT provides students with the opportunity to hear the metacognitive processes used by a proficient problem solver. Students then apply the process with a partner, improving their ability to think through a mathematics problem.

How This Fact Informs Instruction

By listening to students during the partner *Think-Alouds*, teachers can monitor comprehension of concepts, skills, and procedures as well as the ability of students to think about their own thinking.

Design and Administration

Choose a multistep problem and talk through the process of finding the solution. Repeated use of starter statements such as those listed below provides students with a protocol when using the technique with partners.

1. The problem is asking . . .

2. The strategy I will use to solve the problem is . . .

3. The steps to using this strategy to solve the problem are . . .

4. I know this answer makes sense because . . .

General Implementation Attributes

Ease of Use: High   Cognitive Demand: Medium
Time Demand: Medium

Modifications

Model, develop, and use protocols or prompts such as those described above to help students who struggle to describe their thought processes. After sufficient modeling and practice, ask for student *Think-Aloud* volunteers periodically throughout the course of the year to model their thinking processes for others.

Caveats

Avoid using this FACT only during a problem-solving unit. Instead, employ it with a variety of problem types within units focusing on different mathematical topics.

Use With Other Disciplines

This FACT can also be used in science and language arts to think aloud about scientific, reading, or writing processes.

My Notes

_____

_____

_____

#59. THINK–PAIR–SHARE

Description

Think–Pair–Share combines thinking with communication. The teacher poses a question and gives individual students time to think about the question. Students then pair up with a partner to discuss their ideas. After pairs discuss, students share their ideas in a small-group or whole-class discussion.

How This FACT Promotes Student Learning

Think–Pair–Share begins by providing students with an opportunity to activate their own thinking. The pairing strategy allows students to share their ideas and modify them or construct new knowledge as they interact with their peers. When students are asked to share ideas with a larger group, they are more willing to respond after they have had a chance to discuss their ideas with another student. As a result, the quality of their responses improves. This FACT contributes to students' oral communication skills as they discuss their ideas with one another. *Think–Pair–Share* can also be used as an end-of-unit reflection by asking students to think about and discuss their response to a reflective prompt given by the teacher.

How This FACT Informs Instruction

As students share ideas during their paired and larger-group discussions, the teacher notes inaccurate ideas or flaws in reasoning that may need to be addressed in targeted instruction. The "share" part of this FACT provides an opportunity for the teacher to probe more deeply after students have had an opportunity to surface their ideas with a partner. The whole-class discussion also provides an opportunity for the teacher and class to give feedback on students' ideas. When used as an end-of-unit reflection, the teacher can glean useful information about the effectiveness of instruction.

Design and Administration

This FACT can be used during any stage of the mathematics assessment and instruction cycle. It begins by posing an open-ended question and giving students "think time" to activate their own ideas. It can also be administered as a *Think–Ink–Pair–Share* in which students are asked to write down their ideas before sharing with a partner. Following "think time," students pair up with a learning partner to share, discuss, clarify, and provide feedback on each other's ideas. The pair then shares its thinking with a larger group.

General Implementation Attributes

Ease of Use: High   Cognitive Demand: Medium
Time Demand: Low

Modifications

The "share" part of this FACT can be used with *Partner Speaks.* Not limited to pairs, it can also be used in a triad. The FACT can be modified as a *Think–Pair–Do–Share* in an investigative context in which pairs of students use manipulatives or other objects to test out their ideas before sharing with a larger group.

Caveats

Use different pairing strategies to ensure that students have the opportunity to form pairs with students other than the ones who sit next to them in order to avoid having students always interact with the same group of peers.

Use With Other Disciplines

This FACT can also be used in *science*, social studies, language arts, health, foreign language, and visual and performing arts.

My Notes

_____

_____

_____

#60. THOUGHT EXPERIMENTS

Description

A *Thought Experiment* involves solving a problem set in an imaginary context that could not be easily tested using real objects. Students use mathematics to test their ideas and provide an explanation of their problem-solving approach. For example, asking students how many people, standing shoulder to shoulder, would be needed to stretch from Washington, D.C., to San Francisco, California, would be considered a *Thought Experiment*. It probes for students' ideas related to measurement and magnitude of number. It would not be practical to solve this problem and test the solution in a real setting with real people. However, students can use mathematical thinking to solve the problem.

How This FACT Promotes Student Learning

Thought Experiments provide an engaging way for students to activate their thinking and apply their mathematical ideas and use of logic in a novel situation. It generates interest in solving the problem. As a group activity, *Thought Experiments* promote interesting mathematical debate. They can also spark inquiry and connections to other ideas as students think about ways they can test their ideas and calculations in related contexts or with models and simulations.

How This Fact Informs Instruction

Students' solutions to a *Thought Experiment* provide the teacher with access to students' thinking. This is particularly helpful in abstract situations where it is not possible to empirically test a mathematical idea. As students test and explain their ideas using logic, calculations, and problem-solving strategies, the teacher gains information about student thinking that can be used to design and monitor subsequent learning experiences. The FACT also provides an opportunity to transfer conceptual understanding to a novel context.

Design and Administration

Thought Experiments can be designed to address students' commonly held ideas using an interesting imaginary scenario. They can be presented through stories, pictures, text, discussion, or any combination of these. They can be used as an individual or group activity. Present students with the *Thought Experiment* and provide time for them to discuss their ideas. Students should be encouraged to draw diagrams, propose models, and choose procedures or calculations to test their ideas. Results of the *Thought Experiment* are used to engage the class in mathematical discourse. Figure 4.23

used with a *Mathematician's Ideas Comparison* is an example of a classic thought experiment question that draws upon students' ideas related to proportionality and circumference (Arons, 1977; Leiber, 1942).

General Implementation Attributes

Ease of Use: Medium   Cognitive Demand: High
Time Demand: Medium

Modifications

Have students come up with ideas for *Thought Experiments*. Use situations that are less abstract for younger students.

Caveats

Thought Experiments often use hypothetical situations that may not be realistic or that involve multiple variables. For example, consider the following *Thought Experiment* prompt: "How many times would a piece of paper need be folded so that the resulting height is as tall the Empire State Building?" In this situation, you would ask the students to imagine that any number of folds is possible.

Use With Other Disciplines

This FACT can also be used in **science* and social studies.

My Notes

_____

_____

_____

#61. THREE-MINUTE PAUSE

Description

The *Three-Minute Pause* provides a break during a block of instruction in order to provide time for students to summarize, clarify, and self-assess whether they understand the concept or procedure being taught. The teacher takes a three-minute pause during instruction so that students can engage in discussion with a partner or small group. A three-minute pause is especially helpful when large amounts of information need to be processed for understanding.

How This FACT Promotes Student Learning

This FACT provides a short, metacognitive break during a hands-on activity, video, lecture, or reading assignment so that students can think about what they are doing and learning before going on to the next step or chunk of information. By breaking up an information-heavy lesson or complex activity, students are better able to process and retain the important conceptual understandings from the learning experience. The discussion that occurs in pairs or triads provides an opportunity for students to receive feedback that can help them resolve difficulties they may be experiencing in understanding the concept, skill, or procedure targeted in the lesson.

How This FACT Informs Instruction

Since this FACT requires students to monitor their own learning and work together to clarify any difficulties they are having at a given point in time, it allows the teacher to move ahead with instruction without interrupting the flow of a lesson with numerous questions. The responsibility for making sense of the lesson is initially put on the students. The final 3-minute pause provides an opportunity for students to list any lingering questions or concepts and ideas they are having difficulty understanding that were not resolved in their peer discussions. This information can then be used by the teacher to clarify parts of the lesson or to design additional experiences to support student understanding.

Design and Administration

Decide when it is a logical time to break during an information-heavy lesson or a complex activity. The teacher may set a timer or provide pairs or triads of students with a timing device. All students start their timers at the same time on cue. Students discuss the ideas from the lesson or activity for 3 minutes, helping each other process their thoughts and clarify misunderstandings. When 3 minutes are up, students stop talking and direct their attention once again to the teacher, video, lesson, problem, activity, or reading they are engaged in, and the lesson resumes seamlessly. It is remarkable how much students can say in as little as 3 minutes. Anything left unresolved after the time runs out is recorded and saved for the final 3-minute pause at the end of the lesson. The FACT allows the teacher to continue with the lesson or activity rather than interrupting the flow with questions. At the end of the lesson, students have 3 minutes to discuss and resolve any lingering questions. Unresolved questions are then shared with the teacher or the whole class for clarification. The teacher may also choose to have students write down any lingering questions to be collected and addressed at the beginning of the next lesson.

General Implementation Attributes

Ease of Use: High   Cognitive Demand: Medium
Time Demand: Low

Modifications

For difficult topics, it may be necessary to extend the time for discussion or take time to clarify before resuming. Three-minute egg timers can be used to keep track of the time. All students start and end their discussion at the same time, bringing their attention back to the teacher to facilitate the next steps in learning.

Caveats

Use this strategy only when there is a need to process large amounts of information; otherwise it becomes a trivial exercise that can interrupt the flow of learning.

Use With Other Disciplines

This FACT can also be used in *science*, social studies, language arts, health, foreign language, and visual and performing arts.

My Notes

_____

_____

_____

#62. 3-2-1

Description

3-2-1 provides a structured way for students to reflect on their learning. Students respond in writing to three reflective prompts, providing six responses (three for the first prompt, two for the second prompt, and one final response to the last prompt) that describe what they learned from a lesson or instructional sequence.

How This FACT Promotes Learning

3-2-1 is a technique that scaffolds students' reflections. The scaffold activates thinking about key learnings (Lipton & Wellman, 2000). This FACT provides students with an opportunity to share their success in learning difficult or new concepts as well as recognize what was challenging for them.

How This FACT Informs Instruction

3-2-1 provides rich information to the teacher about what students perceive as the key learnings from a lesson or sequence of lessons. The information can be analyzed to see how well the goals of a lesson were met. The FACT also provides information to the teacher about what students are still struggling with so that further instructional opportunities can be provided that target students' learning needs.

Design and Administration

This strategy is best used with difficult concepts or during an instructional sequence when students have learned something new. Figure 4.41 shows an example of a *3-2-1* reflection sheet. Provide students with a copy of the reflection sheet and time to complete their reflection. Students can also be paired up to share their *3-2-1* reflections with their peers.

Figure 4.41   Example of a *3-2-1* Reflection Sheet

3 new things I learned

    1.

    2.

    3.

2 things I am still struggling with

    1.

    2.

1 thing that will help me tomorrow

    1.

General Implementation Attributes

Ease of Use: High   Cognitive Demand: Medium
Time Demand: Low

Modifications

3-2-1 can also be used when students are learning new algorithms, procedures, or skills. For example, the following can be used with elementary students who are learning multiplication facts: *Three facts that I always know, two facts that I still have to think about first*, and *one strategy I can use when I don't know a fact.* If more information is desired for a particular instructional situation, consider using a *5-3-1*.

Caveats

Vary this strategy with other FACTS that encourage reflection, and change the prompts periodically, or students may quickly tire of this technique.

Use With Other Disciplines

This FACT can also be used in **science*, social studies, language arts, health, foreign language, and visual and performing arts.

My Notes

_____

_____

_____

#63. THUMBS UP, THUMBS DOWN

Description

Thumbs Up, Thumbs Down provides a quick visual check on how well students understand a concept, procedure, or skill before the teacher proceeds further with the lesson or activity. Students hold their thumbs up if they feel ready to move on or put their thumbs down if they feel they are not ready.

How This FACT Promotes Student Learning

Thumbs Up, Thumbs Down promotes metacognition and helps students develop self-assessment skills (Black & Harrison, 2004). Students use their thumb signals to indicate to the teacher when they need additional support for their learning.

How This Fact Informs Instruction

Thumbs Up, Thumbs Down is a quick monitoring strategy that can be used at any time during instruction to help the teacher gauge the extent of student understanding, which in turn informs the pace of instruction. When students are asked to hold up their thumbs showing where they are in their current understanding, the teacher can get a quick snapshot of the class as well as individual students' level of understanding. If the majority of students hold up a "thumbs down," this is a clear indication to the teacher that instruction needs to be modified in order to accommodate the needs of the class. Conversely, a majority of "thumbs up" indicates that most of the class is ready to move on. A mixture of thumbs up and thumbs down indicates the need to provide peer and teacher support before moving on. For example, the "thumbs down" students can be matched with "thumbs up" students to help them address difficulties in their understanding. This frees up time for the teacher to circulate and help individuals who are struggling the most.

Design and Administration

At any point during the lesson, ask students to raise their fists with their thumbs out. Ask students to point thumbs up if they "get it" and are ready to move on. Ask them to point thumbs down if they are confused, have questions, or need help before moving on with the lesson or activity. Analyze the ratio of thumbs up to thumbs down to make determinations on how to proceed with the lesson or note individual students that may need further help as you proceed.

General Implementation Attributes

Ease of Use: High   Cognitive Demand: Low
Time Demand: Low

Modifications

Thumbs can be turned sideways if students feel they can move on but may have some questions as they get further into the lesson or activity. *Thumbs Up, Thumbs Down* can also be used with assessment probes to indicate students' confidence level in their commitment to an idea. For example, a "thumbs up" represents confidence, "thumbs sideways" represents some confidence, and "thumbs down" represents no confidence or a guess.

This FACT can also be used to have students evaluate the solutions and arguments of their classmates. Requiring students to signal agreement (thumbs up) or disagreement (thumbs down) sets the expectation that students are actively listening to their classmates' explanations.

Caveats

Make sure the "thumbs up" students who are matched up with "thumbs down" students have an accurate grasp of the content or skill targeted by the lesson so that one student's misunderstandings will not be passed on to another. Choose students carefully for peer assistance and, if possible, listen in on their discussions to determine how well students are able to assist others.

Use With Other Disciplines

This FACT can also be used in science, social studies, language arts, health, foreign language, and visual performing arts.

My Notes

_____

_____

_____

#64. TRAFFIC LIGHT CARDS

Description

Traffic Light Cards are a variation on the popular "traffic lighting" strategy used in the United Kingdom (Black et. al., 2003). The traffic light icons—red-, yellow-, and green-colored "lights"—are used to represent levels of student understanding. Students are given three cards of different colors, asked to self-assess their understanding about a concept or skill they are learning, and hold up the card that best matches their understanding. Green means "I understand this very well," yellow means "I understand most of it but could use a little help," and red means "Help! I don't get it."

How This FACT Promotes Student Learning

Traffic light icons promote metacognition and help students develop self-assessment skills (Black and Harrison, 2004). Students use the cards to indicate to the teacher when they need additional support for their learning.

How This Fact Informs Instruction

Traffic Light Cards are a monitoring strategy that can be used at any time during instruction to help the teacher gauge the extent of student understanding; this, in turn, can inform the pace of instruction. The colors indicate whether students have full, partial, or minimal to no understanding. When students are asked to hold up the card that best represents their current level of understanding, the teacher can get a quick snapshot of the class as well as individual students' level of understanding. If the majority of students hold up *red*, this is a clear indication to the teacher that instruction needs to be modified in order to accommodate the needs of the class. Conversely, a majority of *greens* indicates that most of the class is ready to move on. A mixture of colors indicates the need to provide peer and teacher support before moving on. For example, the yellow-card students can be matched up with green-card students to help them address difficulties in their understanding. This frees up time for the teacher to work with the red-card students, who may have more serious learning difficulties.

Design and Administration

Cut red, yellow, and green squares out of card stock. Provide each student with a set to keep in his or her desk, the inside flap of a notebook, or other accessible area. When the teacher knows the traffic cards will be used in a lesson, students are asked to put them on their desk. When the teacher decides on the right moment to get feedback from students on their understanding, students are asked to hold up the card that represents how well they feel they understand what they have been doing or learning thus far. A traffic light graphic posted in the front of the room can be used to remind students what the colors represent. See the Appendix for a source that explains in detail the use of this strategy.

General Implementation Attributes

Ease of Use: High   Cognitive Demand: Low
Time Demand: Low

Modifications

Traffic Light Cards can be used with assessment probes to indicate students' confidence level in their commitment to an idea. For example, a green card represents confidence, yellow represents some confidence, and red represents no confidence or a guess. Flip cards for readiness can also be made by gluing a red card to a green card. Students hold up the side that represents how ready they are to proceed with the lesson or next step in a procedure. The green side indicates readiness, and the red side indicates that students are not yet ready.

Caveats

Make sure the green-card students who are matched up to help the yellow-card students have an accurate grasp of the content or skill targeted by the lesson so that one student's misunderstandings will not be passed on to another. Choose students carefully for peer assistance and, if possible, eavesdrop on the discussions to determine how well students are able to assist others.

Use With Other Disciplines

This FACT can also be used in *science*, social studies, language arts, health, foreign language, and visual and performing arts.

My Notes

_____

_____

_____

#65. TRAFFIC LIGHT CUPS

Description

Traffic Light Cups are used during group work, including work with manipulatives or other hands-on mathematics investigations to signal to the teacher when students need help or feedback. Red, yellow, and green stackable party cups placed in the center of a group's table or work station represent whether the group is able to proceed without the need for teacher intervention, assistance, or feedback.

How This FACT Promotes Student Learning

Traffic Light Cups promote self-assessment by increasing students' awareness of when they can proceed with a task without assistance or feedback from the teacher.

How This FACT Informs Instruction

During hands-on activities or other small-group problem-solving tasks, the teacher is constantly monitoring groups that need assistance.

Traffic Light Cups provide a visual signal to the teacher that a group may need assistance or would like feedback on their progress. It allows the teacher to use time more efficiently to work with groups that have the greatest needs. *Traffic Light Cups* signal to the teacher when a group is proceeding successfully without the need for assistance (green), when a group might like feedback or assistance from the teacher in order to best continue with their work but are still able to proceed in the meantime (yellow), or when a group is stuck and can't go any further until they get assistance or feedback from the teacher (red).

Design and Administration

Obtain green, orange or yellow, and red stackable party cups of the same size from a party store. Give all groups a set of cups and ask them to stack them, one inside the other, with the green cup on the outside. The stack of cups is placed in the center of their work area where it can be seen by the teacher. All groups should start with green on the outside. As their needs for instructional support from the teacher increase, students change the outer color to yellow or red. As the teacher scans the room, students with red cups on the outside receive assistance first, followed by yellow cups.

General Implementation Attributes

Ease of Use: High   Cognitive Demand: Low
Time Demand: Low

Modifications

Traffic Light Cups can also be used for individual tasks. They can also be used to signal time on task. Green means that the group or individual feels there is plenty of time to finish on schedule. Yellow signifies the need for just a little more time. Red signifies that a group or individual is behind and will need more time to finish.

Caveats

When this strategy is new, students need to be frequently reminded to change their outer cup when their learning needs change. The teacher should check in occasionally with the green cups to keep informed of the groups' progress. Don't assume because the green cup is on the outside that you don't need to check on a group. Some students may use this tactic if they are off task and do not want the teacher to know they are doing something else!

Use With Other Disciplines

This FACT can also be used in *science, social studies, language arts, health, foreign language, and visual and performing arts.

My Notes

_____

_____

_____

#66. TRAFFIC LIGHT DOTS

Description

Traffic Light Dots are used by students to self-assess their work and get feedback from peers or the teacher. Small peel-off colored dots that come in sheets from office supply stores serve as traffic signal icons. Students place the dots in the margins of their work to indicate areas where they feel that they successfully completed the task (green), areas where they aren't sure about their work and would like feedback (yellow), and areas where they feel they didn't understand or perform well on the task and need help (red).

How This FACT Promotes Student Learning

Traffic Light Dots provide a way for students to self-assess areas of their work and seek help in developing understanding. When students exchange a traffic-light-dotted paper with another student, the FACT supports peer assessment and helps students think further about the concepts or problem-solving strategy they used in order to provide feedback to other students on their yellow or red areas.

How This FACT Informs Instruction

Student work submitted to the teacher for feedback that has been traffic-light dotted saves considerable time on the part of the teacher by enabling the teacher to focus on the yellow and red areas for feedback. A quick scan of a collection of student work from a class that contains a majority of red dots signifies to the teacher that students may not have been ready for the assignment or task and require an adjustment in instruction to help them develop the understanding needed to complete the task. Conversely, papers that have a majority of green dots signify that students were generally able to use their understanding to complete the task. A mixture of dots may indicate the need to have students work in groups to help each other. For example, a student who put a green dot in one area of work may help a student with yellow or red in the same area.

General Implementation Attributes

Ease of Use: High   Cognitive Demand: Medium
Time Demand: Low

Modifications

Students can traffic-light-dot other students' papers as a form of peer assessment. Green means good work, yellow means that the work needs some improvement, and red indicates the need for major revision. If peel-and-stick dots are not available, students can create their own dot icons with red, yellow, and green markers, crayon, or colored pencils.

Caveats

Feedback on yellow and red dots should be given soon after students have submitted their work in order for the feedback to be useful. It is also useful to provide feedback on the green dots, letting students know that you acknowledge areas where they feel they have done well; comment on what you found to be good about their work. When using this FACT, avoid assigning grades to assignments, because the purpose is to provide feedback, not judgment.

Use With Other Disciplines

This FACT can also be used in *science, social studies, language arts, health, foreign language, and visual and performing arts.

My Notes

_____

_____

_____

#67. TWO-MINUTE PAPER

Description

The *Two-Minute Paper* is a quick and simple way to collect feedback from students about their learning at the end of a lesson or other learning experience. Students are given two minutes to respond to a predetermined prompt in writing.

How This FACT Promotes Student Learning

The Two-Minute Paper requires students to use more than recall in responding to questions about a learning experience. Students must first think about what they have been learning about and determine how well they feel they learned the concept or skill. The FACT also demonstrates to the students the teacher's respect for their feedback, particularly when they see how it is used to make their learning experiences more student centered.

How This Fact Informs Instruction

The *Two-Minute Paper* allows the teacher to collect feedback on student learning with minimal effort and time. Student responses are read, sorted, and analyzed in order to determine how to make adjustments to the lesson the next day.

Design and Administration

Provide a half sheet of paper to students during the last 3 to 5 minutes of a lesson. Write one or two questions on the board or on a chart that you want students to respond to. For example, use some variation of the following:

- What was the most important thing you learned today?
- What did you learn today that you didn't know before class?
- What important question remains unanswered for you?
- What would help you learn better tomorrow?

Give students 2 minutes to write, and then collect their papers. After their responses have been analyzed, share the results with students the next day, letting them know how you are going to use the feedback they shared with you.

General Implementation Attributes

Ease of Use: High
Time Demand: Low

Cognitive Demand: Low/Medium

Modifications

The *Two-Minute Paper* can be used at the beginning of a day's lesson to reflect on the previous day's lesson in order to inform the teacher about modifications that may be necessary. It can be used after completing homework or a class assignment. This technique has also been used as a *One-Minute Paper* with older students (Angelo & Cross, 1993). Extend the time allowed for younger students or students who have difficulty writing in the English language into a *Three-* or *Four-Minute Paper.*

Caveats

Adjust the time according to students' writing ability so that slower writers feel they have had adequate opportunity to give feedback.

Use With Other Disciplines

This FACT can also be used in **science*, social studies, language arts, health, foreign language, and visual and performing arts.

My Notes

_____

_____

_____

#68. TWO OR THREE BEFORE ME

Description

Two or Three Before Me provides opportunities for more students to share their ideas during class. It prevents individual students from dominating the responses to the teacher's or other students' questions. The rule is that at least two or three students must have an opportunity to talk before the same person can speak again.

How This FACT Promotes Student Learning

This FACT provides opportunities for a greater number of students in a class to share their thinking, particularly when there are dominant voices in a class. It also provides an opportunity for students who tend to be overly responsive to teacher questioning to listen to the ideas of their peers. Taking the time to listen to the ideas of others before voicing their own ideas helps dominant students reconsider their own thinking in light of what others think.

How This Fact Informs Instruction

Two or Three Before Me provides a classroom norm that teachers can use to ensure that more students in a class have an opportunity for their ideas to be heard. When more student voices are heard, the teacher is better able to determine the extent of understanding and range of ideas in the class that can be used to inform instruction.

Design and Administration

Explain the strategy to students, including the purpose of *Two or Three Before Me,* and practice using it during a class discussion. Eventually students will adopt it as a discussion norm.

General Implementation Attributes

Ease of Use: High   Cognitive Demand: Low
Time Demand: Low

Modifications

The strategy can be changed to any number of students such as *One or Two Before Me* or *Three or Four Before Me.* This FACT can also be applied in reverse to the teacher by encouraging two or three students to speak before the teacher will speak again. It can be used by small groups of four to six students to monitor participation within a group.

Caveats

Make sure to accompany this technique with *Wait Time* strategies.

Use With Other Disciplines

This FACT can also be used in *science*, social studies, language arts, health, foreign language, and visual and performing arts.

My Notes

_____

_____

_____

#69. TWO STARS AND A WISH

Description

Two Stars and a Wish is a technique used in *Comments-Only Marking*. It is a way to balance positive comments with the need for improvement when providing students with feedback on their work (Black & Harrison, 2004). The first two sentences provide detailed comments on good features of the student's work. The third sentence provides a detailed comment that encourages revision or further improvement.

How This FACT Promotes Student Learning

Specific comments, both positive ones and those that indicate a need for improvement, provide students with a better understanding of where their strengths and weaknesses are and how to improve their work. These comments provide the student with better insight into ways to improve their work than comments like *Great job, Nice explanation, Needs revision,* or *Unclear.* The balance and tone used with *Two Stars and a Wish* encourages students to take action on their work for the purpose of improving their learning. Providing two positive comments for every area of improvement raises the confidence and self-esteem of students who typically feel discouraged and give up when papers are marked up with wrong answers or given low grades. Because it does not pass judgment by grading, students feel successful, while acknowledging they can do better. This approach is particularly helpful with lower-achieving students in improving their desire to learn and ability to succeed.

How This Fact Informs Instruction

Teachers who use this strategy support the culture needed in a classroom to focus on success and the belief that all students can achieve when given feedback that focuses on the learning target. The comments from *Two Stars and a Wish* also provide a stimulus for students to discuss their work with the teacher so that the teacher can individualize improvements for each student.

Design and Administration

Use with assignments that provide an opportunity for students to demonstrate their conceptual understanding, including solving multi-step problems and explaining solution steps, making and justifying conjectures, and providing examples and nonexamples. Instead of marking students' work right or wrong, look for areas throughout the work where you can identify two good features of the students' work and one area for improvement. Place comments on a sticky note or in the margin of their work. The following are examples of feedback given using *Two Stars and a Wish*:

> Feedback on a high school student's strategy for solving a problem: *You were able to identify the relevant and nonrelevant information from the problem and your answer is clearly labeled. However, you left one piece of relevant information out of your solution steps. Please review what you had labeled as relevant and your solution to determine what is missing.*

> Feedback on homework questions from a middle school lesson on linear equations: *You have graphed each of the problems correctly and have accurately labeled the y-intercepts. Although the process used to determine slope is correct, your choice of points to use sometimes results in a wrong answer. Review your notes to find a method that ensures the points are on the line. Use this process to determine which of your slopes need to be recalculated.*

> Feedback on an elementary student's construction of a bar graph: *Your graph clearly describes the data collected in class yesterday, and you have created two questions that can be answered directly by finding the number of students who liked a particular color. Now you need to write an additional question that relates two or more of the color categories.*

General Implementation Attributes

Ease of Use: High   Cognitive Demand: Medium
Time Demand: Medium

Modifications

This FACT can also be used by students to self-assess their own work or peer-assess the work of other students. Students provide two positive statements about their work or the work of their peers and indicate one area that can be improved.

Caveats

This is a comments-only FACT. Research indicates a less positive effect on student learning when grades are given in addition to comments (Black & Harrison, 2004). Because this strategy reinforces the notion that the teacher wants students to improve their work and that their improvement is being monitored by the teacher, time should be provided in class for students to read and react to the comments. If possible, provide time in class for students to work on their revisions.

Use With Other Disciplines

This FACT can also be used in *science*, social studies, language arts, health, foreign language, and visual and performing arts.

My Notes

#70. TWO THIRDS TESTING

Description

Summative end-of-unit tests often cover a lot of information. This technique provides an opportunity for students to take an ungraded practice test two thirds of the way through a unit (Wiliam, 2006). Students are then provided time to get feedback from their peers and the teacher on their responses, gaps in understanding, or difficulties in arriving at their answers.

How This FACT Promotes Student Learning

Two Thirds Testing provides a metacognitive opportunity for students to identify areas of difficulty or misunderstanding two thirds of the way through an instructional unit so that interventions and support can be provided to help them learn and be prepared for a final summative assessment. It alleviates the pressure of trying to recall all the concepts, procedures, and skills learned throughout an instructional unit by providing an opportunity to practice using what they learned in a nonjudgmental way two thirds of the way through their learning. In addition, working on the test in small groups or sharing and discussing answers afterward through discussions with a partner or in a small group further develops and solidifies conceptual and procedural understanding.

How This Fact Informs Instruction

Examining students' cumulative knowledge and understanding two thirds of the way through a unit may reveal nonreadiness or areas of difficulty for individual students or the class as a whole. The information can be used to differentiate instruction for individuals or revisit difficult concepts with the entire class. This FACT indicates to the teacher whether instruction is on pace in preparation for readiness to take an upcoming summative assessment. It provides an opportunity to give students targeted feedback and assistance in the areas where they need help the most.

Design and Administration

Select an alternative version of a test that will be given at the end of a unit, or create a similar test. Select or make up a new version of questions that were addressed by students' learning experiences two thirds of the way through the instructional unit. Have students work individually, in pairs, or in small groups on the items. Use the results for differentiated feedback or class discussion about items students have the most difficulty with.

General Implementation Attributes

Ease of Use: Medium
Time Demand: Medium/High

Cognitive Demand: Depends
on type of questions

Modifications

Depending on the unit of study, this FACT can be modified to one third testing, one half testing, three quarters testing, etc. It can also be used as a one half or two thirds testing for midterm, semester, or year-end final exams.

Caveats

The use of summative tests with this technique is for formative purposes only. Thus, use comments-only marking for feedback, not grades.

Use With Other Disciplines

This FACT can also be used in *science*, social studies, language arts, health, foreign language, and visual and performing arts.

My Notes

_____

_____

_____

#71. VOLLEYBALL, NOT PING-PONG!

Description

Volleyball, Not Ping-Pong describes a technique that changes the nature of the question-and-answer interaction pattern in the classroom from a back-and-forth teacher-to-student exchange to one of teacher to student A to student B to student C, D, and so on, then back to the teacher. The ping-pong metaphor represents the typical rapid-fire, back-and-forth cycle of questions and responses that take place between the teacher and students. The volleyball metaphor represents the teacher asking a question, a student responding, and other students building off the response until the teacher "serves" another question.

How This FACT Promotes Student Learning

Good questioning techniques that involve all students provide an opportunity for deeper engagement with ideas in mathematics and richer responses to questions. "Volleyball" questioning helps students link, apply, and give reasons for their ideas. It motivates students to consider the ideas of others as they think about how their own ideas may enhance, extend, or challenge other students' thinking. Encouraging several students to put their ideas forth in the public arena of the classroom rather than accepting one answer and moving on enhances the opportunity for sustained, thoughtful discussions that promote student learning.

How This Fact Informs Instruction

This FACT encourages teachers to change their questioning techniques from simple recall questions that can be answered by one student to more open-ended questions that elicit thoughtful, more detailed responses. A consequence of using this technique is that teachers have a greater opportunity to listen to their students in order to learn more about their understandings, gaps, or misconceptions. The information is used to inform their next instructional moves so as to address their students' ideas and needs.

Design and Administration

Share the volleyball and ping-pong metaphor with students before using this strategy. Practice "serving" a question and having several students respond as if they were setting up the ball for the next student and hitting it over the net. When the question becomes exhausted, the "ball" goes back to the teacher for a new "serve." This type of questioning and response takes practice the first few times it is used. It may help to have students sit where they can see each other, such as in a circle, the first time it is used. Encourage students not to look at the teacher when they reply, because they are putting their ideas forth to the class, not just to the teacher. They should look at their classmates when they respond. Students should also be encouraged to ask new questions that build off the responses of others that can sustain the "volleys."

General Implementation Attributes

Ease of Use: Medium
Time Demand: Low/Medium

Cognitive Demand: Depends
  on the question

Modifications

Consider setting a minimum number of times the question and responses must go back and forth among students before the next question is asked or a comment is made by the teacher. The first time the strategy is used, it may be helpful to use a physical prop such as a Koosh ball, beach ball, or other type of soft ball that can be passed from student to student.

Caveats

This strategy also involves the use of *Wait Time*. It may appear that students are not going to respond when in fact, they are using wait time to think and formulate their comments. Be patient, and don't throw out a new question too soon!

Use With Other Disciplines

This FACT can also be used in *science*, social studies, language arts, health, foreign language, and visual and performing arts.

My Notes

_____

_____

_____

#72. WAIT TIME VARIATIONS

Description

Wait Time, also called the "miracle pause," has an extensive body of research behind it (Walsh & Sattes, 2005). Mary Budd Rowe, a former professor at the University of Florida, discovered the value of silence as she conducted research on interactions in K–12 classrooms. Her research found that teachers tend to leave no more than one second of silence before addressing an unanswered question or asking someone to answer it. *Wait Time* is the interval between the time a question is posed and the time either a student or teacher responds to the question. When teachers increase their *Wait Time* to at least 3 seconds, class participation increases, answers are more detailed, complex thinking increases, and science achievement scores increase significantly (Rowe, 1974). *Wait Time II* involves the interval between when a student answers a question and the teacher responds.

How This FACT Supports Student Learning

Complex questions require time for students to formulate an answer. *Wait Time* provides the opportunity students need to think. Research has found numerous benefits of various kinds to students when *Wait Time* of three to five seconds is deliberately practiced (Rowe, 1986; Walsh & Sattes, 2005):

- Students give longer, more detailed responses.
- Students give evidence for their ideas and conclusions.
- Students speculate and hypothesize.
- Students ask more questions.
- Students talk more to other students.
- There are fewer "I don't knows."
- Discipline problems decrease as students become more engaged in the lesson.
- More students respond.
- Students answer with more confidence.
- Achievement improves on cognitively complex items.

How This FACT Informs Instruction

In addition to dramatically increasing the participation of students in a class discussion, this FACT also provides information to the teacher about students' understanding and ways of thinking. Since *Wait Time* encourages longer, richer answers, the teacher gains a better sense of what the students know and the reasoning students use to formulate their ideas. Furthermore, practicing *Wait Time* increases the sample of students from which teachers can gain information about the progress of learning in the class. This information is then used by the teacher to monitor student learning experiences, differentiate individual students, and adjust instruction accordingly to meet the learning needs of the class. In addition to promoting student thinking and informing instruction, *Wait Time* has been shown to have the following effects on teacher practice:

- Teacher responses are more thoughtful and tend to keep the discussion focused and ongoing.
- The quality of teacher feedback improves.
- Teachers ask fewer questions. The questions they do ask increase in cognitive level.
- Teachers expect more from previously nonparticipating students.

Design and Administration

Students are accustomed to rapid-fire questions and answers. Discuss with students what *Wait Time* is and why it is used, so they will understand the reason for your long pause. Establish *Wait Time* as a classroom norm practiced by both teachers and students. Practice *Wait Time* by silently counting to at least 3 seconds ("one – one thousand, two – one thousand, three – one thousand") before calling on a student. Continue to use 3- to 5-second *Wait Time* after a student answers and before you respond to the student's answer so that both the student and the rest of the class have time to think about the response. Use lead-ins that encourage the overeager students to wait, such as "I want everyone to think carefully about their own ideas before we tackle this question" or "I'm going to wait until everyone has had a chance to think before I ask you to share your thinking." Teachers can also try deliberately pausing, indicating thinking time, and then asking for no hands to be raised until the teacher gives a signal. Sometimes it helps to give students a chance to jot their own ideas down on paper first before asking for responses. Another way is to have students discuss the proposed question with a partner, using FACTS such as *Think–Pair–Share* before taking responses from the whole class.

The following example shows how *Wait Time* can be used:

"Who can remember why common dominators are important when adding and subtracting fractions?" Silently count to 4 seconds before selecting a student to respond. Kerry responds with "So that there are the same number of pieces for each bar." Include a 4-second wait time before responding to the student or calling on another student. "Kerry pointed out that common denominators have something to do with the same number of pieces. I want you think about what she said, and then I'd like to hear who agrees, disagrees, or would like to add to what Kerry said." Wait time . . .

General Implementation Attributes

Ease of Use: High   Cognitive Demand: Medium
Time Demand: Low

Modifications

Wait Time between students can also be encouraged and practiced with a variety of FACTs in which students interact in pairs or small groups. Remind students to practice pausing before responding to another student or building upon someone else's response so that everyone has a chance to think and process his or her ideas. Consider using a chart like the one in Figure 4.42 to help students practice wait time. See the Appendix for more details on using *Wait Time* and the timeless research that supports it.

Figure 4.42   *Wait Time* Classroom Poster

Wait Time

When the teacher asks a question:

- Listen carefully.
- Silently think about your own ideas.
- Don't raise your hand.
- Wait to be called on.
- Answer in a clear voice so everyone can hear.
- Remember all ideas are important.
- If you are not called on, listen to others' responses.
- Think about how your ideas are similar to or different from the answers you hear.

When a student answers a question and other students can add their ideas:

- Use the silent time to think about your own ideas.
- Be prepared to build on others' responses.
- Think about what others have said before it is your turn to talk.
- Respect others' ideas when you challenge them.
- Make eye contact with the class, not just the teacher.

Source: Adapted from Walsh & Sattes (2005). Used with permission.

Caveats

Three to five seconds of silence can seem agonizingly long! Don't succumb to the silence or students' strategy of waiting out the teacher. Students have learned in the past that if they wait long enough, the teacher will answer his or her own question. Don't give up, and if there are no takers, use the *No Hands Questioning* strategy. Keep quiet, and don't inter-ject comments during *Wait Time*, such as "Think about it," that distract student thinking.

Use With Other Disciplines

This FACT can also be used in **science*, social studies, language arts, health, foreign language, and visual and performing arts.

My Notes

_____

_____

_____

#73. WHAT ARE YOU DOING AND WHY?

Description

If a visitor walked into your classroom and asked students what they were doing and why they were doing it, you would hope all students could answer. This FACT helps teachers find out if their students know the goal of an activity-based mathematics lesson and how or why the activity can help them learn. This technique "models" the visitor who walks into the room scenario.

How This FACT Promotes Student Learning

What Are You Doing and Why? activates students' thinking about the purpose of the activity they are engaged in. It asks students to describe what they are supposed to be learning about and how the task they have been working on will help them learn. Students are more engaged in their learn-ing when they understand the learning goal and purpose of an activity.

How This FACT Informs Instruction

This short, simple monitoring strategy can be quite an eye-opener to teachers, especially if students are highly engaged in an activity yet show they do not know what the purpose of the activity is or how it is helping them learn. It encourages teachers to be clear and explicit about the learn-ing targets for the activity and explain to the students how the activity will help them develop new skills or understandings. When this question is used as a spot check during an activity, teachers can get a quick read from the class on whether the purpose of the activity is understood by students. If not, teachers can readjust to make sure the activity's purpose and goals are clearly communicated to the students and understood by all. This FACT helps avoid "activitymania" in mathematics, which occurs when teachers use hands-on activities that are fun and engaging even though students have no understanding of the purpose of the activity and what they will learn from it. Rather, they are merely following teacher directions with no or minimal learning gains.

Design and Administration

At any point partway into an activity, the teacher gets the class's attention and asks a "What are you doing and why are you doing it?" question. Responses can be shared with the class, discussed between partners, or recorded in writing as a *One-Minute Paper* to be passed in to the teacher. The data are analyzed by the teacher to determine whether the students understand the purpose of the activity they are involved in and how it may or may not be supporting student learning.

General Implementation Attributes

Ease of Use: High   Cognitive Demand: Medium
Time Demand: Low

Modifications

This FACT can also be used with non-hands-on learning experiences such as assigned readings, homework, videos, and problem-solving tasks. Any instructional task a student is asked to engage in should be clear about the purpose and intended outcomes.

Caveats

Do not use this FACT as a substitute for explicitly addressing the purpose and outcome of a learning activity. Make sure the purpose and outcome are addressed before students start the activity.

Use With Other Disciplines

This FACT can also be used in *science,* social studies, language arts, health, foreign language, and visual and performing arts.

My Notes

_____

_____

_____

#74. WHITEBOARDING

Description

Whiteboarding is used in small groups to encourage students to pool their individual thinking and come to a group consensus on an idea or problem-solving approach that is then shared with the teacher and the whole class. The use of whiteboards supports a classroom environment that encourages student-generated ideas and solutions. Researchers have found that when students use whiteboards their discussions are more animated and on task and draw upon higher-level thinking (Henry, Henry, & Riddoch, 2006). The technique involves using portable 24-by-32-inch whiteboards and dry-erase markers. Students work collaboratively around the whiteboard to draw and record their ideas and solutions in response to a prompt given by the teacher. Students use the whiteboard during class discussion to communicate their ideas to their peers and the teacher, thus modeling an essential feature of mathematics: communication supported by evidence and reasoning.

How This FACT Promotes Student Learning

Whiteboarding can be used at the beginning of an instructional unit or throughout a sequence of instruction to elicit students' prior knowledge and problem-solving strategies. It activates their thinking and construction of new understandings through interaction with their peers. As students collaborate on getting their ideas and solutions down on a whiteboard and sharing them with the class, they reveal their own thinking. They accept, discard, or modify their own ideas and solutions based on their consideration of alternative ideas and the problem-solving approaches of others. Unlike writing on chart paper, what is written on the whiteboards is erasable, allowing students to easily modify their work as new ideas emerge through discussion. The nonpermanent nature of the writing surface encourages students to draw or write something that they may not be sure of, because they know it can be easily changed or modified. *Whiteboarding* can also be used to help students design approaches to solving problems as well as analyze data and draw conclusions from mathematical investigations.

How This Fact Informs Instruction

The size of the whiteboards allows teachers to quickly see and examine a group's thinking, providing students with feedback when necessary. As students are working on the whiteboards, the teacher is able to circulate through the class, asking questions, probing more deeply, and encouraging students to make their thinking visible. The teacher can observe their drawings, writing, and discussions to note areas where additional instructional support might be needed. As students present their whiteboards to the class, the teacher can help students clarify and solidify their understandings. In addition, the whiteboard presentations provide an opportunity for teachers to give feedback to students on their communication skills, such as how to share ideas so that others can understand their reasoning, how to listen carefully to critique others' ideas, how to look for commonalities in thinking, and how to engage in mathematical argumentation in a constructive way, including coming to consensus when there are differences in opinions and ideas.

Design and Administration

Whiteboards can be purchased from suppliers but they are less expensive and a more suitable size when cut from 4-by-8-foot sheets of white economy tile board, available from home building supply stores. Many of these stores will custom-cut them for teachers and even cut handles into the top and round off the edges. You will also need low-odor dry-erase markers (four colors, preferably black, red, green, and blue), an eraser, and cleaners for dry-erase surfaces. Inexpensive tube socks can be used as erasers and also provide a handy storage receptacle for the markers. Provide students with a prompt that encourages them to work together in groups of two to four, huddled around the whiteboard, to draw and write about their ideas so that they can use the whiteboard to present their thinking to the class. For example, a prompt for a middle school lesson on perimeter and area might be as follows:

Draw and label at least three figures that each have a perimeter of 30 units but have different areas.

Encourage students to use different colors to differentiate parts of their drawing and solution. When groups have finished with their boards, use them to facilitate a whole-class discussion, revealing the variety of ideas in the class. Sometimes it is helpful to line up the whiteboards and allow students an opportunity to do a "walk-through" first, silently walking around to look at other groups' work. During whole-class discussion with the whiteboards, it is important to allow the student group to be the center of attention, with other students' eyes on them and their whiteboard. Position students so that everyone can see the whiteboard that is being presented. Encourage the students to interact and exchange ideas, using strategies like *Volleyball, Not Ping-Pong* so that the conversation is between the students, with the teacher as listener. After students have had an opportunity to take turns describing and discussing their boards, the teacher may choose to photograph each board for a digital record of students' thinking.

General Implementation Attributes

Ease of Use: High   Cognitive Demand: Medium/High
Time Demand: Medium/High

Modifications

Smaller individual whiteboards can be used but are not as effective for promoting group thinking as the larger sizes. If whiteboards are not available, shiny-sided freezer paper also works with dry-erase markers and allows the teacher to keep a record of the group's ideas. Depending on the prompt and the size of the whiteboards, they can be divided into four sections, with each student in a group contribute to one of the four sections.

Caveats

As with any new technique, students should be introduced to the use of *Whiteboarding* by modeling the first time it is used for group work and presentation, including ways to use features such as bullets, diagrams, symbols, arrows, color, and text size. Make sure there is enough room to accommodate the larger whiteboards either on a table or on the floor, including room for three to five students to work on the board simultaneously.

Use With Other Disciplines

This FACT can also be used in **science*.

My Notes

_____

_____

_____

#75. WORD SORT

Description

This FACT is a variation of *Concept Card Mapping*. Students are given cards with words written on them. They move the cards around to determine categories in which to groups the words.

How This FACT Promotes Student Learning

Students need to develop an appreciation of the need for precise definitions and for the communicative power of conventional mathematical terms by first communicating in their own words. Allowing students to grapple with their ideas and develop their own informal means of expressing them can be an effective way to foster engagement and ownership. (National Council of Teachers of Mathematics, 2000, p. 62)

This FACT activates prior knowledge of mathematical terms. Moving the cards during a *Word Sort* provides an opportunity for students to explore what they know about a mathematical term and to think about various relationships to other words in the set.

How This Fact Informs Instruction

This FACT can be used at the beginning of a unit of instruction to elicit students' initial ideas and to motivate them to want to learn more about the mathematical words and their relationships. Students' descriptions of categories provide insight into prior knowledge and can help teachers plan for instruction that will build on or clarify misunderstandings that have been uncovered.

Design and Administration

Select no more than 12 key mathematical words that students will learn and use during the unit of instruction or encounter in their instructional materials. Figure 4.43 shows an example of a *Word Sort* list for an elementary class on area and perimeter. You can place the words on index cards or make cards from preprinted matchbook-size squares on a sheet of paper, cut out and sorted into zip-lock bags (or have students cut out the squares). Have students work in small groups to discuss each of the words and brainstorm possible categories. Provide students with blank cards on which to write their categories once agreement has been reached. Listen carefully to students as they discuss and argue for their ideas about how to sort the words. Note examples where you may need to provide additional instructional opportunities to address students' misunderstandings. If a record of student thinking is needed, provide individual students or small groups with a recording sheet to note where each word was placed, along with a justification for its placement, or glue the cards onto a sheet of paper.

Figure 4.43　*Word Sort* for Area and Perimeter Unit

tiling	unit	square unit
dimension	side	length
width	height	decompose
measure	cover	surround

General Implementation Attributes

Ease of Use: High　　　　　　　　　　Cognitive Demand: Medium
Time Demand: Medium

Modifications

Rather than calling for an open sort, provide the number of categories you would like students to generate, or provide some of the categories and have students generate additional categories.

Caveats

The cognitive demand of this FACT depends on the concrete or abstract nature of the words selected and the number of cards to be categorized. Choose the appropriate level of demand that matches the grade level of the students and complexity of the topic they are learning about.

Use With Other Disciplines

This FACT can also be used in science, social studies, language arts, health, foreign language, and visual and performing arts.

My Notes

_____

_____

_____

Appendix

Annotated Resources for Mathematics Formative Assessment

T he following resources provide sources of supplementary material to use in designing or informing your use of the FACTs. In addition, several of the listed resources provide the FACT numbers for those that are referred to in the *FACT Design and Administration* descriptions provided in Chapter 4.

Annenberg Videos. Several of the Annenberg video series show examples of students being interviewed about their ideas in mathematics. They also show teachers using various formative assessment techniques. These videos are available online as streaming videos by going to www .learner.org and selecting the mathematics link.

Assessment for Common Misunderstandings. These assessment tools are based on a series of highly focused, research-based Probe Tasks. The *Probe Task Manual* also includes a number of additional tasks and resources that have been organized to address common misunderstandings. http://www .education.vic.gov.au/studentlearning/teachingresources/maths/common/ default.htm

Assessment for Learning. This book provides an excellent description of the rationale for formative assessment, the research that supports it, and information on specific techniques teachers have used. This resource is referenced in FACTs 6, 34, 64, and 70.

Black, P., Harrison, C., Lee, C., Marshall, B., & Wiliam, D. (2003). *Assessment for learning.* Berkshire, UK: Open University Press.

Concept Cartoons. The Concept Cartoon Web site at www.conceptcartoons .com gives examples of concept cartoons and ordering information. The cartoons can be ordered as a book or on a CD. There are posters and big books that use the concept cartoon format to stimulate discussion. The site also contains selected research studies done in the United Kingdom to examine the impact of concept cartoons on student learning. This resource is referenced in FACT 10.

Early Mathematical Thinking (EMT). This set of diagnostic assessment tools can be used as a formative assessment strategy to uncover students' current level of thinking in mathematics and guide instruction. Funded by the Maine Department of Education for use in a project at the Maine Mathematics and Science Alliance, its professional development component focused on the use of the EMT tools and relevant cognitive research to enhance student achievement in mathematics. EMT was developed from state, national, and international math research as well as cognitive research on how students learn math. The EMT diagnostic tools were derived and adapted from Australia's Early Numeracy Research Project (ENRP). Information about ENRP can be found at http://www.education .vic.gov.au/studentlearning/teachingresources/maths/enrp/default.htm.

For additional information on EMT professional development and diagnostic tools, contact the Maine Mathematics and Science Alliance at www.mmsa.org.

How Students (Mis)understand Science and Mathematics: Intuitive Rules. This book provides an explanation and examples of intuitive rules students use to reason in science and mathematics and instructional strategies for addressing students' use of these rules. This resource is referenced in FACTs 32 and 34.

Stavy, R., & Tirosh, D. (2000). *How students (mis)understand science and mathematics: Intuitive rules.* New York: Teachers College Press.

Interactive Technology Applets. Some concepts elicited by the FACTs can be addressed through available online resources. Keep in mind that most of these applets were developed as instructional resources or to provide practice and were not developed to address a specific misconception. When searching for available applets that meet students' needs as elicited by a FACT, be sure to review the applet carefully to consider the range of examples and nonexamples that can be modeled using the tool. Before using with students, prepare a scaffolded set of questions designed specifically to highlight the misunderstandings elicited by the probe items.

Sample list of sites to look for freely available interactive applets:

National Library of Virtual Manipulatives: http://nlvm.usu.edu/en/nav/vlibrary .html

NCTM's Illuminations: http://illuminations.nctm.org

Educational Development Center: http://maine.edc.org

Interactive applets are referenced in FACT #40.

Mathematics Curriculum Topic Study: Bridging the Gap Between Standards and Practice. This book was funded by a grant from the National Science Foundation. It provides a process for using national standards and cognitive research to deeply examine K–12 teaching and learning in 92 mathematics topics. The vetted readings included in the Curriculum Topic Study guides point out areas of the cognitive research where teachers can learn more about students' misconceptions. Chapter 4 includes a process for developing formative assessment probes similar to the ones described in several of the FACTs. The book is available through Corwin (www.corwin.com). This resource is useful in designing FACTs 4, 9, 13, 19, 24, 28, 36, 37, and 40. There is also a website at www.curriculumtopicstudy.org that includes a supplementary database where you can access a variety of articles that inform teaching and learning.

Keeley, P., & Rose, C. (2006). *Mathematics curriculum topic study: Bridging the gap between standards and practice.* Thousand Oaks, CA: Corwin.

Note: In addition, *A Leader's Guide to Mathematics Curriculum Topic Study* (Keeley, Mundry, Rose-Tobey, & Carroll, in press), also available through Corwin, provides facilitation materials for guiding professional development sessions in which teachers design their own formative assessment probes as well as strategies for examining student work.

National Center on Response to Intervention. The tools chart provided on the website reflects the results of the second annual review of research studies of screening tools by the Center's Technical Review Committee. Many of these tools are interview based and can be used to supplement FACT 54. http://www.rti4success.org/chart/screeningTools/screeningtools chart.html

Online Interviews. These can be used to support the use of FACT 54. The Australian website listed below provides examples of student interviews. *The Fractions and Decimals Online Interview* is designed to help teachers better understand their students' knowledge, skills, and behaviors with regard to fractions and decimals, a known area of difficulty for many students. *The Mathematics Online Interview* consists of appropriate hands-on assessment tasks in which students demonstrate mathematical understanding and preferred strategies for solving increasingly complex tasks. http://www.education.vic.gov.au/studentlearning/teachingresources/maths/assessment.htm

Quality Questioning. This book provides a wealth of information on asking good questions. In addition to the FACTs described in Chapter 4, this book provides additional techniques for asking questions, prompting students' responses, and generating, preparing, and processing questions. This resource is referenced in FACTs 14, 46, and 72.

Walsh, J., & Sattes, B. (2005). *Quality questioning: Research-based practice to engage every learner.* Thousand Oaks, CA: Corwin.

The Rational Number Project (RNP). This project advocates teaching fractions using a model that emphasizes multiple representations and connections among different representations. Important outcomes from early RNP work include a deeper understanding of children's thinking as they develop initial fraction ideas and a curriculum module for teaching students fractions using a multiple representation approach. The materials include assessment and interview questions.

http://www.cehd.umn.edu/rationalnumberproject/rnp1-09.html

SALG—Student Assessment of Learning Gains. This website (http://www.salgsite.org/) was developed with funding from the National Science Foundation to help college course instructors evaluate their courses in terms of how well their students think the course components advanced their learning. The site, which can be also used by middle and high school teachers, has an online instrument so that teachers can develop their own surveys and provide access to students to take the survey online. This resource is referenced in FACT 53.

Science Formative Assessment: 75 Practical Strategies for Linking Assessment, Instruction, and Learning. This is the science version of this FACTs book. It is a parallel resource that provides 75 examples of FACTs science teachers can use. Several of the FACTs in the science version overlap with this book. The book is available through both Corwin and NSTA at nsta.org.

Keeley, P. (2008). *Science formative assessment: 75 practical strategies for linking assessment, instruction, and learning.* Thousand Oaks, CA: Corwin.

Uncovering Student Ideas Website. Visit uncoveringstudentideas.org to get information and updates on science and mathematics formative assessment and to share tools and resources with other educators.

Uncovering Student Thinking in Mathematics Series. This multivolume series contains ready-to-use formative assessment probes that can be used as is or adapted for use with several of the FACTs described in this book. Each book contains a set of probes along with extensive teacher background notes. The books are available through Corwin at corwinpress.com

or through the Maine Mathematics and Science Alliance at www.mmsa
.org. This resource is referenced in several of the assessment probe FACTs.

Rose, C., Minton, L., & Arline, C. (2007). *Uncovering student thinking in mathematics: 25 formative assessment probes.* Thousand Oaks, CA: Corwin.

Rose, C., & Arline, C. (2009). *Uncovering student thinking in mathematics, grades 6–12: 30 formative assessment probes for the secondary classroom.* Thousand Oaks, CA: Corwin.

Rose Tobey, C., & Minton, L. (2009). *Uncovering student thinking in mathematics, grades K–5: 25 formative assessment probes for the elementary classroom.* Thousand Oaks, CA: Corwin.

Workshops and Professional Development on Formative Assessment.
Both of the authors of this book provide professional development on formative assessment for mathematics and science educators. Page Keeley
and Cheryl Rose Tobey have worked extensively with school districts,
math-science organizations, math-science partnership projects, leadership
institutes, and curriculum developers throughout the United States to build
teachers' capacity to use formative assessment. Professional development
ranges from invited talks to half-day, full-day, and multiday sessions. To
arrange for professional development or invited presentations, contact the
authors at pagekeeley@gmail.com or pkeeley@mmsa.org, or cheryltobey@
gmail.com or ctobey@edc.org, or visit the website www.uncoveringstudent
ideas.org, to learn where and when the authors are presenting at state,
regional, and national conferences.

References

Ainsworth, L., & Viegut, D. (2006). *Common formative assessments.* Thousand Oaks, CA: Corwin.

Angelo, T., & Cross, K. P. (1993). *Classroom assessment techniques: A handbook for college teachers.* San Francisco: Jossey-Bass.

Arons, A. (1977). *The various language: An inquiry approach to physical science.* New York: Oxford University Press.

Ausubel, D., Novak, J., & Hanesian, H. (1978). *Educational psychology: A cognitive view* (2nd ed.). New York: Holt, Rinehart, & Winston.

Black, B., & Harrison, C. (2004). *Science inside the black box: Assessment for learning in the science classroom.* London: NFER/Nelson.

Black, P., Harrison, C., Lee, C., Marshall, B., & Wiliam, D. (2003). *Assessment for learning.* Berkshire, UK: Open University Press.

Black, P., & Wiliam, D. (1998). Inside the black box: Raising standards through classroom assessment. *Phi Delta Kappan, 80*(2), 139–148.

Bransford, J., Brown, A., & Cocking, R. (1999). *How people learn: Brain, mind, experience, and school.* Washington, DC: National Academy Press.

Bruner, J. S., Goodnow, J. J., & Austin, G.A. (1956). *A study of thinking.* London: Chapman & Hall.

Buehl, D. (2001). *Classroom strategies for interactive learning.* Newark, DE: International Reading Association.

Buffington, P., Tierney-Fife, P., & Todd-Brown, B. (n.d.) Bag of marbles: Probability simulation. Retrieved from http://maine.edc.org/file.php/1/tools/BagOf Marbles.html

Burns, M. (2010). Snapshots of student misunderstandings. *Educational Leadership, 67*(5), 18–22.

Carey, S. (2000). Science education as conceptual change. *Journal of Applied Developmental Psychology, 21*(1), 13.

Carlson, M., Humphrey, G., & Reinhardt, K. (2003). *Weaving science inquiry and continuous assessment.* Thousand Oaks, CA: Corwin.

Carre, C. (1993). Performance in subject-matter knowledge in science. In N. Bennet & C. Carre (Eds.), *Learning to teach* (pp. 18–35). London: Routledge.

Clarke, S. (2005). *Formative assessment in the secondary classroom.* London: Hodder Murray.

Cobb, P., Wood, T., & Yackel, E. (1991). A constructivist approach to second grade mathematics. In E. Von Glasersfeld (Ed.), *Radical constructivism in mathematics education.* Dordrecht, Netherlands: Kluwer.

Common Core State Standards Initiative (CCSSI). (2010). The standards: Mathematics. Available at http://www.corestandards.org/the-standards/mathematics

Council of Chief State School Officers. (2008). Attributes of effective formative assessment. Retrieved November 23, 2010, from http://www.ccsso.org/publications/details.cfm?PublicationID=362

Dabell, J., Keogh, B., & Naylor, S. (2008). *Concept cartoons in mathematics education.* Chesire, UK: Millgate House.

Donovan, S., & Bransford, J. (2005). *How students learn mathematics in the classroom.* Washington, DC: National Academy Press.

Erickson, L. (1998). *Concept-based curriculum and instruction.* Thousand Oaks, CA: Corwin.

Fennema, E., & Romberg, T. (1999). *Mathematics classrooms that promote understanding.* London: Psychology Press.

Fleener, M., Westbrook, S., & Rogers, L. (1995). Learning cycles for mathematics: An investigative approach to middle-school mathematics. *The Journal of Mathematical Behavior, 14*(4), 437–442.

Flick, L., & Tomlinson, M. (2006). Helping students understand the minds-on side of learning science. In M. McMahon, P. Simmons, R. Sommers, D. DeBaets, & F. Crawley (Eds.), *Assessment in science: Practical experiences and education research* (pp. 183–196). Arlington, VA: NSTA Press.

Gunning, T. (1997). *Assessing and correcting reading difficulties.* Boston: Allyn & Bacon.

Hall, K., & Burke, W. (2003). *Making formative assessment work: Effective practice in the primary classroom.* Berkshire, UK: Open University Press.

Hammer, D., & Van Zee, E. (2006). *Seeing the science in children's thinking.* Portsmouth, NH: Heinemann.

Hattie, J., & Timperley, H. (2007). The power of feedback. *Review of Educational Research, 77*(1), 81–112.

Henry, D., Henry, J., & Riddoch, S. (2006, April). Whiteboarding your way to great student discussions. *Science Scope,* pp. 50–53.

Heritage, M. (2010). *Formative assessment: Making it happen in the classroom.* Thousand Oaks, CA: Corwin.

Hodgen, J., & Wiliam, D. (2006). *Mathematics inside the black box: Assessment for learning in the mathematics classroom.* London: NFER/Nelson.

Joyce, B., Weil, M., & Calhoun, E. (2009). *Models of teaching* (8th ed.). Boston: Pearson Education.

Keeley, P. (2008). *Science formative assessment: 75 practical strategies for linking assessment, teaching, and learning.* Thousand Oaks, CA: Corwin.

Keeley, P., Eberle, F., & Tugel, J. (2006). *Uncovering student ideas in science: 25 more formative assessment probes* (Vol. 2). Arlington, VA: NSTA Press.

Keeley, P., & Harrington, R. (2010). *Uncovering student ideas in physical science: 45 new force and motion assessment probes.* Arlington, VA: NSTA Press.

Keeley, P., & Rose, C. (2006). *Mathematics curriculum topic study: Bridging the gap between standards and practice.* Thousand Oaks, CA: Corwin.

Leiber, L. (1942). *The education of T. C. Mits [the celebrated man in the street]: What modern mathematics means to you.* Brooklyn, NY: Long Island University and the Galois Institute of Mathematics and Art.

Leinhardt, G., Zaslavsky, O., & Stein M. (1990). Functions, graphs and graphing: Tasks, learning and teaching. *Review of Educational Research, 60*(1), 37–42.

Lipton, L., & Wellman, B. (1998). *Pathways to understanding: Patterns and practices in the learning-focused classroom.* Sherman, CT: Mira Via.

Love, N. (2002). *Getting data/getting results: A practical guide for school improvement in mathematics and science.* Norwood, MA: Christopher-Gordon.

McDermott, M., Rosenquist, L., & Van Zee, E. (1987). Student difficulties in connecting graphs and physics: Examples from kinematics. *American Journal of Physics, 55*(6), 503.

Mestre, J. (1989). Hispanic and Anglo students' misconceptions in mathematics. *ERIC Digest.* Charleston, WV: ERIC Clearinghouse on Rural Education and Small Schools. (ERIC Document Reproduction Service No. ED313192)

National Council of Teachers of Mathematics. (2000). *Principles and standards for school mathematics.* Reston, VA: Author.

Naylor, S., & Keogh, B. (2000). *Concept cartoons in science education.* Cheshire, UK: Millgate House Publisher.

Naylor, S., Keogh, B., & Goldsworthy, A. (2004). *Active assessment: Thinking, learning and assessment in science.* London: David Fulton.

Novak, J. (1998). *Learning, creating, and using knowledge: Concept maps as facilitative tools in schools and corporations.* Mahwah, NJ: Lawrence Erlbaum.

Organisation for Economic Co-operation and Development. (2003). *The PISA 2003 assessment framework: Mathematics, reading, science and problem solving knowledge and skills.* Paris: Author.

Perkins, D. (1992). *Smart schools.* New York: Free Press.

Rittle-Johnson, B., & Star, J. R. (2007). Does comparing solution methods facilitate conceptual and procedural knowledge? An experimental study on learning to solve equations. *Journal of Educational Psychology, 99*(3), 561–574.

Rose, C., & Arline, C. (2009). *Uncovering student thinking in mathematics, grades 6–12: 30 formative assessment probes for the elementary classroom.* Thousand Oaks, CA: Corwin.

Rose, C., Minton, L., & Arline, C. (2007). *Uncovering student thinking in mathematics: 25 formative assessment probes.* Thousand Oaks, CA: Corwin.

Rose Tobey, C., & Minton, L. (2010). *Uncovering student thinking in mathematics, grades K–5: 25 formative assessment probes for the secondary classroom.* Thousand Oaks, CA: Corwin.

Rowe, M. (1974). Wait time and rewards as instructional variables: Their influence on language, logic, and fate control. *Journal of Research in Science Teaching, 11,* 81–94.

Rowe, M. (1986). Wait time: Slowing down may be a way of speeding up! *Journal of Teacher Education, 37*(1), 43–50.

Sadler, D. R. (1989). Formative assessment and the design of instructional systems. *Instructional Science, 18,* 119–140

Sato, M. (2003). Working with teachers in assessment-related professional development. In M. Atkin & J. Coffey (Eds.), *Everyday assessment in the science classroom* (pp. 109–119). Arlington, VA: NSTA Press.

Shapiro, B. (1994). *What children bring to light: A constructivist perspective on children's learning in science.* New York: Teachers College Press.

Shute, V. (2008). Focus on formative feedback. *Review of Educational Research, 78*(1), 153–189.

Siegel, M., Borasi, R., & Fonzi, J. (1998). Supporting students' mathematical inquiries through reading. *Journal for Research in Mathematics Education, 29*(4), 378–413.

Stavy, R., & Tirosh, D. (2000). *How students (mis-)understand science and mathematics.* New York: Teachers College Press.

Stepans, J. I., Schmidt, D. L., Welsh, K. M., Reins, K. J., & Saigo, B. W. (2005). *Teaching for K–12 mathematical understanding using the Conceptual Change Model.* St. Cloud, MN: Saiwood Publications.

Vygotsky, L. (1978). *Mind in society.* Cambridge, MA: Harvard University Press.

Walsh, J., & Sattes, B. (2005). *Quality questioning: Research-based practice to engage every learner.* Thousand Oaks, CA: Corwin.

Waring, S. (2000). *Can you prove it? Developing concepts of proof in primary and secondary schools.* Leicester, UK: The Mathematical Association.

White, B., & Frederiksen, J. (1998). Inquiry, modeling, and metacognition: Making science accessible to all students. *Cognition and Instruction, 16,* 3–118.

White, R., & Gunstone, R. (1992). *Probing understanding.* London: Falmer.

Wiliam, D. (2005, November 9). *Science assessment: Research and practical approaches for grades 3–12 teachers and school and district administrators.* Remarks made at the closing Plenary Session of the NSTA Assessment Conference, Chicago.

Wiliam, D. T., & Thompson, M. (2006). Integrating assessment with learning: What will it take to make it work? In C. A. Dwyer (Ed.), *The future of assessment: Shaping, teaching and learning.* Mahwah, NJ: Lawrence Erlbaum.

Index